MW00849985

WINTER LIGHTNING

BOOKS BY MATT SPRUILL

Guide to the Battle of Chickamauga

Storming the Heights: A Guide to the Battle of Chattanooga

Echoes of Thunder: A Guide to the Seven Days Battles
with Matt Spruill IV

Winter Lightning: A Guide to the Battle of Stones River
with Lee Spruill

WINTER LIGHTNING

A Guide to the Battle of Stones River

MATT SPRUILL AND LEE SPRUILL

The University of Tennessee Press / Knoxville

Copyright © 2007 by The University of Tennessee Press / Knoxville.
All Rights Reserved. Manufactured in the United States of America.
First Edition.

This book is printed on acid-free paper.

Published in cooperation with the Tennessee Civil War National Heritage Area,
which is a partnership unit of the National Park Service.

Library of Congress Cataloging-in-Publication Data

Spruill, Matt.
  Winter lightning : a guide to the Battle of Stones River / Matt Spruill
and Lee Spruill. − 1st ed.
     p. cm.
  Includes index.
  ISBN-13: 978-1-57233-598-1 (pbk. : alk. paper)
  ISBN-10: 1-57233-598-X (pbk. : alk. paper)
  1. Stones River, Battle of, Murfreesboro, Tenn., 1862-1863.
  2. Stones River National Battlefield (Tenn.)−Tours.
  I. Spruill, Lee.
  II. Title.
  E474.77.S68 2007
  976.8'57−dc22   2007021246

To those who make life wonderful

Kathy and Nicole
our present

Jeanne, Christine, and David
our future

CONTENTS

FIGURES

MAPS

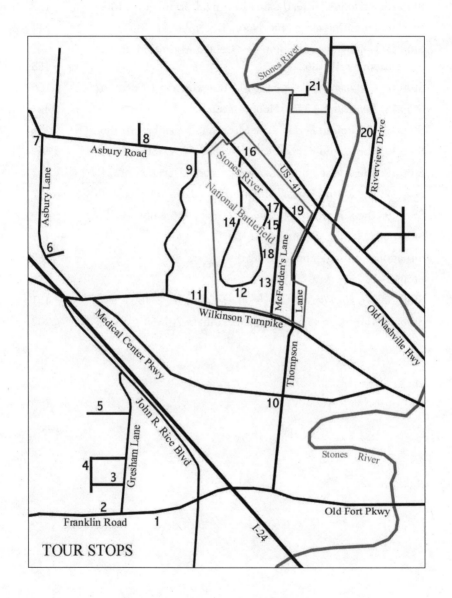

TOUR STOPS

INTRODUCTION

The Civil War year of 1862 began as one of promise and high expectations for the Union. In the eastern and western theaters, Union forces were positioned to strike deadly blows against the Confederacy.

In the east, on January 9, a Union division-sized force commanded by Brigadier General Ambrose E. Burnside departed Annapolis, Maryland, by ship and in early February landed inside the North Carolina Outer Banks. Burnside's operation secured a lodgment from which future operations against eastern North Carolina and southeastern Virginia could be conducted. This was followed in March by the revitalized and reorganized Army of the Potomac, under command of Major General George B. McClellan, landing on the tip of the Peninsula in Virginia. From there McClellan began a campaign up the Peninsula designed to capture the Confederate capital, Richmond. Although movement was not as rapid as planned, by the middle of June the army was on the eastern outskirts of Richmond. It appeared that it was only a matter a time before the Confederate capitol and major manufacturing center would fall into Union hands.

In the west Union armies and naval forces gained early and decisive victories. Middle Tennessee was opened, and the Confederate defensive line from the mountains west to the Mississippi River was broken when Brigadier General Ulysses S. Grant on February 6 captured Fort Henry on the Tennessee River and then ten days later captured Fort Donelson on the Cumberland River. This was followed with Grant's victory at Shiloh in early April and the Union navy's capture of New Orleans, the Confederacy's largest city, on April 25.

By late summer the euphoria from these victories was gone as Confederate armies went on the offense and diminished the early Union successes.

In the east, General *Robert E. Lee* took command of the Confederate army defending Richmond. During the Seven Days Battles, June 25 to July 1, he drove McClellan's army away from Richmond and eventually forced its departure from the Peninsula. *Lee* followed this by moving the center of conflict to northern Virginia. On August 29 and 30 he defeated the Union Army of Virginia commanded by Major General John Pope at the Second Battle of Bull Run and then invaded northern territory. On September 17 he fought McClellan to a tactical draw along Antietam Creek in Maryland. Electing to retreat from Maryland, *Lee* finished the year with the dramatic defeat of the Army of the Potomac, now commanded by Major General Ambrose E. Burnside, at Fredericksburg, Virginia, in mid-December.

In the west things did not go well for Union forces. In the first week of November, Grant commenced his offensive to capture Vicksburg and open the Mississippi River. After suffering reverses at Holly Springs and Chickasaw Bluffs in late December, Grant terminated his initial operations and was forced to develop new avenues of approach.

In late summer a two-pronged Confederate offense was launched into Kentucky. Major General *Edmund Kirby Smith* led a force north from Knoxville, Tennessee, which eventually captured Lexington, Kentucky, on September 1. A second Confederate force joined *Smith's* invasion when, on August 28, General *Braxton Bragg* led his army from Chattanooga, Tennessee, into Kentucky. On September 23 *Bragg's* army was at Bardstown, Kentucky. The invasion of Kentucky by these two Confederate armies brought Major General Don Carlos Buell's Army of the Ohio north from southern Tennessee.

Buell's army reached Louisville, Kentucky, on September 29 and on October 1 moved to locate and attack the Confederate forces. In the meantime *Bragg* had ordered his and *Smith's* army to concentrate in the Harrodsburg-Perryville area. As Buell approached Perryville, *Bragg*, even though his force was not concentrated, seized the initiative and attacked him on October 8. Buell's mismanagement of the battle prevented him from gaining a significant victory, and the perception in the north was that of a Union defeat. *Bragg* retreated into Tennessee and eventually placed his army just south of Nashville at Murfreesboro, Tennessee, along Stones River.

As the year drew to a close, *Bragg's* newly named Army of Tennessee and what would shortly become the Union Army of the Cumberland, previously the Army of the Ohio, now under the command of Major General William S. Rosecrans, fought a bloody battle from December 31, 1862, to January 2,

1863, along Stones River. Although hard pressed at first, Rosecrans would eventually win the Battle of Stones River and *Bragg* would retreat farther south toward Chattanooga. Coming at the end of a series of Union defeats, this victory gave the Lincoln presidency and the populace in the North a bright ray of hope during a fall and winter of Union defeats and Confederate victories.

The Confederate army that fought at Stones River came into existence in the spring of 1862 as the Army of the Mississippi when General *Albert S. Johnston* concentrated Confederate forces at Corinth, Mississippi, for the attack on Grant's army at Shiloh. *Johnston* was killed at Shiloh, and his deputy, General *P. G. T. Beauregard*, took over command of the army and retreated back to Corinth.

General *Braxton Bragg*, having assumed command of the Army of the Mississippi on June 27, on July 20 began transferring the army to Chattanooga. From Chattanooga, in conjunction with Major General *Kirby Smith's* Army of Kentucky, he launched an invasion of Kentucky. After the Battle of Perryville, *Bragg* and *Smith* retreated from Kentucky to Middle Tennessee. On November 20 *Smith's* army was absorbed into *Bragg's*, which was renamed the Army of Tennessee. The army was organized into two infantry corps, of three and two divisions, and a cavalry division

The Union army that came to Stones River was the Army of the Cumberland. It was constituted on November 15, 1861, under the command of Major General Don Carlos Buell as the Army of the Ohio. Under Buell it fought at Shiloh, pursued *Bragg* and *Smith* into Kentucky, and fought the Battle of Perryville.

Major General Rosecrans replaced Buell on October 30 and the army was renamed the Fourteenth Corps. This force was further divided into three wings: Left, Center, and Right, with three, four, and three infantry divisions, respectively. The cavalry was organized into a division. Unofficial practice was to call it the Army of the Cumberland, and seven days after the Battle of Stones River this became its official title. In this book we have used this name for Rosecrans's force.

The Army of Tennessee had 37,317 soldiers at Stones River, while the Army of the Cumberland had 43,400. In the winter of 1862 the soldiers in these two armies unleashed a lightning storm in Middle Tennessee.

Normal practice for Civil War armies was to cease major campaigns during the winter months. This pause in operations was caused by the adverse road conditions during winter and the extreme difficulty, if not impossibility, of moving supply and ammunition wagons and artillery in addition to the difficulty in just marching large formations of soldiers. *Bragg* was preparing to place his army in winter quarters and thought that Rosecrans was doing the same at Nashville. When Rosecrans marched his army south out of Nashville in late December, he caught *Bragg* by surprise.

Stones River was fought in some of the most adverse weather of any of the Civil War battles. When Rosecrans began his march from Nashville on December 26, it was in a cold rain. From that day until the end of the battle, and during *Bragg's* retreat except for one day, weather conditions were early morning cold mists or fog, usually followed by rain, which sometimes turned to sleet, and nighttime temperatures close to or at the freezing mark. Roads became quagmires of mud during the day and froze over at night.

With the Battle of Stones River, the Army of the Cumberland and the Army of Tennessee began a twenty-two-month conflict that took them through Middle Tennessee to Chickamauga and Chattanooga and eventually to Atlanta, Georgia. Matt Spruill's *U.S. Army War College Guide to the Battle of Chickamauga* and *Storming the Heights: A Guide to the Battle of Chattanooga* provides detail studies and tours of these battles.

U.S. Army doctrine recognizes four types of offensive operations: movement to contact, attack, exploitation, and pursuit. A movement to contact is conducted by a force when the commander is unsure of the exact enemy location and force. An attack, which uses various forms of maneuver, is conducted to destroy or render combat ineffective an enemy force or to capture key terrain. An exploitation often follows a successful attack, its purpose to prevent the enemy from reestablishing its defenses and to capture objectives deep in the enemy rear area. A pursuit, like the exploitation, follows a successful attack or a successful exploitation. Where the exploitation orients on capture of terrain, the pursuit orients on the enemy force. The purpose of the pursuit is to cut off, capture, or destroy an enemy force that is attempting to escape. [*Field Manual 3-0* (Washington, D.C.: GPO, June 14, 2001), chap. 7 (hereafter cited as *FM 3-0*, chap. 7).]

The Battle of Stones River provides the opportunity to study movement to contact as used by Rosecrans and attack as employed by *Bragg.* Rosecrans's operation from December 26 to December 29 was a movement to contact as he deployed his army south and southeast from Nashville. During this movement he was attempting to gain definitive information on the location, strength, and deployment of *Bragg's* army.

On December 30 Rosecrans had brought his army into position in front of *Bragg's* at Murfreesboro. He then prepared to shift to the attack followed by a pursuit. However, *Bragg* was slightly faster, and at dawn on December 31 he regained the initiative as he changed from defensive to offensive operations and attacked.

There are five forms of maneuver that can be used when conducting an attack: envelopment, turning movement, infiltration, penetration, and frontal attack. The envelopment avoids the enemy front and maneuvers against one or both flanks. The single envelopment is against one flank, whereas the double envelopment is against both flanks. Some authors refer to these as "flank attacks." The ultimate purpose of the envelopment is to gain the enemy rear area, to isolate him, and to control his lines of communication and his ability to logistically support his force. An attacking force uses a turning movement to avoid the enemy's principal defensive position by seizing objectives in the enemy rear and causing him to move out of his current position or divert major forces against a new threat. The presence of a force in the enemy's rear turns him out of his position. The infiltration is a form of maneuver in which an attacking force moves undetected through or into an area occupied by the enemy to a position of advantage in the enemy rear area. The penetration is used to cause a break in the enemy's defensive position. This maneuver will create assailable flanks at the point of penetration and provide access to enemy rear areas. A frontal attack strikes the enemy across a wide front and over the most direct approaches. Success with this form of maneuver depends on achieving an advantage in combat power throughout the attack. It can be the most costly form of maneuver. [*FM 3-0,* chap. 7.]

Rosecrans's plan called for the envelopment of *Bragg*'s right flank on December 31, but it was not carried through as *Bragg* preempted with his earlier maneuver against Rosecrans's right flank. The forms of maneuver used by *Bragg* were the envelopment against Rosecrans's right and a frontal attack against his center. The envelopment was the maneuver designed to cut Rosecrans's line of communication to Nashville; the frontal attack fixed his army in position. *Bragg*'s attack on Rosecrans's right was not a turning movement, as it is some times called. Rosecrans's maneuvering of his army in September 1863, which forced *Bragg* to retreat from Chattanooga or be cut off, was a turning movement. On January 2, 1863, *Bragg* conducted a frontal attack against the Union Left Wing at McFadden's Ford.

In recounting the story of the Battle of Stones River, we have relied heavily on the *Official Records of the Union and Confederate Armies.* The gathering and publishing of these records was a monumental task. It was initially begun in 1864 as commanders' reports were collected. In the late 1860s a start was made in putting the thus-far-collected reports into book form. In 1877 Captain Robert L. Scott, a Civil War aide to General Henry W. Halleck, was placed in charge of the project. Scott developed the organizational plan for the material. Until his death in 1887 he supervised the compilation and publication of a large part of the reports. The first book of what was to be a series of 128 books was published in 1880, and the last one was published in 1901. Where *Official Records* were not available, we have used other original source material.

In several instances you will find differences in the spelling of certain words. For example, in the 1860s you will find "reenforcement" or "re-enforcement" as the correct spelling, while today the spelling is "reinforcement." Or you might find "Nashville road" while today you would find it written as "Nashville Road." We have left the spelling as we found it in anything written by the participants. The names of Confederate soldiers and civilians are in italic. This is for the convenience of identifying who was Confederate and who was Union.

The book is organized so that you may follow the battle from its start to finish in chronological order. Driving instructions will move you from stop to stop along the same routes taken by many of the Union and Confederate units. However, each chapter also is designed to stand alone so that, if you wish, you may visit only the west, center, or east portion of the battlefield.

To assist the reader we have included three different types of maps in the book. There are twenty-seven tactical maps that show the ground as it was in the 1860s and are designed to show specific unit deployments during a short time frame. Union units are shown in black and Confederate units are shown in gray. A unit is shown as a bar, which represents the approximate location of the unit's battle line. Unless otherwise indicated, all units shown are brigades. If otherwise, the unit name and size will be listed. Union brigades were officially designated by number, for example, 1st Brigade, 1st Division. However, for clarity and ease of use we have shown them with the commander's name. By late 1862, Confederate brigades, divisions, and corps were designated by their commander's name, which is how we have shown them on the maps. On some tactical maps we have shown modern roads to help with orientation. Where this was done, the road name is followed by the notation "(today)." For example, "Medical Center Parkway (today)." In addition to the tactical maps, there are operational maps to show the general situation and planned movements and modern-day road maps to assist in moving around the battlefield.

We are greatly indebted to many people for their assistance and support as we developed this book. Dr. Jay Luvaas and Brigadier General Hal Nelson taught us the value of the *Official Records* and how to use them on a battlefield. Without them, earlier books, *Guide to the Battle of Chickamauga, Storming the Heights: A Guide to the Battle of Chattanooga,* and *Echoes of Thunder: A Guide to the Seven Days Battles,* would not have been done. This book has been modeled on them and similar books that have been done for the Army War College.

Our thanks go to Jennifer Siler, director of the University of Tennessee Press, and her editing, production, and marketing team. Foremost among them are Scot Danforth, who has guided and supported us in the editing and publishing process, Gene Adair, Thomas Wells, Stephanie Thompson, Tom Post, and Cheryl Carson. To our son and brother, Matt Spruill, special thanks for reading and providing suggested changes to the manuscript. We also would like to thank our friends and fellow Civil War enthusiasts Sandy White, Bob Moulder, Mike Lang, Nick Kurtz, and Larry Peterson, who provided helpful suggestions, research assistance, and support. A big thanks goes to Karin Kaufman for her excellent copyediting of the original manuscript.

Gib Backlund, Jim Bosse, and Bill Lynch provided valuable research assistance at Stones River National Battlefield. Scott Pawlowski at the Denver National Park Service Technical Information Center assisted us in finding movement maps, research documents, and studies on the Battle of Stones River.

We are honored to have had National Park Service rangers Dr. Timothy B. Smith at Shiloh National Military Park and James B. Lewis at Stones River National Battlefield read our manuscript. Their depth of knowledge and insights provided us with a wealth of usable suggestions and comments.

Our greatest thanks goes to our wives, Kathy and Nicole, without whose constant support and encouragement this work would not have developed from concept to book.

One final but very important comment. Of the 4.1 million who wore the blue and the gray from 1861 to 1865, a little over 600,000 gave their lives in a war that determined what the United States would become. What our country is today is because of their commitments and sacrifices.

Those veterans who survived have passed on. The generation that followed them, who personally knew them, has also gone. The personal contact that later generations had to these veterans and their war is now gone forever. The only contact we and future generations have are the writings, the artifacts, and the ground upon which they stood, fought, and died. The battlefields themselves provide the most direct contact we have with those veterans and the Civil War. Indeed, one of the reasons this and other guidebooks are written is to provide that connection with past events on the actual spot where they happened.

Fortunately, national, state, and local governments have preserved some of this ground. However, a crisis in battlefield preservation is upon us. Urban development in our country is growing at an exponential rate. In the past, where we may have had a generation or a decade to protect battlefields, we now have only a few years or, in some very threatened places, only a few months. If you believe in saving this vital part of our heritage, we encourage you to become active in battlefield preservation.

One of the most successful organizations in preserving battlefields is the nonprofit Civil War Preservation Trust (CWPT). We strongly urge you to become a member of the CWPT and leave a legacy that will be passed to future generations of your family. The CWPT can be contacted by writing Civil War Preservation Trust, 1331 H Street NW, Suite 1001, Washington, D.C., 20005; by calling 202-367-1861; or via the Internet at www.civilwar.org.

MATT SPRUILL
Littleton, Colorado

LEE SPRUILL
Red Oak, Texas

Chapter 1

PRELUDE

Braxton Bragg and *Edmund Kirby Smith's* invasion of Kentucky came to an abrupt end after the inconclusive Battle of Perryville. Confronted by Buell's Army of the Ohio, on October 13 both Confederate armies began to retreat south. A week later the Confederates were passing through the Cumberland Gap, and in the last week of October they were at Knoxville. At the same time he began his retreat, *Bragg* ordered Major General *John C. Breckinridge* to move his division from Knoxville to Murfreesboro.

Upon arriving at Knoxville, *Bragg* departed for Richmond for a conference with *Jefferson Davis*. While he was gone, his army kept moving through Knoxville on to Chattanooga and then north toward Tullahoma and Murfreesboro. By the time of *Bragg's* return, his army was deployed into Middle Tennessee, with his headquarters at Tullahoma.

On November 20 *Bragg* issued an order that absorbed *Kirby Smith's* army into his army as a corps, reorganized the army, re-naming it the Army of Tennessee, and deployed it to specific areas of Middle Tennessee.

GENERAL ORDERS No. 151   Tullahoma, November 20, 1862

IV. The three army corps, as at present organized for active operations, will be designated by the names of their respective permanent commanders, viz, *Smith's, Polk's,* and *Hardee's;* the whole to constitute the Army of Tennessee.

V. *Polk's* corps will take position near Murfreesboro; *Smith's* in front of Manchester; *Hardee's* near Shelbyville. The cavalry brigades for these three corps (except one regiment for each) will take position in front of our lines, under the direction of the chief of cavalry.

VI. Brigadier-Generals *Morgan's* and *Forrest's* brigades of cavalry will, as soon as practicable after being relieved by *Wharton's* command, proceed to the special service assigned them by the commanding general. Much is expected by the army and its commander from the operations of these active and ever-successful leaders.

VII. The foregoing dispositions are in anticipation of the great struggle, which must soon settle the question of supremacy in Middle Tennessee. The enemy in heavy force is before us, with a determination, no doubt, to redeem the fruitful country we have wrested from him. With the remembrance of Richmond, Munfordville, and Perryville so fresh in our minds, let us make a name for the now Army of Tennessee as enviable as those enjoyed by the armies of Kentucky and the Mississippi.

Braxton Bragg

[*The War of the Rebellion: A Compilation of the Official Records of the Union and Confederate Armies* (Washington, D.C., 1880–1901), ser. 1, vol. 20, pt. 2, pp. 411–12 (hereafter cited as *OR* followed by volume number, part number, and pages).]

With *Polk's* Corps deployed in a forward position at Murfreesboro, *Bragg* now blocked the direct approach into Middle Tennessee and the railroad from Nashville to Chattanooga. His other two corps, *Smith's* and *Hardee's,* were located twenty-five miles south, where they could be moved forward to reinforce or to either side of the Murfreesboro position as the situation might require. In their present position, these two corps foraged for food in the Duck and Elk River Valleys.

On November 24, Bragg sent a letter to *Jefferson Davis* giving the condition of his army, efforts to resupply, troop movements, deployment of forces, and an outline of his future operational intentions.

Tullahoma, Tenn., November 24, 1862

His Excellency *Jefferson Davis:*

Since reaching my command again, we have been constantly engaged in preparing the troops for the operations intended, and in their transportation to the field of action. The process has been slow, for several reasons, but especially from the condition of the railroads. The Georgia and East Tennessee road is greatly deficient in rolling stock. The Nashville and Chattanooga had but a very limited supply this side the Tennessee [River], and was unwilling to risk more until the bridge [across the Tennessee River at Bridgeport, Alabama] was finished. The increased force now here has given confidence, and they are adding to the supply. The bridge is progressing well, and, if we are not disappointed in getting iron from the Tredegar Works, in Richmond, and timber promised from Georgia, will be finished in three weeks. Many of my troops were bare-footed and ragged, inducing me to spare them as much as possible from marching. More than half, however, marched from Bridgeport forward. I am happy to find the deficiency in clothing, shoes, and blankets is being rapidly supplied, and even now we are in very fair condition in that respect, and are daily improving. The health and general tone of my old Army of the Mississippi (now *Polk's* and *Hardee's* corps) were never better. The Tennesseans especially are in fine condition, having been fitted out by their friends. The ranks of those from this section, too, are rapidly filling. Having felt the heel of the tyrant, the people of this region are determined to resist, and nobly furnishing us men and means. *Smith's* corps is just coming up—nearly all being this side of the [Tennessee] river. Composed mostly of new troops, it has suffered much more from sickness than the others, so that he brings only about 11,000 infantry, instead of 15,000, as he expected. Our whole effective force of infantry and artillery will, therefore, be about 40,000, with 5,000 cavalry (or, rather, mounted gun-men) in the three regular brigades; 5,000 more I send, under *Forrest* and *Morgan,* on partisan service, for which, and which alone, their commanders are peculiarly and specially suited.

My present dispositions are: *Morgan* to operate with his cavalry brigade north of the Cumberland [River], on the enemy's lines of communication, which, I am confident, will prevent the enemy from using the Louisville Railroad, which is not yet in running order, and their wagon trains will be in constant danger. *Forrest,* with his cavalry brigade, is to work south of the Cumberland and west of Nashville. With a fine battery of rifle guns, he will destroy their transports on both rivers. He is instructed now to seek a crossing, which he is confident of finding; throw his command rapidly over the Tennessee River, and precipitate it upon the enemy's lines, break up railroads, burn bridges, destroy depots, capture hospitals and guards, and harass him generally. Thus we may create a diversion in favor of *Pemberton,* and, if successful, force the enemy to retire from Mississippi.

My infantry and artillery is concentrating in three corps at Murfreesboro, and on the turnpikes leading thereto, on the right and left, within supporting distance, and ready for any move. The three regular cavalry brigades are in front of the advanced infantry, and always in sight of the enemy, giving me daily information. He is thus kept from foraging this side of the Cumberland [River]. From the best information we get, the enemy numbers not less than 60,000 in and about Nashville. This we are prepared to meet at any time, and are confident of beating in the open field, and we shall spare no effort to draw him out. But it is a serious matter to assail such a force behind strong intrenchments, garnished with the heaviest artillery, with one much inferior in numbers. My troops, however, are ready for any work assigned them, and will move to this, if I require it, with alacrity and confidence.

I shall go forward to-morrow with General *Polk*, who has just arrived, and remain with the front, as the slightest change with either party may precipitate an engagement at any moment. A rise in the rivers, of which there is yet no indication, might render necessary a modification of my plans and a change in my dispositions.

We are securing a rich harvest of supplies. Subsistence is abundant, not only for us, but a surplus may be had. Forage is abundant. Some horses and mules are to be had, and material for clothing and tents, and leather are also found in considerable quantities. It should be borne in mind, however, that we are now gleaning the country, and many of these articles, especially salt meat, will not be reproduced during the war.

We have not been enabled, with the limited means of transportation at our disposal, to move the stores as rapidly as obtained; but hope soon to supply the want, and make up lost time. All are safe, however, unless the enemy detests us in a battle. On this subject it may not be improper for me to remark, that economy and efficiency would, in my judgment, be consulted if the agents of the subsistence department were to operate in concert with my own. By the present independent arrangement, competition and collision will occur, in spite of all I can do, for it is human. The Government may rest assured that whatever is subject to my control will be divided, to the last pound, in promotion of the whole cause.

Most respectfully and truly, yours,

Braxton Bragg

[*OR* 20, pt. 2, pp. 421–22.]

On December 4, *Bragg*, sensing a possible Union move south from Nashville, issued orders to move *Kirby Smith's* and *Hardee's* Corps farther north. This move placed these corps in closer proximity to *Polk's* Corps at Murfreesboro. Further changes took place within the army in mid-December when Major General *Carter*

Stevenson's division was ordered to Mississippi and sent away and *Kirby Smith* was reassigned to the Trans-Mississippi Department. The five remaining infantry divisions were organized into two corps with *Hardee* and *Polk* as corps commanders. It is with this latest reconfiguration of the Army of Tennessee that *Bragg* fought at Stones River.

After Perryville, Lincoln had expressed his desire that Buell would move into eastern Tennessee to provide support and show the flag to a population largely loyal to the Union. Buell followed the retreating Confederates as far as London, Kentucky, forty miles north of the Cumberland Gap, and there he turned southwest, abandoned a march into eastern Tennessee, and moved toward Nashville.

If Union troops had continued on through the Cumberland Gap and occupied Knoxville, they would have gained a strategic advantage. The railroad running through Knoxville connected western Virginia with the railroad hub at Chattanooga, and this hub provided additional rail lines to points in the Deep South. The rail line from Chattanooga through Knoxville to western and central Virginia provided the Confederacy with a major lateral communications route to move troops and supplies. Loss of this rail link would have forced Confederate movements to take a longer route south through the Carolinas to Atlanta then on to other points such as Chattanooga. This in fact happened in September 1863, when Lieutenant General *James Longstreet's* corps, moving from Virginia to reinforce *Bragg* before the Battle of Chickamauga, had to take the longer Atlanta route. This prevented all of his artillery and a significant part of his infantry from arriving in time to participate in the battle.

Frustrated with Buell, Lincoln had him relieved and on October 24 Major General William S. Rosecrans was ordered to assume command of his army. Rosecrans took command on October 30, and the Army of the Ohio was renamed the Fourteenth Corps. Immediately after the Battle of Stones River, the Fourteenth Corps was renamed the Army of the Cumberland, a term that had been in use unofficially before then. Throughout this book, "Army of the Cumberland" is the name that will be used for this corps.

On October 24, Major General Henry W. Halleck, general-in-chief in Washington, sent Rosecrans a letter setting forth the strategic and operational objectives for the Army of the Cumberland.

Washington, October 24, 1862

Maj. Gen. W. S. Rosecrans:

You will receive herewith the order of the President placing you in command of the Department of the Cumberland and of the army of operations now under Major-General Buell.

You will immediately repair to General Buell's headquarters and relieve him from the command.

The great objects to be kept in view in your operations in the field are: First, to drive the enemy from Kentucky and Middle Tennessee; second, to take and hold East Tennessee, cutting the line of railroad at Chattanooga, Cleveland, or Athens, so as to destroy the connection of the valley of Virginia [the Shenandoah Valley] with Georgia and the other Southern States. It is hoped that by prompt and rapid movements a considerable part of this may be accomplished before the roads become impassable from the winter rains.

Two means of reaching East Tennessee have been proposed. First, to push a small force on the rear of *Bragg's* army to drive him into Tennessee and move the main army on such lines as to cover Nashville; second, to go directly to Nashville and make that the base of your operations, by McMinnville or Cookville. Adopting the first plan, the route by Somerset to Montgomery, if practicable, would be the most direct; if not practicable, it would then be necessary to move by Columbia or Glasgow to Sparta, &c. If the second plan be adopted, you will be obliged to move twice the distance in order to reach your objective point and at the same time afford the enemy an opportunity to resume his raids into Kentucky. Moreover, it would give the appearance of a retreat, which would encourage the enemy, while it would discourage our own troops and the country. Nevertheless, the difficulty of the roads, the pressure of the enemy upon Nashville, the position in which you find General Buell's army, and the difficulty of supplying it in a mountainous and sparsely populated country may compel you to adopt this line. In either case it will be necessary for you to repair and guard the railroad, so as to secure your supplies from Louisville until the Cumberland River becomes navigable.

You will fully appreciate the importance of moving light and rapidly, and also the necessity of procuring as many of your supplies as possible in the country passed over. Where you cannot obtain enough by purchase of loyal men or requisitions upon the disloyal you will make forced requisitions upon the country, paying or receipting, as the case may be, for the supplies taken. The time has now come when we must apply the sterner rules of war, whenever such application becomes necessary, to enable us to support our armies and to move them rapidly upon the enemy. You will not hesitate to do this in all cases where the exigencies of the war require it.

Moreover, if the enemy's forces in Mississippi now operating against General Grant should be drawn east to re-enforce *Bragg* or to operate in Tennessee General Grant may be able to render you important assistance.

Although the Department of the Ohio covers a portion of your theater of operations this will in no respect interfere with your movements in the field nor the command of your army. Moreover, you will call upon General Wright [commander of the Department of the Ohio, in Cincinnati, Ohio] for any assistance or supplies, which you may require.

It is possible that *Bragg,* having failed of his object in Kentucky, may leave only a small force in East Tennessee and throw his main army into Mississippi against General Grant. His railroad communications from Knoxville to Holly Springs and Tupelo will enable him to make this movement with great rapidity. In that case a part of your forces must be sent to the assistance of General Grant, either by railroad to Decatur or by water, should the Cumberland be navigable, to Columbus or Memphis. Every effort should be made to ascertain *Bragg's* movements by pressing him closely.

I need not urge upon you the necessity of giving active employment to your forces. Neither the country nor the Government will much longer put up with the inactivity of some of our armies and generals.

Very respectfully, your obedient servant,

H. W. Halleck,
General-in-Chief

[*OR* 16, pt. 2, pp. 640–41.]

In the last paragraph of his letter Halleck warned Rosecrans about allowing his army to remain inactive. This warning was repeated several times in November and December.

Rosecrans's first concern after assuming command was the securing and repairing of his railroad supply line from Louisville to Nashville. This was completed on November 26. At the same time he reconfigured the eleven infantry divisions of his army into three wings (later to be corps). The wings were designated the Right Wing, Center Wing, and Left Wing and were commanded by Major Generals Alexander McD. McCook, George H. Thomas, and Thomas L. Crittenden. Rosecrans then spent the rest of November and the first half of December accumulating ammunition and supplies for a move south against *Bragg's* army.

During this period of time he received several telegrams from Halleck urging him to begin operations. A December 4 communication from Halleck informed Rosecrans that "the President is very impatient at your long stay in Nashville. The favorable season for your campaign will soon be over. You give *Bragg* time to supply himself by plundering the very country your army should have occupied. Twice have I been asked to designate some one else to command your army. If you remain one more week at Nashville, I cannot prevent your removal. As I wrote you when you took the command, the Government demands action, and if you cannot respond to that demand some one else will be tried." [*OR* 20, pt. 2, pp. 117–18.]

The same day Rosecrans sent off a fiery response, telling Halleck, "I have lost no time. Everything I have done was necessary, absolutely so; and has been done as rapidly as possible. Any attempt to advance sooner would have increased our difficulty both in front and rear. In front, because of greater obstacles, enemies in greater force, and fighting with better chances of escaping pursuit, if overthrown in battle. In rear, because of insufficiency and uncertainty of supplies, both of subsistence and ammunition, and no security of any kind to fall back upon in case of disaster. If the Government which ordered me here confides in my judgment, it may rely on my continuing to do what I have been trying to—that is, my whole duty. If my superiors have lost confidence in me, they had better at once put some one in my place and let the future test the propriety of the change. I have but one word to add, which is, that I need no other stimulus to make me do my duty than the knowledge of what it is. To threats of removal or the like I must be permitted to say that I am insensible." [*OR* 20, pt. 2, p. 118.]

Ignoring Rosecrans's ultimatum, the next day Halleck sent a more reconciling telegram urging action—but also providing a political reasoning as to why immediate action was required.

Washington, December 5, 1862

Maj. Gen. W. S. Rosecrans:

Your telegram of last evening, in explanation of your delay at Nashville, is just received. My telegram was not a threat, but merely a statement of facts. The President is greatly dissatisfied with your delay, and has sent for me several times to account for it. He has repeated to me time and again that there were imperative reasons why the enemy should be driven [south] across the Tennessee River at the earliest possible moment. He has never told me what those reasons were, but I imagine them to be diplomatic, and of the most serious character. You can hardly conceive his great anxiety about it. I will tell you what I guess it is, although it is only a guess on my part. It has been feared that on the meeting of the British Parliament, in January next, the political pressure of the starving operatives [from a lack of cotton] may force the [British] Government to join France in an intervention. If the enemy be left in possession of Middle Tennessee, which we held last July, it will be said that they have gained on us. We have recovered all they gained on us in Kentucky, Virginia, Missouri, Arkansas, and Mississippi, and in North Carolina, South Carolina, Florida, Louisiana, and Texas we have gained on them. Tennessee is the only State which can be used as an argument in favor of intervention by England. You will thus perceive that your movements have an importance beyond mere military success. The whole Cabinet is anxious, inquiring almost daily. "Why don't he move?" "Can't you make him move?" "There must be no delay." "Delay there will be more fatal to us than anywhere else." You will thus perceive that there is a pressure for you to advance much greater than you can possibly have imagined. It may be, and perhaps is, the very turning-point in our foreign relations. It was hoped and believed when you took the command that you would recover all lost ground by, at furthest, the middle of December, so that it would be known in London soon after the meeting of Parliament. It is not surprising that our Government should be impatient and dissatisfied under the circumstances of the case. A victory or the retreat of the enemy before the 10th of this month would have been of more value to us than ten times that success at a later date.

No one doubted that General Buell would eventually have succeeded, but he was too slow to be in time. It was believed that you would move more rapidly. Hence the change.

Yours, truly,

H. W. Halleck,
General-in-Chief

[*OR* 20, pt. 2, pp. 123–24.]

Halleck in the summer of 1863 would again try to have coordinated action by all three main Union armies. Although Rosecrans conducted the successful Tullahoma Campaign in central Tennessee, he was not able to sustain his operations beyond June 30 and take full advantage of Confederate preoccupation with Vicksburg and Gettysburg. When Rosecrans began his operation against Chattanooga in August, it was *Bragg* who received reinforcements from the west and the east prior to the Battle of Chickamauga.

Historian Thomas Connelly named that area of Tennessee, north-central Alabama, north-central Georgia, and northeast Mississippi the Confederate "Heartland." Within this geographical area was a concentration of food, livestock, mules, horses, iron, raw materials, and the facilities for manufacturing weapons and equipment. Through this area ran the major east-west railroads that provided the links between Virginia and the western Confederacy. The loss of all or part of this area would deprive the Confederacy of a vast source of materials and food. In addition, such a loss would split the South in two and have a devastating effect on southern morale.

Any Union army located in East or Middle Tennessee must have Atlanta, Georgia, as its strategic objective. In late 1862, Atlanta, located one hundred miles south of Chattanooga, was one of the Confederacy's most important population centers. Located in the Deep South, it was a major railroad hub with railroad lines radiating to the four points of the compass. In addition, it was a vital manufacturing and supply center, providing clothing, food, and weapons needed to sustain the armies of the Confederacy.

The most direct, and practical, avenue of approach for a Union army located in northern Middle Tennessee would be along the axis Nashville-Chattanooga-Atlanta. Chattanooga was vital as a supply base for any army advancing into northern Georgia. Therefore, a Union army in Middle Tennessee using Nashville as a supply base would have two options for an advance to Chattanooga. The first was the Nashville-Murfreesboro-Tullahoma-Stevenson-Chattanooga axis. This 140-mile avenue of approach was the most direct route, and the Nashville-Chattanooga Railroad provided a supply and communications link to the Nashville base. The second option was the Knoxville-Chattanooga axis. Before this could be attempted, however, the army would have to move from Kentucky through the Cumberland Gap and into eastern Tennessee. Although providing the relief to a loyal Union population that Lincoln wanted, it was the most difficult avenue of approach for a large force. The logical decision for Rosecrans was to take the more direct avenue of approach to Chattanooga.

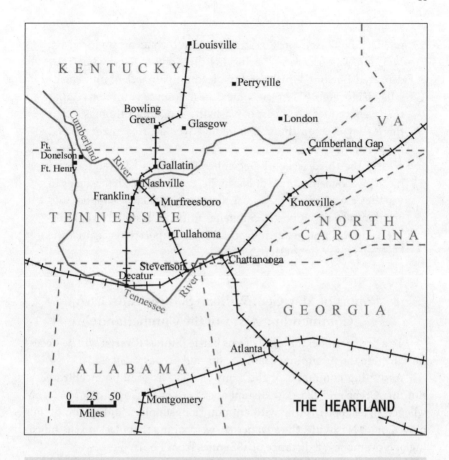

KENTUCKY

Louisville

Perryville

Bowling Green

Glasgow

London

VA

Cumberland River

Ft. Donelson
Ft. Henry

Cumberland Gap

Gallatin

Nashville

Franklin

Murfreesboro

Knoxville

TENNESSEE

NORTH CAROLINA

Tullahoma

Stevenson

Chattanooga

Decatur

Tennessee River

GEORGIA

Atlanta

ALABAMA

0 25 50
Miles

Montgomery

THE HEARTLAND

In the early part of the winter of 1862–63, Union armies were on the move east and west of the Appalachian Mountains. To the east, Major General Ambrose Burnside, now commanding the Army of the Potomac, marched into central Virginia in an operation designed to capture Richmond. Meanwhile, to the west Grant had begun a move against Vicksburg on the Mississippi River. To prevent Confederate forces from being shifted from the Tennessee area to reinforce either the east or the west, Rosecrans need to put his army in motion. However, he was unable to do this until late in December. On December 16, Major General *Carter Stevenson's* division was detached from *Bragg's* army and sent to reinforce *Pemberton* in Mississippi. The ability to laterally move forces would benefit *Bragg* in the late summer of 1863. But in December 1862 it was a determent to him as it reduced his strength by one division at a critical time.

During November Rosecrans began to concentrate his army. McCook was ordered to bring his divisions to Nashville. They departed Bowling Green, and the lead units marched into Nashville on November 7. At the same time Crittenden moved to Gallatin, twenty miles northeast of Nashville and joined Thomas. From there they crossed the Cumberland River on November 18 and then marched to Nashville.

By the third week of December Rosecrans had reorganized his army, concentrated it at Nashville, made up the deficiencies in supplies and equipment, and accumulated sufficient supplies and ammunition to support a campaign until at least early February 1863. He was now ready to begin offensive operations against the Confederate army south of Nashville.

Report of Maj. Gen. William S. Rosecrans, USA, Commanding Army of the Cumberland

To a proper understanding of this battle [Stones River] it will be necessary to state the preliminary movements and preparations:

Assuming command of the army . . . it was found concentrated at Bowling Green and Glasgow, distant about 113 miles from Louisville, from whence, after replenishing with ammunition, supplies, and clothing, they moved on to Nashville, the advance corps reaching that place on the morning of November 7, a distance of 183 miles from Louisville.

At this distance from my base of supplies [Louisville, Kentucky], the first thing to be done was to provide for the subsistence of the troops and open the Louisville and Nashville Railroad. The cars commenced running through on November 26, previous to which time our supplies had been brought by rail to Mitchellsville, 35 miles north of Nashville, and from thence, by constant labor, we had been able to haul enough to replenish the exhausted stores for the garrison at Nashville and subsist the troops of the moving army.

From November 26 to December 26 every effort was bent to complete the clothing of the army; to provide it with ammunition, and replenish the depot at Nashville with needful supplies; to insure us against want from the largest possible detention likely to occur by the breaking of the Louisville and Nashville Railroad, and to insure this work the road was guarded by a heavy force posted at Gallatin. The enormous superiority in numbers of the rebel cavalry kept our little cavalry force almost within the infantry lines, and gave the enemy control of the entire country around us. It was obvious from the beginning that we should be confronted by *Bragg's* army, recruited by an inexorable conscription, and aided by clans of mounted men, formed into a guerrilla-like cavalry, to avoid the hardships of conscription and infantry service. The evident difficulties and labors of an advance into this country, and against such a force, and at such distance from our base of operations, with which we were connected but by a single precarious thread, made it manifest that our policy was to induce the enemy to travel over as much as possible of the space that separated us, thus avoiding for us the wear and tear and diminution of our forces, and subjecting the enemy to all this inconvenience, besides increasing for him and diminishing for us the dangerous consequences of a defeat. The means taken to obtain this end were eminently successful. The enemy, expecting us to go into winter quarters at Nashville, had prepared his own winter quarters at Murfreesboro, with the hope of possibly making them at Nashville, and had sent a large cavalry force into West Tennessee to annoy Grant, and another large force into Kentucky to break up the railroad.

In the absence of these [Confederate cavalry] forces, and with adequate supplies in Nashville, the moment was judged opportune for an advance on the rebels. [*OR* 20, pt. 1, p. 189.]

In late 1862 a Union army was poised on the northern perimeter of the Heartland. The fighting begun in the winter of 1862–63 would culminate in late 1864 with the capture of Atlanta, then Savannah and the splitting of the Confederacy.

In the third week of December, *Bragg's* army was deployed along a twenty-six-mile-long line that covered the main roads from Nashville into Middle Tennessee.

Report of Gen. *Braxton Bragg*, CSA, Commanding Army of Tennessee

On December 26, last, the enemy advanced in force from Nashville to attack us at Murfreesboro. Before night on that day the object of the movement was developed by our dispositions in front, and orders were given for the necessary concentration of our forces, then distributed as follows: *Polk's* corps and three brigades of *Breckinridge's* division, *Hardee's* corps, at Murfreesboro; the balance of *Hardee's* corps near Eagleville, about 20 miles west of Murfreesboro; *McCown's* division at Readyville, 12 miles east of

Murfreesboro, the three cavalry brigades of *Wheeler, Wharton,* and *Pegram* occupying the entire front of our infantry, and covering all approaches to within 10 miles of Nashville; *Buford's* small cavalry brigade, of about 600, at McMinnville. The brigades of *Forrest* and *Morgan* (about 5,000 effective cavalry) were absent on special service in West Tennessee and Northern Kentucky. . . . *Jackson's* small infantry brigade was in rear, guarding the railroad from Bridgeport, Ala., to the mountains. [*OR* 20, pt. 1, p. 663.]

Rosecrans's plan was to conduct a movement to contact to determine the location and strength of *Bragg's* force. Initially the forward movement was planned for December 25, but it was delayed one day and operations commenced on the twenty-sixth.

Major General Alexander McD. McCook's Right Wing advanced southward toward Nolensville with Brigadier General Jefferson C. Davis's division and Brigadier General Philip H. Sheridan's division marching on the Nolensville Pike and a converging road to the west. As the Right Wing reserve, Brigadier General Richard W. Johnson's division followed. Davis made contact with Brigadier General *John A. Wharton's* pickets north of Nolensville and the pickets fell back upon their main body. As soon as Davis deployed, *Wharton* fell back to a new delaying position south of Nolensville. Davis followed, deployed again, and *Wharton* withdrew to Triune. Darkness brought a halt to McCook's march. The Right Wing bivouacked in the vicinity of Nolensville.

Thomas had five divisions in the Center Wing. However, Brigadier General Joseph J. Reynolds's division and two brigades of Brigadier General Speed S. Fry's division were left at Gallatin, Tennessee, twenty miles northeast of Nashville, to protect this critical point and other parts of the railroad to Louisville from Brigadier General *John H. Morgan's* raid. Brigadier General Robert B. Mitchell's small division was left as the garrison force at Nashville.

On McCook's right (west), Major General George H. Thomas with two divisions and a separate brigade marched south on the Franklin Pike to Brentwood, where he then followed the Wilson Pike. His lead division, Brigadier General James S. Negley's, marched to Nolensville, where it bivouacked. The remainder of Thomas's Center Wing, the division of Major General Lovell H. Rousseau and Colonel Moses B. Walker's brigade, stopped farther back along the Wilson and Franklin Pikes.

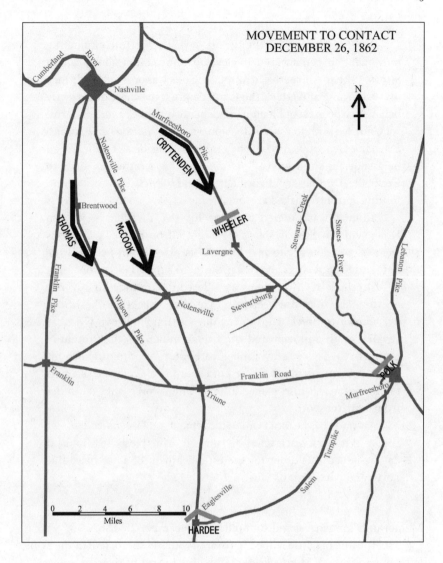

MOVEMENT TO CONTACT
DECEMBER 26, 1862

N

Major General Thomas L. Crittenden's Left Wing, preceded by cavalry, made contact with Brigadier General *Joseph Wheeler's* cavalry two miles north of Lavergne, where Hurricane Creek crosses the Nashville-Murfreesboro Pike. Brigadier General John M. Palmer's division moved forward and attacked the Confederates, driving them back to Lavergne before darkness brought a halt to the attack.

Rosecrans's plan for the twenty-seventh was to continue the movement to contact and to develop information about *Bragg's* forces. With this objective in mind, McCook was ordered to advance toward Triune and attack the Confederate force there, incorrectly believed to be most of Lieutenant General *William J. Hardee's* corps. McCook led with Johnson's division against *Wharton's* cavalry and Brigadier General *S. A. M. Wood's* infantry brigade at Triune. Faced by a superior-sized force, *Wharton* and *Wood* retreated south to Eagleville. Darkness again brought an end to McCook's attack, and his divisions bivouacked around Triune.

Thomas was ordered to move his two divisions east from Nolensville to Stewartsburg. By nightfall both of his divisions were in position at Stewartsburg. This placed him between the Left and Right Wings and in a position to support either one.

On the left, Crittenden was ordered to continue his advance on the Nashville-Murfreesboro Pike and to capture the bridge over Stewarts Creek. During the day Crittenden drove *Wheeler's* cavalry south and captured the bridge intact. As the ground at Stewarts Creek was a favorable location for *Bragg* to establish his defense, the securing of the ground south of the creek was a plus for Rosecrans. It also placed a large Union force only ten miles from Murfreesboro.

Alarmed by the rapid Union movement, on December 27 *Bragg* began to move his scattered divisions to Murfreesboro. The next day he issued this order for the establishment of a defensive line north and northwest of Murfreesboro.

Memoranda for general and staff officers, December 28, 1862

1st. The line of battle will be in front of Murfreesboro; half of the army, left wing, in front of Stone's River; right wing in rear of river.

2d. *Polk's* corps will form left wing; *Hardee's* corps, right wing.

3d. *Withers'* division will form first line in *Polk's* corps; *Cheatham's*, the second line. *Breckinridge's* division forms first line *Hardee's* corps; *Cleburne's* division, second line *Hardee's* corps.

4th. *McCown's* division to form reserve, opposite center, on high ground, in rear of *Cheatham's* present quarters.

5th. *Jackson's* brigade reserve, to the right flank, to report to Lieutenant-General *Hardee*.

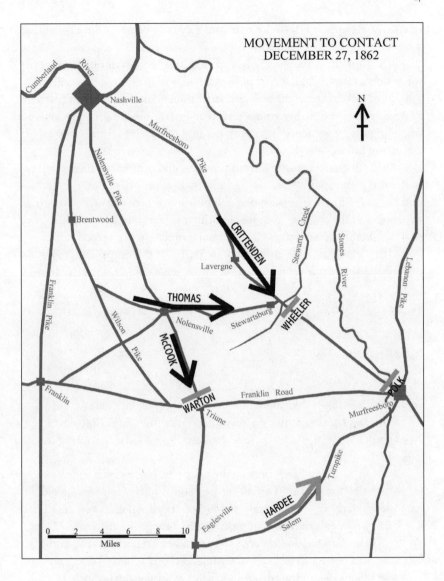

MOVEMENT TO CONTACT
DECEMBER 27, 1862

6th. Two lines to be formed from 800 to 1,000 yards apart, according to ground.

7th. Chiefs of artillery to pay special attention to posting of batteries, and supervise their work, seeing they do not causelessly waste their ammunition.

8th. Cavalry to fall back gradually before enemy, reporting by couriers every hour. When near our lines, *Wheeler* will move to the right and *Wharton* to the left, to cover and protect our flanks and report movements of enemy; *Pegram* to fall to the rear, and report to commanding general as a reserve.

9th. Tonight, if the enemy has gained his position in our front ready for action, *Wheeler* and *Wharton,* with their whole commands, will make a night march to the right and left, turn the enemy's flank, gain his rear, and vigorously assail his trains and rear guard, blocking the roads and impeding his movements every way, holding themselves ready to assail his retreating forces.

10th. All quartermasters, commissaries, and ordnance officers will remain at their proper posts, discharging their appropriate duties. Supplies and baggage should be ready, packed for a move forward or backward as the results of the day may require, and the trains should be in position, out of danger, teamsters all present, and quartermasters in charge.

11th. Should we be compelled to retire, *Polk's* corps will move on Shelbyville and *Hardee's* on Manchester pike; trains in front; cavalry in rear.

> *Braxton Bragg,*
> General,
> Commanding

[*OR* 20, pt. 1, pp. 672–73.]

On Sunday, December 28, Rosecrans stopped for a day of rest. However he sent units on reconnaissance missions that developed enough information to indicate *Bragg* was concentrating at Murfreesboro.

On Monday Rosecrans again began to move toward *Bragg's* army. On the left Crittenden pushed south from Stewarts Creek and by dark was just outside of Murfreesboro. Thomas remained on Crittenden's right and in position to support either wing.

In midafternoon Rosecrans had received a report that the Confederates were retreating from Murfreesboro. These were probably troops belonging to *Wheeler's* cavalry brigade, who were falling back before Crittenden's advance. Acting upon this erroneous information, Wood was ordered to advance, cross Stones River, and occupy Murfreesboro. Shortly after the order was issued, the mistake was realized and the movement was cancelled. But before the new instructions reached Colonel Charles G. Harker, his brigade crossed the river and moved toward Wayne's Hill. Harker attacked up the hill and was able to gain the top but was stopped when the defenders received reinforcements. After dark Harker was ordered to retreat and recrossed Stones River. Had Union forces been able to hold Wayne's Hill on the night of December 29 and through the next day, the entire character of the Battle of Stones River would have been different.

McCook marched east from Triune and by night had reached a position along Overall Creek, just four and a half miles from

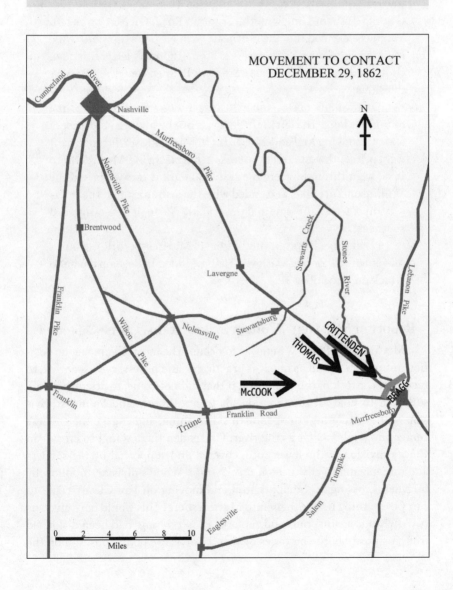

MOVEMENT TO CONTACT
DECEMBER 29, 1862

Murfreesboro. He failed, however, to make contact with the right flank of Thomas's Center Wing. On December 30 McCook began to move forward in order to tie-in his left with Thomas's right. As he moved forward he began to run into increased resistance from the Confederate skirmish line and eventually the left of *Bragg's* main line of defense.

By dark McCook had contacted Thomas's right. McCook's line ran southward across the Wilkinson Turnpike to the intersection of Gresham Lane with the Franklin Road. On McCook's left, Thomas extended the line northeast with Negley's division, while maintaining Rousseau in reserve. From Thomas's left Crittenden continued the line northeastward with Palmer's and then Wood's divisions.

On the night of December 30 Rosecrans's army occupied a line four miles long. The left of the line was on the high ground west of and overlooking McFadden's Ford of the Stones River. From there it went in a southwest direction, crossed the Nashville-Murfreesboro Pike, went through where the National Park is today, crossed the Wilkinson Turnpike, and ended with the army's right at the intersection of Gresham Lane and the Franklin Road. It generally faced southeast.

Having fixed *Bragg's* army in front of Murfreesboro, Rosecrans's movement to contact was over. He proceeded to develop a plan to attack on December 31.

Report of Maj. Gen. William S. Rosecrans, USA—Continued

McCook [the Right Wing] was to occupy the most advantageous position, refusing his right as much as practicable and necessary to secure it, to receive the attack of the enemy; or, if that did not come, to attack himself, sufficient to hold all the force on his front; Thomas and Palmer's [division of the Left Wing] to open with skirmishing, and engage the enemy's center and [right] as far as the river; Crittenden [Left Wing] to cross Van Cleve's division at the lower ford, covered and supported by the sappers and miners, and to advance on *Breckinridge;* Wood's division to follow by brigades, crossing at the upper ford and moving on Van Cleve's right, to carry everything before them into Murfreesboro. This would have given us two divisions against one, and, as soon as *Breckinridge* had been dislodged from his position, the batteries of Wood's division, taking position on the

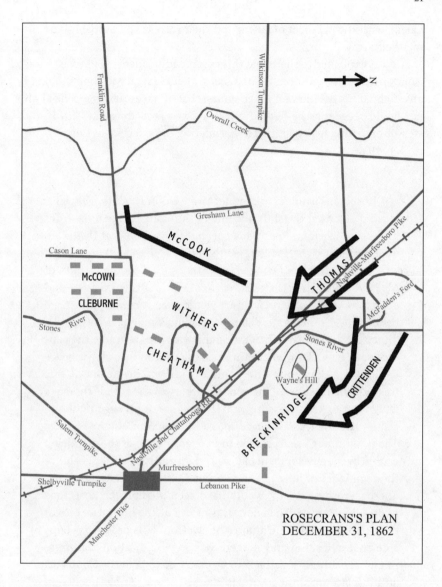

ROSECRANS'S PLAN
DECEMBER 31, 1862

heights east of Stones River, in advance, would see the enemy's works in reverse, would dislodge them, and enable Palmer's division to press them back, and drive them westward across the river or through the woods, while Thomas, sustaining the movement on the center, would advance on the right of Palmer, crushing their right, and Crittenden's corps, advancing, would take Murfreesboro, and then, moving westward on the Franklin road, get in their flank and rear and drive them into the country toward

Salem, with the prospect of cutting off their retreat and probably destroying their army.

It was explained to them that this combination, insuring us a vast superiority on our left, required for its success that General McCook should be able to hold his position for three hours; that, if necessary to recede at all, he should recede, as he had advanced on the preceding day, slowly and steadily, refusing his right, thereby rendering our success certain. [*OR* 20, pt. 1, p. 192.]

Rosecrans planned to conduct an envelopment of *Bragg's* right. Having observed the shift of some of the Confederate units from his left to his right, Rosecrans correctly surmised that they were weak on their right, his left. He therefore planned a two-division attack by Crittenden's wing across Stones River in the vicinity of McFadden's Ford. This attack was to overpower the defenders and push into Murfreesboro, where it would then turn west and move behind the Confederate defenses, forcing *Bragg* to fight in two directions or retreat. An additional advantage would be the capture of Wayne's Hill, where Union artillery would be able to place flanking fire along the entire length of the Confederate line. While this was in progress, Crittenden's other division and Thomas's wing were to keep pressure on the remainder of *Bragg's* right and center, holding them in place, and at the appropriate time attack. Thomas's attack was designed to take advantage of the confusion caused by the envelopment of *Bragg's* right and to destroy or capture the remainder of his right and center. With both Crittenden and Thomas pushing west it would have been possible for Rosecrans to present *Bragg* with a major disaster by cutting his line of retreat to Tullahoma. On the Union right, McCook was order to occupy a defensive position and as there was some indication that *Bragg* might be planning an attack, to be prepared to hold the Confederates in place until they were outflanked or cut off by the attacks of Crittenden and Thomas. Depending on developments, McCook could change over from the defense to the offense and attack if the opportunity presented itself.

On December 28 *Bragg* began moving his divisions into defensive positions on either side of Stones River to the west, northwest, and north of Murfreesboro. The position was not a good one, as Stones River divided *Bragg's* army. In a defensive battle, if the need arose to shift forces left or right, the river, although shallow and narrow, could make such moves time-consuming.

The left of *Bragg's* defensive line stopped on the Franklin Road. As McCook's divisions moved into position on December 29 and 30, *Bragg* became concerned that he was about to be attacked on and beyond his left flank. On Tuesday, December 30, he decided to take the initiative and go on the offense. He began shifting forces to his left in preparation to outflank the Union right and then conduct an envelopment designed to drive Rosecrans's right northward and back to and beyond the Nashville-Murfreesboro Pike. Such an attack, if successful, would not only destroy much of the Union army but also cut the remaining divisions' lines of communication and supply to Nashville.

Report of Gen. *Braxton Bragg*, CSA, Commanding Army of Tennessee

Late on Monday it became apparent the enemy was extending his right, so as to flank us on the left. *McCown's* division, in reserve, was promptly thrown to that flank and added to the command of Lieutenant General *Polk.* The enemy not meeting our expectations of making an attack on Tuesday, which was consumed in artillery firing and heavy skirmishing, with the exception of a dash late in the evening on the left of *Withers'* division, which was repulsed and severely punished, it was determined to assail him on Wednesday morning, the 31st. For this purpose, *Cleburne's* division, *Hardee's* corps, was moved from the second line on the right to the corresponding position on the left, and Lieutenant General *Hardee* was ordered to that point and assigned to the command of that [*Cleburne's* division] and *McCown's* division. This disposition, the result of necessity, left me no reserve, but *Breckinridge's* command on the right, now not threatened, was regarded as a source of supply for any re-enforcements absolutely necessary to other parts of the field. Stones River, at its then stage, was fordable at almost any point for infantry, and at short intervals perfectly practicable for artillery. [*OR* 20, pt. 1, pp. 663–64.]

His troop movements for the attack complete, *Bragg's* army was deployed from south of the Franklin Road to the high ground, Wayne's Hill, northwest of Murfreesboro then east to the

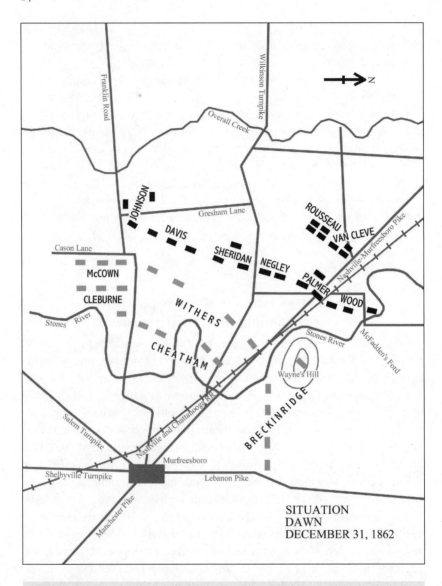

SITUATION
DAWN
DECEMBER 31, 1862

Lebanon Pike. The left of *Bragg's* line of battle was Major General *John P. McCown's* three-brigade division, which was deployed south of the Franklin Road and facing west. Directly behind *McCown* were the four brigades of Major General *Patrick R. Cleburne's* division. *McCown* and *Cleburne* were under the command of Lieutenant General *William J. Hardee.* North of the Franklin Road were deployed the divisions of Lieutenant General *Leonidas Polk's* corps.

The four brigades of Major General *Jones M. Withers's* division were deployed from just north of the Franklin Road, across the Wilkinson Turnpike to the Nashville-Murfreesboro Pike. *Withers's* line covered 3,100 yards (1.75 miles). Major General *Benjamin F. Cheatham* placed his four-brigade division behind *Withers's* left and center. Cheatham's line was 1,700 yards long and touched the Franklin Road and the Wilkinson Turnpike. To *Polk's* right, across Stones River, Major General *John C. Breckinridge's* division was placed to protect the Confederate right and to be available to provide reserves where needed. *Breckinridge's* left was on Wayne's Hill, where the golf course is today. This predominate terrain feature anchored *Bragg's* right. From Wayne's Hill, *Breckinridge's* line went east for two miles to the Lebanon Pike.

Report of Gen. *Braxton Bragg*, CSA—Continued

These dispositions completed, Lieutenant-General *Hardee* was ordered to assail the enemy at daylight on Wednesday, the 31st, the attack to be taken up by Lieutenant-General *Polk's* command in succession to the right flank, the move to be made by a constant wheel to the right, on *Polk's* right flank as a pivot, the object being to force the enemy back on Stone's River, and, if practicable, by the aid of the cavalry, cut him off from his base of operations and supplies by the Nashville pike. The lines were now bivouacked at a distance in places of not more than 500 yards, the campfires of the two being within distinct view. *Wharton's* cavalry brigade had been held on our left to watch and check the movements of the enemy in that direction, and to prevent his cavalry from gaining the railroad in our rear, the preservation of which was of vital importance. In this he was aided by Brig. Gen. *A. Buford,* who had a small command of about 600 new cavalry. The duty was most ably, gallantly, and successfully performed. [*OR* 20, pt.1, p. 664.]

At dawn on the last day of 1862, both armies were poised to attack from their left into the right flank of the other. Whoever moved first with the greater combat power would be the attacker, forcing the other to assume the defense. In preparation for his attack, Rosecrans had units crossing Stones River on his left. However, by the smallest of margins *Bragg* launched his attack first, and Rosecrans recalled his units as he assumed the role of defender.

Chapter 2

THE WEST FLANK
WEDNESDAY, DECEMBER 31, 1862

The start point for your on-the-ground tour and study of the Battle of Stones River is Exit 78 of Interstate 24. If you are driving north or south on I-24, at Exit 78 leave the interstate and drive west on the Franklin Road, Tennessee Highway 96, for 0.6 mile if you are driving south on I-24 or 0.8 mile if you are driving north on I-24. From Exit 78 drive the prescribed distance and turn left into a parking lot. Park in this area, get out of your car, and face west, the direction you were driving. Be careful of traffic.

If you are at the Stones River National Battlefield Visitor's Center, exit the National Battlefield and take a right on to the Old Nashville Highway, which was the Nashville-Murfreesboro Pike in 1862, and drive south for 0.7 mile to the entry road for Thompson Lane (the overpass). Turn right and drive for 0.1 mile to Thompson Lane. Turn left on to Thompson Lane and drive for 1.7 miles to the intersection with Old Fort Parkway, Tennessee Highway 96. Turn right on to Old Fort Parkway, drive for 0.9 mile, and turn left into a parking lot. Park in this area, get out of your car and face west, the direction you were driving. Be careful of traffic.

Stop 1—*McCown's* Attack

The road you have been driving on was the Franklin Road in 1862. The ground on both sides of the road was farmland and cornfields. To your right front was a wood line of cedar trees.

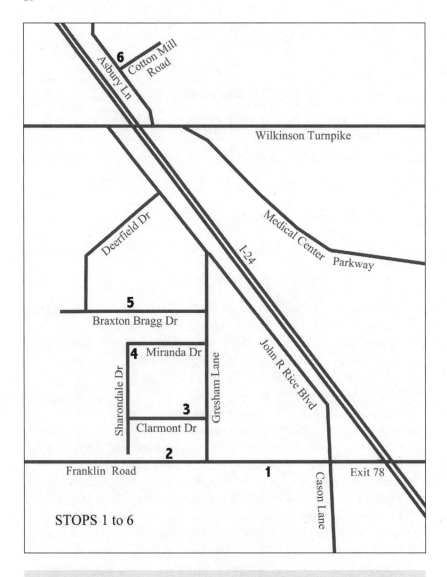

STOPS 1 to 6

You are in the vicinity of the Confederate left flank and the Union right flank. The Confederate first line of battle was 300 yards behind you. To the left, south, of the Franklin Road were the three brigades of Major General *John P. McCown's* division. *McCown's* right touched the Franklin Road, was perpendicular to the road, and went south along Cason Lane, which is there today, for 900 yards. His division faced west. Behind *McCown's* Division between

Cason Lane and Stones River, Major General *Patrick R. Cleburne* deployed the four brigades of his division, so they also faced west. These two divisions were positioned to envelope, outflank, the Union right and drive it back to the Nashville-Murfreesboro Pike.

To *McCown's* right and your right rear was Major General *Jones M. Withers's* division. *Withers's* left flank brigade, commanded by Colonel *J. Q. Loomis,* was 400 yards to your right rear, its left flank touching the Franklin Road. The other three brigades of *Withers's* Division were deployed on line to *Loomis's* right. This line went for 3,100 yards (1.75 miles) to the Nashville-Murfreesboro Pike. The left two brigades of *Withers's* Division faced west, while the right two brigades faced northwest. Major General *Benjamin F Cheatham's* division was deployed behind and facing in the same direction as *Withers's* Division. The left of both of these divisions were positioned to assist in driving back the Union right while their right brigades maintained pressure on the Union center and left.

Report of Lieut. Gen. *William J. Hardee,* CSA, Commanding *Hardee's* Corps, Army of Tennessee

In the afternoon of [December 30] I received instructions from the commanding general to proceed to the left, to take command of *McCown's* division, to place it in position, and to move *Cleburne's* division from our extreme right in the same direction. The order was communicated to *Cleburne,* and I proceeded at once to the left. I found *McCown's* division, consisting of three brigades, in two lines—*Ector's* and *Rains'* brigades in the first, and *McNair's* in the second line, with *Rains'* brigade so situated as to be enfiladed by a battery from the enemy. Orders were given to rectify the position of *Rains,* and to place *McNair* on the first line. *Cleburne's* division was brought forward and placed 500 yards in rear of *McCown,* as a second line. During the night, the commanding general having determined to attack the enemy on our left, Brigadier-General *Wharton* was ordered to report to me, and I was instructed, with the two divisions mentioned and *Wharton's* cavalry, to commence the attack at dawn the next morning. The new position, which my command now occupied, was embraced in the angle between the Salem turnpike and the Triune [Franklin] road. About half a mile from Murfreesboro, on the Nashville road, the Wilkinson turnpike diverges to the left, passing nearly equidistant between it and the Triune [Franklin] road. Each of these roads crosses Stones River about 1½ miles west of the town. The river makes a bend in the shape of a horseshoe to the west, and the roads cross at the bases of the bend. The enemy's right was about three-quarters of a mile beyond the river, with their line [on] the Triune [Franklin] road, and extending almost northwardly toward the Wilkinson pike and the Nashville road. The force under my immediate command Wednesday morning was 10,045 infantry and artillery, under *McCown* and *Cleburne*, and 2,000 cavalry, under Brigadier-General *Wharton*.

Major-General *McCown* having failed to get *McNair's* brigade on the line of battle Tuesday night, as directed by me, the brigade was moved into position early the next morning, and *McCown* advanced with his division against the enemy, about 600 yards distant, with *McNair* on the right of *Ector* and with *Rains'* brigade on the left. The division of Major-General *Cleburne* was about 500 yards in rear of *McCown*, as a second line. The two divisions were posted on the left of Lieutenant-General *Polk's* command. The troops advanced with animation and soon became hotly engaged. The enemy were broken and driven through a cedar brake after a rapid and successful charge by *McCown's* command, in which Brigadier-General [August] Willich and many prisoners were taken.

I had ordered *McCown* and *Cleburne*, as they crushed the line of the enemy, to swing round by a continued change of direction to the right, with [Lieutenant General *Leonidas*] *Polk's* left as a pivot, while *Wharton* was to make a diversion on their flank and rear. This was done by *Cleburne*, but was not so promptly executed by *McCown*, on account of the position of the enemy in his front. *McCown* continued westwardly, fighting toward Overall's Creek, far to our left, while *Cleburne*, executing the maneuver, changed his direction northeastwardly toward the Wilkinson turnpike, which placed him on the right of *McCown* and filled the interval between *McCown* and [Lieutenant General *Leonidas*] *Polk*. The line, now single and without support, engaged and drove the enemy with great carnage through the fields and cedar brakes which lie between the Triune [Franklin] and Wilkinson roads. Before this gap in the line was filled by *Cleburne*, *McCown's* right flank was exposed. *McNair* halted his brigade, while *Liddell* advanced gallantly, filling the interval, covered *McNair's* unprotected right, and engaged a superior force of the enemy posted behind a rail fence. These two brigades charged the enemy with impetuosity, took their battery, and pursued their broken and fleeing regiments before *Ector* and *Rains* could be brought into action. [*OR* 20, pt. 1, pp. 773–74.]

The right flank of Rosecrans's army was 500 yards in front of you and just to the right, north, side of the Franklin Road. Near the Union flank a small road, Gresham Lane, began and went directly north, where it intersected with the Wilkinson Turnpike. Brigadier General Richard W. Johnson's three-brigade division was deployed at the intersection and was the right flank division. Brigadier General August Willich's brigade, the extreme right brigade, was in position just west of Gresham Lane and north of the Franklin Road. Willich's brigade faced south and west. Brigadier General Edward N. Kirk's brigade was to Willich's left. Kirk's line faced southeast and went at a 45-degree angle from Willich's left. Colonel Philemon P. Baldwin's brigade was in a reserve position 1,800 yards behind Willich and west of Grisham Lane.

From Johnson's left, Brigadier General Jefferson C. Davis's three-brigade division extended the line 1,300 yards to the northeast. On Davis's left, Brigadier General Philip H. Sheridan's division extended the Union line 1,400 yards north to the Wilkinson Turnpike.

Johnson's left and Davis's right were 400 yards to your right front. The ground to your right was a cornfield and, beyond that, a woods. The Union line was along the southeast edge of the woods.

The first Confederate force to attack here was *McCown's* Division.

Report of Maj. Gen. *John P. McCown*, CSA, Commanding *McCown's* Division, *Hardee's* Corps, Army of Tennessee

At the dawn of day, in obedience to orders from Lieutenant-General *Hardee*, I moved my reserve brigade (*McNair's*) and placed it on my right, and moved upon the enemy in my front, about 600 or 800 yards distant. I will here state that Major-General *Cleburne's* division was placed in rear of my command as a second line. The Triune [Franklin] road turned square to the left about 150 yards in front of Lieutenant-General *Polk's* left, and again square to the right about 400 yards from the first turn. An open field [was] on my entire front; on the right of the field and in front of Lieutenant-General *Polk's* left was a cedar brake.

As I advanced, my right flank received a galling fire from this brake, as well as in my front, from both infantry and artillery. My men advanced steadily, reserving their fire until they were but a short distance from the

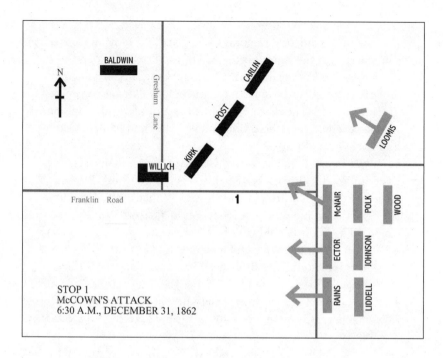

STOP 1
McCOWN'S ATTACK
6:30 A.M., DECEMBER 31, 1862

enemy's position. A volley was delivered, and their position and batteries taken with the bayonet, leaving the ground covered with his dead and wounded, leaving also many prisoners in our hands; among them Brigadier General [August] Willich, captured by Mr. *James Stone* volunteer aide to General *McNair.* The enemy made several attempts to rally, but failed, being closely pressed by my men, their defeat becoming almost a rout. The enemy was pressed near a mile. The force of the enemy in my front prevented me throwing forward my left wing as soon as instructed by Lieutenant-General *Hardee.*

About this time a heavy force was brought against my right flank. Brigadier-General *McNair,* commanding the brigade on my right, discovered their movements and halted his brigade. I directed General *McNair* to face his brigade to the right, and file it to the right to check this movement. The moment was critical. I sent the same order to Generals *Ector* and *Rains,* which was promptly obeyed by them, leaving a strong body of the enemy in their front. Seeing General *Liddell's* brigade [of *Cleburne's* Division] in the rear, I brought it forward and placed it on my right to cover this change of front. General *Liddell* became at once engaged with a largely superior force, the enemy under shelter of a fence, General *Liddell* in an open field. He gallantly maintained his ground until General *McNair's* brigade was placed on his left. General *McNair* at once moved upon the enemy, pushing his right on his center and forcing him from his position for half a mile. The enemy was here posted behind a rail fence. Again General *McNair* advanced across an open field for nearly 400 yards, and drove them from their position, capturing all but two guns of their battery—one of those afterward captured. General *Liddell's* brigade cooperated in this action. The enemy was actively pursued for about three-quarters of a mile, where the division was halted and ammunition issued—40 rounds having been nearly exhausted. [*OR* 20, pt. 1, p. 912.]

McCown's attack took his division from behind you through your location and to your right front to the intersection of Gresham Lane with the Franklin Road and beyond. Here *McCown's* line turned to the right, north, and, reinforced with *Liddell's* Brigade, continued his attack. This turn north began the envelopment of the Union right for which *Bragg* had planned.

McCown's right brigade was Brigadier General *Evander McNair's*. This brigade began its attack from a position 300 yards behind you and to the left of the Franklin Road. As the brigade advanced, it angled to its right front, which brought it across to the right side of the road. As it passed by where you are, it was to your right.

Report of Brig. Gen. *Evander McNair,* CSA, Commanding *McNair's* Brigade, *McCown's* Division, *Hardee's* Corps, Army of Tennessee

At 6 a.m. on December 31, I moved forward about 150 yards, and joined Brigadier-General *Ector's* brigade on the right. We then moved forward together to meet the enemy, who was in force, immediately in front of us. We had advanced but a short distance before the enemy's pickets and sharpshooters opened fire upon us. At this point I cautioned my brigade to reserve their fire and push forward. I had advanced but a short distance when the fire became general along the line, indicating that we were near the enemy in position; and at that moment he opened upon us with a six-gun battery a most terrific fire of shell and grape shot. I then ordered a charge, which was responded to with alacrity and good will. It was but a moment until his battery was ours, his long line of infantry routed and dispersed, and the strong position which he held in security but a moment before covered with his dead and wounded. My command continued to pursue the enemy for three-quarters of a mile, pouring a destructive fire into his broken and scattered ranks, strewing the ground with his killed and wounded. At this point, discovering that the support on my right had not come up as expected by me, and the enemy having thrown a heavy force partly in my rear, their sharpshooters having already commenced to fire upon my wounded men, I halted my brigade and moved them to the rear by the flank, for the purpose of protecting my wounded men. After having moved but a short distance, I discovered Brigadier-General *Liddell* advancing with his brigade on my right, thus obviating any further movement on my part in the direction in which I was then moving. I then immediately wheeled my brigade; thus changing my front and joining Brigadier-General *Liddell* on his left. Again I ordered a forward movement, pushing the enemy back upon his center in a direction due north from that point. Here a heavy skirmish commenced with fresh forces of the enemy, supposed to be about one division [actually one brigade]; they were driven from every position for the distance of half a mile. Here they took position, protecting themselves behind a rail fence to the right-oblique of my line of battle. The enemy [Baldwin's brigade] had already engaged General *Liddell's* brigade, on my right, holding them in check and pouring a destructive fire into their ranks. Discovering his critical position, I immediately ordered a forward movement, and had to advance across an open field a distance of about 400 yards. Again I directed my brigade to reserve their fire, which was done, until we had advanced within about 300 yards. Though the enemy poured a heavy fire upon my line from behind their cover, yet not a man faltered, but pushed forward with the stern determination of veterans. Here I ordered a charge, and, as before, officers and men seemed to vie with each other in performing acts of gallantry, and one simultaneous shout rent the air. The enemy, made bold by his front being protected by the fences, held his position with more tenacity than usual; but the terrific fire poured upon his ranks, and the velocity with which my men charged, drove him from his position in confusion, thus relieving Brigadier-General *Liddell's* brigade, which was already faltering under the heavy fire of the enemy, thus for the second time driving the foe from his choice and strong position. This was perhaps the hardest contested engagement of the day. Here my loss in killed and wounded was heavy, though small compared with that of the enemy. [*OR* 20, pt. 1, pp. 944–45.]

McNair's initial attack was against Kirk's brigade. This brigade was Johnson's left brigade and was located to your right front. After the collapse of Kirk's defenses, *McNair* began to turn north and was the pivot point on which the Confederate force to his left began to wheel to the right.

To *McNair's* left was Brigadier General *Matthew D. Ector's* brigade. This brigade was the center unit of *McCown's* line. It was also located to the left of the Franklin Road. *Ector's* attack struck the Union defenses west of the Gresham Lane–Franklin Road intersection.

Report of Brig. Gen. *Matthew D. Ector,* CSA, Commanding *Ector's* Brigade, *McCown's* Division, *Hardee's* Corps, Army of Tennessee

During the night of the 30th ultimo, I was ordered to have my command in readiness to move upon the enemy at daylight on the next morning. General *McNair's* brigade was to move up in position on my right and General *Rains'* brigade on my left. The enemy were known to be in strong force immediately in front of us, supported by several batteries. These were posted near the edge of the timber. There was a level field between us, about 500 yards across it. A few minutes after 6 a.m. on December 31, the two brigades had arrived in the position indicated, and the command "Forward march," was given. The three brigades moved off together. When we had arrived within about 200 yards of the enemy's batteries in front of my brigade, they opened fire upon us. Immediately the order was given to charge. The enemy were not expecting such a movement on our part. Their infantry fired into us about this time. None of the three brigades faltered for a moment. When we had arrived within about 100 yards of their batteries, I ordered my men to fire. We poured a hot and deadly fire into them and continued to advance. Such determination and courage was perfectly irresistible. My brigade was within 30 yards of their cannon when they fired the second round. Quite a number of my brigade were killed and wounded, but the gaps made by the canister and small-arms closed up in an instant. In this charge Col. *J. C. Burks,* commanding the Eleventh Texas Regiment, received a mortal wound. Their infantry gave way about the time we reached their batteries. They attempted to form again behind a second battery. We pressed upon them so rapidly they soon gave way the second time. At a fence they made a short stand, but were driven from it.

We passed over two cannon which they had attempted to get off with. They continued to keep up a running fight for awhile, taking shelter behind the farm-houses which lay in the line of their retreat. The rout soon, however, became complete. I soon discovered that we had separated from General *McNair's* brigade. After pursuing the enemy 2½ miles, I halted my command, faced it to the right, intending to proceed with it in the direction of a heavy firing of small-arms; in that direction I supposed General *McNair's* brigade had gone. We had captured quite a number of prisoners, who had been sent to the rear. The enemy in their hasty retreat had left their camp equipage; and guns, blankets, overcoats, and knapsacks marked the line of their retreat. General *Wharton's* cavalry brigade continued in pursuit of those we had been after, and killed and captured (as I have since learned) many of them. [*OR* 20, pt. 1, pp. 926–27.]

Ector's attack struck the extreme right of the Union defense, Willich's brigade. Added by *McNair's* successful attack on his right, *Ector* was able to overrun and break up Willich's defense. However, instead of turning north, right, as *McNair* had, *Ector,* with *Rains's* Brigade on his left, continued to pursue the retreating defenders to the northwest. This pursuit took these two brigades 2.1 miles to Overall Creek and beyond. This opened up a gap in the left of the Confederate line and removed combat power from the Confederate envelopment at a critical time.

Return to your car for the drive to Stop 2.

Depart your present location by turning left and continuing to drive west on the Franklin Road for 0.3 mile to the parking lot of the Franklin Road Baptist Church. After you have driven 0.1 mile, you will go through the intersection with Gresham Lane. Gresham Lane will be on your right. Turn right in to the parking lot of the Franklin Road Baptist Church. Be extremely careful of children as you drive in this parking lot. Park, get out of your car, walk to within 10 yards of the Franklin Road, and face the road. You are facing south. You are parking here courtesy of the church's pastor, Dr. Mike Norris, and his congregation. This is all private land, so keep noise to a minimum and respect their privacy.

Stop 2–The Union Right Flank

The ground to your right and in front of you, across the road, was an open field. To your left, in the angle formed by the intersection of Gresham Lane and the Franklin Road, there was a square-shaped open wood.

Willich's brigade occupied the ground where you are. This brigade generally was lined up on the north side of the Franklin Road and facing south. The intersection of the Franklin Road and Gresham Lane is 200 yards to your left. Willich's left flank regiment, the Thirty-ninth Indiana, was to your left and just on the other side of Gresham Lane. To that regiment's right, still to your left, was the Thirty-second Indiana. To the right of the Thirty-second Indiana and to your right was the Forty-ninth Ohio. You are between the positions of the Thirty-second Indiana and the Forty-ninth Ohio. Just behind you, in a reserve position, was the Eighty-ninth Illinois. To the right of the Forty-ninth Ohio and Eighty-ninth Illinois and facing west was the Fifteenth Ohio. Between the Forty-ninth Ohio and the Fifteenth Ohio was Battery A, First Ohio Artillery. To the left of Willich's brigade and on the other side of Gresham Lane was Kirk's brigade.

Sunrise was at 7:00 a.m., but there was intermittent ground fog and haze, so visibility was reduced when the attack struck this position.

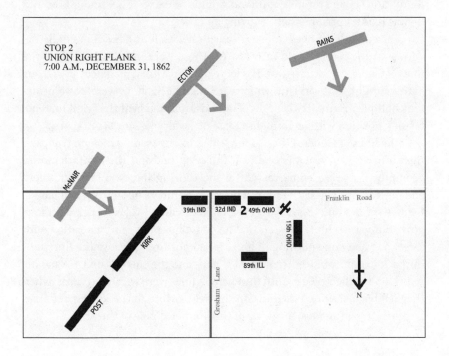

> Willich's brigade was attacked by *Ector's* Brigade and out-flanked by *Rains's* Brigade. During this attack Willich was captured. He was exchanged and returned to command his brigade in time to fight at Chickamauga. Command of the brigade was passed to Colonel William Wallace of the Fifteenth Ohio and then to Colonel William H. Gibson of the Forty-ninth Ohio, who wrote the brigade report.

Report of Col. William H. Gibson, USA, Commanding First Brigade, Second Division, Right Wing, Army of the Cumberland

At dawn of day [December 31] orders were received to build fires and make coffee. In a few moments after I met General Willich, who remarked that he would be absent a few moments at the headquarters of General Johnson, and in case anything occurred in front of our pickets he directed me to rally the Thirty-ninth and Thirty-second to their support.

At 6:25, and soon after meeting the general, firing was heard on General Kirk's right. The brigade was instantly ordered to take arms, and Lieutenant Miles, of the staff, was dispatched for General Willich. He was found, and started for his command, but his horse was shot under him, and he was made a prisoner before giving an order.

The enemy advanced upon our position with four heavy lines of battle, with a strong reserve held in mass. All these were in full view before the lines of General Kirk gave way. His left extended a great distance beyond our extreme right, and was thrown forward, so that his lines were, to some extent, oblique to ours. To the right of our position, and near the Franklin road, he took position with an immense force of cavalry [*Wharton's* Brigade].

The lines of General Kirk soon yielded to an assault which no troops in the world could have withstood. The Thirty-second and Thirty-ninth moved promptly, but were embarrassed by the retiring forces, and their safety endangered by an assault in overwhelming numbers upon front and flanks. Lieutenant Belding [Battery A, First Ohio Artillery] moved back with four guns, but was so hotly pressed that he could not put them in position with safety. He had done nothing in his original position, because the lines falling back in our front were between his guns and the enemy's line. He and his men stood at their pieces until the enemy's lines were within 50 yards, when they fell back, leaving two guns on the field, owing to the killing of horses attached to one and the breaking of the [limber's] pole of the other.

Colonel William H. Gibson, USA. Massachusetts Commandery Military Order of the Loyal Legion and the U.S. Army Military History Institute.

The Forty-ninth remained in its position until ordered to retire, and fought desperately at every rod. The Fifteenth Ohio, Colonel Wallace, delivered six rounds [volleys] before falling back, while the Thirty-second and Thirty-ninth Indiana bravely contested the ground on the right. The courage and activity of these regiments kept the enemy in check until our artillery horses could be hitched, and the dead of the foe showed the telling effect of their fire. With cavalry on their right, infantry assailing them on the left, and heavy masses rushing to the assault in front, these regiments were directed to retire as the only escape from annihilation or capture.

Edgarton's battery [Battery E, First Ohio Artillery], after being uncovered by the lines of General Kirk, opened fire, but before three rounds were delivered the enemy reached the guns and captured the pieces. Unchecked, the foe rushed on, and as his advance reached Goodspeed's battery, his second line reached Edgarton's battery, and that gallant officer being wounded and made prisoner, his men continued to defend themselves with their gun-swabs. The Fifteenth Ohio, Colonel Wallace, had got into position and, under cover of its fire, the Forty-ninth Ohio and Eighty-ninth Illinois were directed to retire by the flank. The Thirty-second and Thirty-ninth were now retiring in good order.

At this juncture, learning nothing of General Willich, I felt it my duty to exert myself as far as possible to save the command. Goodspeed's battery, [Battery A, First Ohio Artillery] under command of Lieutenant Belding, was ordered to retire to a position beyond an open field, and Lieutenant-Colonel Drake was directed to place the Forty-ninth Ohio in position at the same point.

Here I had hoped to rally the whole brigade, but Lieutenant-Colonel Drake was killed, and Major Porter, of the Forty-ninth, was severely wounded. My horse was shot, and most of our field officers were disabled or dismounted by the enemy's fire. From my position, looking to our center, I could see our whole line fall back rapidly in some disorder, though a constant fire was kept up to the right. [*OR* 20, pt. 1, pp. 304–5.]

The Confederate attack was successful in using surprise and overwhelming combat power against the Union defenders at this point. The result was a collapse of the Union right flank. Kirk's defenses collapsed first, his troops retreating west and northwest through Willich's position. This assisted the Confederate attack against Willich and caused his defense to collapse. His troops also retreated in a northwesterly direction.

However, their success would also cause the attacking Confederates problems. *McNair's* Brigade made a right wheel through this vicinity and continued the attack to the north. *Ector's* and *Rain's* Brigades continued to pursue the fleeing troops from Willich's and Kirk's brigades to the northwest. This caused a large gap to develop between *McNair* and the brigades on his left and drew off Confederate combat power that was needed to continue the attack north.

Return to your car for the drive to Stop 3

Drive to the Franklin Road, turn left, and drive 0.1 mile to the intersection with Gresham Lane. Turn left on to Gresham Lane and drive north for 0.3 mile to Clarmont Drive. As you turn left and drive on Gresham Lane, Willich's brigade was on your left and Kirk's brigade was on your right. Turn left on to Clarmont Drive and drive for 25 yards, pull over to the right, and stop. Get out of your car and face back toward the intersection of Clarmont Drive and Gresham Lane, which is east. Be careful, as this is a residential area. There are children playing here, and when school is in session there may be school busses present. All the land around you is private property; do not trespass.

Stop 3—*Johnson's* Attack

As you look back toward Gresham Lane, you are facing east. In 1862, where you are was a large open field that extended west from Gresham Lane. Five hundred yards north of you, to your left, the field turned into cornfields and then woods. To your right was a cornfield then the square, open wood that was next to the Franklin Road. On the other side of Gresham Lane was a large woods.

You are located directly behind the two right flank Union brigades. Willich's brigade was 500 yards to your right. This brigade was on the right, west, side of Gresham Lane and was facing south and west. To Willich's left and 400 yards to your right front, on the east side of Gresham Lane, was Kirk's brigade. Both of these brigades were part of Johnson's division. Johnson's other brigade, Baldwin's, was located 1,000 yards to your left in a reserve position. Davis's three-brigade division was to the left of Johnson's.

The day before, December 30, Davis, along with Sheridan's division, had moved in a southeasterly direction, which brought his division into this area. Rosecrans ordered the move so that the left of McCook's Right Wing would have flank contact with Thomas's Center Wing. This move also made *Bragg* believe he was about to be attacked on his left flank. At dawn on December 31 Davis had deployed his three brigades into a defensive line. From right to left they were Post's, Carlin's, and Woodruff's brigades.

Report of Brig. Gen. Jefferson C. Davis, USA, Commanding First Division, Right Wing, Army of the Cumberland

Receiving directions at this time from General McCook to desist from any further offensive demonstration further than what might be necessary to hold my position, I ordered the troops to rest for the night on their arms. Two brigades of General Johnson's division, heretofore held in reserve, arrived and took position on my right, about sunset, thus extending our line of battle beyond the old Franklin and Murfreesboro road. These brigades were commanded by Generals Willich and Kirk.

The night passed off quietly until about daylight, when the enemy's forces were observed by our pickets to be in motion. Their object could not, however, with certainty, be determined until near sunrise, when a vigorous attack was made upon Willich's and Kirk's brigades. These troops seemed not to have been fully prepared for the assault, and, with little or no resistance, retreated from their position, leaving their artillery in the hands of the enemy. This left my right brigade [Post's] exposed to a flank movement, which the enemy was now rapidly executing, and compelled me to order Post's brigade to fall back and partially change its front. Simultaneous with this movement the enemy commenced a heavy and very determined attack on both Carlin's and Woodruff's brigades. [*OR* 20, pt. 1, 263–64.]

Turn left and face to the north. Gresham Lane is to your right, east.

Davis's right brigade was Colonel Sydney Post's. This brigade was initially located 350 yards to your right. When Willich's and Kirk's brigades collapsed and retreated, Post's right flank was exposed. Davis ordered Post to bring his line back so that it faced south. In that location, Post's brigade was 200 yards in front of you and facing you. All four regiments of the brigade were deployed on line. The center regiment was the Fifty-ninth Illinois. This regiment was directly in front of you and on this side Gresham Lane. To the left of the Fifty-ninth and on the other side of Gresham Lane were the Seventy-fourth Illinois and Seventy-fifth Illinois. To the right of the Fifty-ninth Illinois was the Fifth Wisconsin Battery. To that battery's right were the Twenty-second Indiana and from Kirk's brigade the Seventy-seventh Pennsylvania. The report of the commander of the Fifty-ninth Illinois is representative of the fighting by all these regiments.

Report of Capt. Hendrick E. Paine, USA, Commanding Fifty-ninth Illinois Infantry, First Brigade, First Division, Right Wing, Army of the Cumberland

At daylight, on the morning of the 31st, we were in line of battle, in full view of the enemy, who appeared to be moving in strong force to our right. [This is the first position occupied by the brigade.] I was then ordered, together with Captain Pinney's [Fifth Wisconsin] battery, to hold ourselves as a reserve, and were moved a short distance to the rear; at the same time

Grisham Lane today.

the line of battle was formed in our front, and the firing became heavy both on our right and left.

It soon became evident that the enemy was closely pressing our right, and our lines were rapidly extended in that direction. [This is the second position. The one in front of you.] At the same time my regiment and Captain Pinney's battery were ordered to the front to engage the enemy across an open field. I immediately faced my command in the direction indicated, and moved forward in good order. At the same time the long lines of the enemy appeared on the opposite side of the field, moving directly to our front. When we approached within short musket range, I gave the order to fire, and lie down and load, which order was promptly responded to; at the same instant the enemy's balls came whistling over us in awful proximity to our heads. I do not know how long we remained in that position, but my men poured a deadly and destructive fire upon the enemy, who had laid down to avoid its terrible effects, until regiment after regiment on our right gave way, when I, reluctantly, received the order to fall back. At the same instant Captain Pinney was severely wounded, and the horses from two of his guns were either disabled or killed, when my men gallantly took hold and assisted to haul the guns from the field by hand, exposed all the while to a deadly fire of the enemy's musketry and grape and canister shot. We continued to move to the rear in reasonably good order, forming twice and firing upon the pursuing enemy, until we were beyond the range of his fire. [*OR* 20, pt. 1, p. 273.]

The unit attacking Post at this location was Brigadier General *Bushrod Johnson's* brigade of *Cleburne's* Division. *Johnson's* Brigade, with the other three brigades of *Cleburne's* Division, had begun the morning deployed east of Cason Lane and behind *McCown's* Division. They were in a supporting line to *McCown's* Division and expected to follow *McCown* until called forward to reinforce the attack or to conduct a pursuit of retreating Union forces.

Report of Major General *Patrick R. Cleburne,* CSA, Commanding *Cleburne's* Division, *Hardee's* Corps, Army of Tennessee

Before daylight I formed line, placing *Polk's* brigade, with [*Key's*] battery, on the right; *Johnson's* brigade, with *Darden's* battery, in the center, and *Liddell's* brigade, with the Warren Light Artillery, commanded by Lieutenant *Shannon,* on the left. *Wood's* brigade I placed a short distance in rear of *Polk's.*

It was not yet clear day when I received orders from General *Hardee* to advance. Swinging to the right as I moved forward, I rapidly communicated these instructions to brigade commanders, caused my division to load, and moved forward, stepping short upon the right and full upon the left, so as to swing round my left as directed. General *Cheatham's* left did not move forward at the same moment as my right, and my division, inclining to the left as it advanced, a gap was soon left between us, which General *Hardee* directed General *Wood's* brigade to fill. My whole division was now advancing in line of battle, gradually wheeling to the right as it advanced. My left had not moved half a mile when heavy firing commenced near its front, supposed to be *McCown's* division engaging the enemy. A few moments more, and the enemy's skirmishers opened fire along the right and left center of my division, indicating that instead of being a second line supporting *McCown's* division, I was, in reality, the foremost line on this part of the field, and that *McCown's* line had unaccountably disappeared from my front. Skirmishers were immediately thrown forward, and I pressed on, continuing the difficult wheel under fire, through a country cut up with numerous fences and thickets. There was a great deal of crowding and improper opening out in the center of my line. Driving back the enemy's skirmishers in the face of a heavy fire of shot and shell, I encountered his first solid line of battle at an average distance of three-fourths of a mile from the scene of my bivouac of last night. The left of this line (opposite *Wood's* and *Polk's* brigades) stretched through a large cedar brake; the right (opposite *Liddell's* and *Johnson's*) through open ground. In many parts of the brake the enemy found natural breastworks of limestone rock. In the open ground he covered most of his line behind a string of fence. Opposite my left, where the ground was open, a second line of the enemy, supported by artillery, could be seen a short distance in rear of his first. Here was my first important fight of the day. It extended along my whole line, and was participated in by *McNair's* brigade, of *McCown's* division, which had been placed on my left. [*OR* 20, pt.1, pp. 844–45.]

The development of the gaps between *McCown's* brigades brought *Cleburne's* Division into the front line without warning and before expected. After the left of *Cleburne's* Division complete its right wheel, *Johnson* and *Liddell* were committed to action in the area where you are. *Liddell* attacked across the ground to your left, while *Johnson's* attack went through where you are now.

When *Johnson* completed his change of direction to the north, his line was 200 yards behind you. *Johnson's* Brigade was composed of five Tennessee Infantry Regiments. All five were deployed on line. They were, from left to right, the Twenty-third and Seventeenth, this side of Gresham Lane, and the Twenty-fifth, Forty-fourth, and Thirty-seventh on the other side of the lane. The Jefferson Artillery Battery was assigned the mission of direct support and went into position to the right rear of the Twenty-third Tennessee.

Report of Brig. Gen. *Bushrod R. Johnson,* CSA, Commanding *Johnson's* Brigade, *Cleburne's* Division, *Hardee's* Corps, Army of Tennessee

My brigade moved first over open fields up a gentle ascent for about 1,200 yards, when we reached the summit of the slope, with my [right] within about 150 yards of the Triune [Franklin] road. Here the enemy's balls from cannon and small-arms fell around and in our ranks. Though we had moved out on the second line to support Major-General *McCown's* division, it became evident that there was here nothing before us but the enemy, whose sharpshooters were posted at the fence and in the woods along the north side of the Triune [Franklin] road. We therefore prepared to take our place in the first line. I ordered out skirmishers in front of each

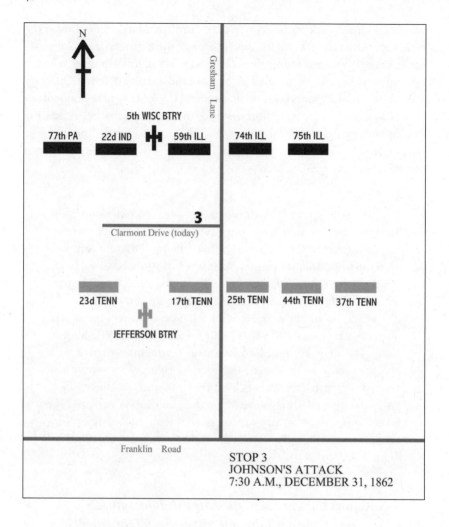

N

Gresham Lane

5th WISC BTRY

77th PA 22d IND 59th ILL 74th ILL 75th ILL

3

Clarmont Drive (today)

23d TENN 17th TENN 25th TENN 44th TENN 37th TENN

JEFFERSON BTRY

Franklin   Road

STOP 3
JOHNSON'S ATTACK
7:30 A.M., DECEMBER 31, 1862

regiment, halting and correcting the right of my line, which had been somewhat broken in passing through a small thicket in the field.

Our skirmishers now drove the enemy from the fence and border of the woods, and the brigade advanced to the Triune [Franklin] road in a beautiful line, completing the wheel to the right. My command was here moved to the left on the road, to give room to Brigadier-General *Polk's* brigade.

In front of the left wing of the Twenty-fifth Regiment Tennessee Volunteers there was, at this time, a lane [Gresham Lane] running nearly perpendicular to the Triune [Franklin] road; and with a narrow opening on the right of this lane there was on either side a cedar glade. The brigade advanced into the glade, and, passing it under a warm fire on the right wing, it entered a wide corn-field on the left and a narrow field on the right of the lane. The conflict now became very severe—perhaps as much so as at any period during the day.

Immediately in front of the Seventeenth Tennessee Regiment, and to the right of a small thicket, was a battery of four guns supported by a heavy force of infantry. As soon as the brigade entered upon the open ground it was exposed to a very heavy fire of grape, shells, and bullets. The Twenty-fifth Regiment, on the right of the lane, was especially exposed to a flank fire of the enemy's battery. The Seventeenth advanced steadily to within 150 yards of the battery, halted, and engaged the enemy most gallantly and efficiently for some time. Captain *Darden's* [Jefferson] battery at the same time took position on the south side of the field, and with admirable skill poured in a well-directed fire of shell, shrapnel, and solid shot over the heads of our men upon the battery and infantry in front of my left wing, which soon silenced the enemy's pieces. The Seventeenth then charged and took the battery of four guns in front of it, having, with the aid of the artillery, killed eight men of the battery and many horses, and having wounded the captain and a number of his men and damaged one of his pieces.

As our men advanced, Captain *Darden* moved his battery to the left and engaged the enemy's battery on the left of the small thicket, which finally moved back from its position. After continuing the fire for a time from the open fields upon the enemy now in the woods beyond, the Seventeenth again charged and gained the woods, where a stubborn resistance continued to be offered by the enemy, who took shelter behind trees and logs. Still the Seventeenth pushed rapidly forward, driving the enemy until its left was exposed to an enfilading fire from the enemy, who occupied a fence some 60 yards to the left. The Twenty-third Tennessee Regiment, in conjunction with the right of Brigadier-General *Liddell's* brigade, now approached in good time, and gallantly relieved the Seventeenth from this flank fire, enabling it to pass forward and drive the enemy from the woods.

On the right of the lane, where the Twenty-fifth, Forty-fourth, and Thirty-seventh Tennessee Regiments passed, there was much less open ground than on the left. When the enemy gave way in the field on the left of the lane, they fell rapidly back to the woods, and were soon driven from this cover; but on the right of the lane my right wing had to advance much more slowly against artillery and infantry, and gradually drive the enemy step by step, without the aid of artillery, through woods almost equal in extent to the woods and open ground on the left.

The first serious conflict in which my brigade was engaged in this battle may be considered as closing here. More than half of the whole loss of this brigade, in my opinion, occurred in this conflict. [*OR* 20, pt. 1, pp. 875–77.]

Brigadier General *Bushrod R. Johnson,*
CSA. Library of Congress.

Supporting *Johnson, Darden's* battery went into firing posi-
tion 300 yards to your left rear. From this location it engaged the
Fifth Wisconsin Battery and the Union regiments on this side of
Gresham Lane.

Report of Capt. *Putnam Darden,* CSA, Commanding Jefferson Artillery Battery, *Cleburne's* Division, *Hardee's* Corps, Army of Tennessee

We formed in rear of the center of [*Johnson's*] brigade and followed on.
We moved on for nearly a mile, when we came to a halt on the [Franklin]
road. The brigade moved by the left flank for a short distance, then by the
right through a small skirt of woods. Emerging from the woods we entered
a corn-field, when the firing became general along the lines of the brigade.
I moved the battery into the field, but could not engage the enemy without
endangering our men, who were in front. I immediately moved by the left
flank to an elevated position, and came into battery to the right under a
murderous fire of canister from one of the enemy's batteries, posted about
400 yards distant. We opened fire with shell, shrapnel, and solid shot (we

could not use canister without injuring our own men), and in about twenty minutes had the satisfaction of knowing that we had silenced their guns. Shortly after this a battery on the left opened on the brigade on our left (General *Liddell's,* I think). We immediately threw our guns into position, bearing on the battery, but could not open fire for our infantry, which was in front of us. But this obstacle was soon removed by moving by the flank to a position where they were not in our way. We then opened fire on the battery, and in a few minutes it limbered and retired with its supporting infantry through an open field nearly a mile in length. We played on their retreating columns until they were out of the reach of our guns. We then refilled our chests with ammunition and moved on as rapidly as possible. [*OR* 20, pt.1, pp. 894–95.]

Return to your car for the drive to Stop 4.

Continue to drive west on Clarmont Drive for 150 yards to the T-intersection with Sharondale Drive. Turn right on to Sharondale Drive and drive north for 0.2 mile, pull off to the side of the road, stop, and get out of your car. Face north, which is the direction you were driving. Be careful of traffic and children playing. All the land around you is private property; do not trespass.

Stop 4—*Liddell's* Attack

You are standing in the vicinity of where the right half of *Liddell's* Brigade passed through as it attacked Baldwin's brigade of Johnson's division. The ground to your left and right and in front of you were cornfields. Beyond the cornfields was a woods. The large open field is behind you.

When Willich and Kirk went into position on either side of the Franklin Road and Gresham Lane intersection, Baldwin was ordered into a reserve position 700 yards in front of you. As the Confederate attack developed, he was ordered to move forward, and his brigade moved into position 200 yards in front of you. After the collapse of the extreme Union right, Baldwin was the only uncommitted unit west of Gresham Lane to face the Confederate attack.

Like *Johnson's* Brigade, *Liddell's* had been in the supporting line of the attack. But with the opening of the gaps between *McCown's* brigades he quickly found himself in the front line of the attack.

As *Liddell* complete his right turn to the north, he went into position on *Johnson's* left with *McNair's* Brigade to his left. *Liddell* deployed all four of his Arkansas infantry regiments in his first line. They were, from right to left, the Second, Fifth, Sixth, and Seventh Combined and Eighth Arkansas Regiments. The Second Arkansas was to the right of where you are standing; the Fifth Arkansas was to your left. To the left of the Fifth Arkansas were the Sixth and Seventh Arkansas and the Eighth Arkansas.

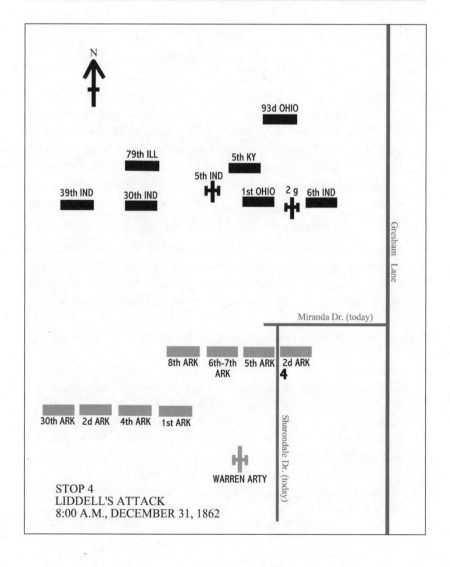

STOP 4
LIDDELL'S ATTACK
8:00 A.M., DECEMBER 31, 1862

Report of Brig. Gen. *St. John R. Liddell*, CSA, Commanding *Liddell's* Brigade, *Cleburne's* Division, *Hardee's* Corps, Army of Tennessee

In a moment's conversation with General *McCown*, he wished me to take position in advance, as his men were somewhat exhausted by the fight. I proposed, instead, that he should move by the left flank and allow me to move up in line with his command, thus placing [*McNair's* Brigade] on my left, which was readily consented to and done. We then moved forward in line, and almost immediately engaged the enemy. My battery [Lieutenant *Shannon's* Warren Light Artillery] was immediately placed in position on an eminence in rear of the line, and opened fire upon the enemy, who were posted behind a fence in front of us, about 75 yards distant, with another line 150 yards farther in their rear, in the woods, from which position they had heavy batteries playing upon our line. After a contest lasting about half an hour, we repulsed the front line, driving it back upon the second, which also gave way upon our approach, after a short struggle. Here I lost sight of Brigadier-General *Johnson's* left, and continued to move straight forward against the enemy, with General *McCown* still on my left. We continued

the pursuit, constantly skirmishing, until we reached a house, which was afterward found to be a hospital, where we re-engaged and drove back the enemy's second line of defense. My battery was here pushed forward within 60 yards of the hospital, and fired upon the retreating foe, now crossing the Wilkinson turnpike. My men continued the pursuit across the turnpike, when they were halted to wait for ammunition, to obtain which I dispatched Lieutenant *J. L. Bostick,* my aide-de-camp, to General *McCown,* who was near a house some 300 yards to the left of the hospital, with his command. Meanwhile my own ammunition arrived and supplied me. [*OR* 20, pt. 1, pp. 856–57.]

Brigadier General *St. John R. Liddell*, CSA. Library of Congress.

The commander of the Fifth Arkansas, who was to your left, gives a good representation of the attack from the regimental level.

Report of Lieut. Col. *John E. Murray*, CSA, Commanding Fifth Arkansas Infantry, *Liddell's* Brigade, *Cleburne's* Division *Hardee's* Corps, Army of Tennessee

At about the hour of 7.30 a.m. we came in sight of the enemy, strongly posted with artillery and infantry in the edge of a piece of woods about 200 yards in our front, who immediately opened a well-directed and most deadly fire upon our advancing line. My command halted and immediately commenced returning the fire, and for about twenty minutes the command remained in an open field, exposed to a most deadly fire of artillery and infantry. At the end of this time the command to charge was given, and, as the men arose and started forward with a yell, the enemy gave way, falling back in good order to near the [Wilkinson] pike, [1.1 mile north of this location] when a short stand was made, but, as our men showed no signs of wavering or halting for their fire, the enemy soon gave way again. [*OR* 20, pt. 1, pp. 865–66.]

Lieutenant *Shannon's* battery provided direct support to *Liddell's* attack by engaging Union artillery while changing position twice.

Report of Lieut. *H. Shannon*, CSA, Commanding Warren Artillery Battery, *Cleburne's* Division, *Hardee's* Corps, Army of Tennessee

After advancing about 1 mile, crossing a lane, and passing through a narrow strip of timber, I posted the battery on an eminence in an open field to the right of the brigade, and within 600 yards of one of the enemy's batteries, in front of Brigadier-General *Johnson's* brigade, and opened with a well-directed fire of round shot and shrapnel, causing the enemy to retire. Our loss was one horse killed.

I then moved the battery rapidly to the front and left, and took position 100 yards in rear of [*Liddell's*] brigade, in front of and within 600 yards of one of the enemy's rifle batteries, firing about 20 rounds to the piece with good effect, when the brigade gallantly charged and captured the battery, consisting of one rifle brass 6-pounder and one 10-pounder Parrott steel gun. From some unknown cause a shrapnel shot lodged about half way down one of the howitzers, thus temporarily disabling the piece, which was at once ordered a short distance to the rear. The limber being brought forward, I substituted the brass rifle piece just captured for the disabled howitzer, getting a good supply of ammunition from the enemy's chests. Our loss at this position was, Corpl. *Martin Green,* killed by a rifle shell; Sergt. *John McMullen,* severely wounded in the chest by a minie ball; Artificer *Charles McDermit,* severely wounded in the arm and chest by a minie ball; Private *Peter Hogan,* severely wounded in the foot by a minie ball; Private *Frank Bonengal,* slightly wounded in the hand by a minie ball; Private *E. H. Duggar,* slightly wounded on the hip by the fragment of a shell; also one wheel disabled by the enemy's rifle shot. [*OR* 20, pt. 1, pp. 871–72.]

Return to your car for the drive to Stop 5.

Continue to drive north on Sharondale Drive for 25 yards to the intersection with Miranda Drive. Turn right on to Miranda Drive and drive east for almost 0.1 mile to the intersection with Gresham Lane. Turn left on to Gresham Lane and drive north for 0.1 mile to the intersection with *Braxton Bragg* Drive. Turn left on to *Braxton Bragg* Drive and drive west for 0.2 mile, pull over to the side, and stop. Get out of your car and face south, which is to your left as you drove on *Braxton Bragg* Drive. Be careful of traffic and children playing. All the land around you is private property; do not trespass.

Stop 5—Baldwin's Defense

You are in the center of the position occupied by Baldwin's brigade of Johnson's division. You are on the other side of the cornfields that were north of Stop 4. To your left and behind you was a large woods.

Initially, Baldwin's brigade had been in a reserve position 500 yards north of where you are. As the Confederate attack south of this position began to make progress, Baldwin commenced to deploy his infantry regiments and artillery battery into a defensive line. Before this was accomplished, he was ordered to move his brigade forward and deploy at the location where you are now.

You are at the position of the First Ohio. To that regiment's left was part of the Fifth Indiana Battery, and to its left was the Sixth Indiana. The rest of the battery was on the First Ohio's right. The Fifth Kentucky was positioned within supporting distance of the First Ohio. During the fighting it moved forward and attempted to deploy to the right of the First Ohio's position. The Ninety-third Ohio was held in a reserve position behind the First Ohio. The attack on this position was so overwhelming that the Ninety-third did not have time to reinforce the defensive line. To the right of Baldwin's brigade, the Thirty-ninth Indiana of Willich's brigade and the Seventy-ninth Illinois and Thirtieth Indiana of Kirk's brigade were attempting to re-form and fight alongside Baldwin.

Report of Col. Philemon P. Baldwin, USA, Commanding Third Brigade, Second Division, Right Wing, Army of the Cumberland

I was informed by stragglers, who were running across the open field in my front, of the attack on Generals Willich's and Kirk's brigades.

I immediately ordered the brigade under arms, and proceeded to form line of battle in the edge of timber facing the large open fields over which I knew the enemy must come to attack me.

I deployed the Louisville Legion [Fifth Kentucky Infantry] on the right, and was proceeding to post the First Ohio in the center, and the Sixth Indiana on the left, holding the Ninety-third Ohio in reserve, to protect either flank, when [Johnson] ordered me to move the First Ohio across the open field and post it at the fence. The Sixth Indiana was moved forward and posted in the edge of a skirt of timber to the left of the First Ohio, the Thirtieth Indiana and Seventy-ninth Illinois being posted on the right; a section of the Fifth Indiana Battery was posted between the First Ohio and Sixth Indiana, The Louisville Legion moved to within supporting distance of the First Ohio, and the Ninety-third Ohio held in reserve in the woods near the edge of the field.

These dispositions were scarcely made when the enemy, in immense masses, appeared in my front at short range, their left extending far beyond the extreme right of my line. My infantry and artillery poured a destructive fire into their dense masses, checking them in front, but their left continued to advance against my right. Here four pieces that Captain Simonson had

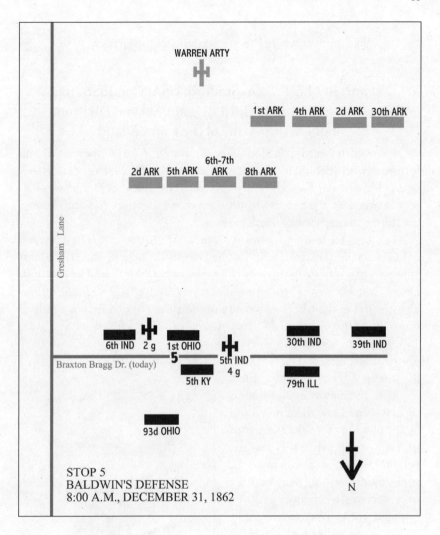

WARREN ARTY

1st ARK   4th ARK   2d ARK   30th ARK

6th-7th
ARK

2d ARK   5th ARK   8th ARK

Gresham Lane

6th IND   2 g   1st OHIO   30th IND   39th IND

5th IND
4 g

Braxton Bragg Dr. (today)

5th KY   79th ILL

93d OHIO

STOP 5
BALDWIN'S DEFENSE
8:00 A.M., DECEMBER 31, 1862

N

posted near the woods, in rear of my first line, poured in a terrible fire; but the enemy came in such overwhelming numbers that, after half an hour's stubborn resistance my line was compelled to retire, not, however, until the enemy had flanked my right and were pouring in an enfilading fire. Had my line stood a moment longer it would have been entirely surrounded and captured. Falling back to the edge of the woods. I endeavored to make a stand. I moved the Ninety-third Ohio up to the left of the Louisville Legion, but my line was again forced back, almost before I had got the Ninety-third in position. [*OR* 20, pt. 1, p. 337.]

The regiment where you are located was the First Ohio.

Report of Maj. Joab A. Stafford, USA, Commanding First Ohio Infantry, Third Brigade, Second Division, Right Wing, Army of the Cumberland

I moved forward at a double-quick across, a large open field, and formed my line behind a rail fence, on a line with the Sixth Indiana (they occupying a piece of woods to my left), with two pieces of Simonson's battery between us, the Seventy-ninth Illinois and Thirtieth Indiana occupying the right, the Seventy-ninth in reserve.

I ordered Lieutenant Hayward, Company D, to deploy the first platoon of his company as skirmishers. This had hardly been done when the enemy appeared in our front in three distinct lines of battle, followed by columns, closed in mass, several batteries of artillery, and a large amount of cavalry, the left of their lines extending not less than one-fourth of a mile to the right of the Thirtieth Indiana. As soon as they arrived within about 150 yards of my line, I opened fire, which checked their advance for about fifteen minutes. Their line then in front of me seemed to separate, and I saw them marching by the flank to the right and left of us. Immediately after this maneuver, the two regiments on my right gave way, and left my flank entirely unprotected. The enemy's left then changed their front to the right and marched diagonally toward my right. At this moment the Sixth Indiana was forced from their position, the enemy immediately taking possession of the fence they occupied. They then again appeared in my front and opened an enfilading fire on my regiment.

Finding it was impossible to hold my position without being annihilated, I ordered my regiment

Major Joab A. Stafford, USA. Massachusetts Commandery Military Order of the Loyal Legion and the U.S. Army Military History Institute.

to fall back, intending to take a position in the rear of the Louisville Legion, which was at that time supporting me. My regiment started back in good order, but coming in contact with the Louisville Legion (Colonel Berry having just ordered a change of front forward on first company, to protect our right), we became entangled with them, as we did also with the Ninety-third Ohio, which had [been] ordered to our support. I then fell back in some confusion to the woods occupied by me some half an hour previous.

Here I tried to form my line, but again became entangled with a part of the First Brigade. My regiment became scattered, and it was impossible to get them into line until we had fallen back through the woods into a cotton-field and into another piece of woods. Here, by your [Baldwin's] help and the united efforts of my officers, I succeeded in rallying part of my regiment, and took position on the left of Colonel Berry, who had also succeeded in rallying part of his regiment. Here the enemy was checked and driven back a short distance, but soon rallied and came down in a solid mass, and we were obliged again to retire. [*OR* 20, pt. 1, p. 343.]

To the left of the First Ohio and your left, under command of First Lieutenant Henry Rankin, was positioned a two-gun section of the Fifth Indiana Battery. The remainder of the battery was deployed to the right rear of the First Ohio.

Report of Capt. Peter Simonson, USA, Commanding Fifth Indiana Battery, Second Division, Right Wing, Army of the Cumberland

At about 7.30 a.m. two light 12-pounder guns were ordered out to a position about 800 yards southeast from the camp, facing a large cornfield, the enemy appearing in a very heavy force. I was then ordered to return and get the other four guns in position as quickly as possible, which was done, placing them to the right and rear of the first pieces posted. The light 12-pounder guns in the advanced position were under command of First Lieut. H. Rankin. The brigade commander is better informed as to their actions than I am, as they were under his immediate eye. I simply noticed that they fired very rapidly, and were the last troops which passed to the rear upon my left. They fired in that position 17 rounds from one piece, and 23 from the other—nearly all canister. Some of the rounds were double charges. The four guns under my immediate command commenced firing shell. We had fired about 15 rounds when a very large body of our own troops appeared to our right-oblique, retreating rapidly; it was the remains of Kirk's brigade. Colonel Dodge [now commanding Kirk's brigade] had hardly time to inform me that a very large body of the enemy was in close pursuit, when they appeared. Three of the four guns opened upon them with canister, and checked them in front and to the right-oblique, but more appearing almost directly on our right flank (our infantry were out of sight to the rear), the order was given to leave the field. The command succeeded in getting away with but two of the four pieces. At these two positions there were 3 men killed and 21 wounded; also 23 horses disabled. We retreated through dense woods, and had great difficulty in getting our carriages through. [*OR* 20, pt. 1, p. 298.]

Baldwin's brigade, and others, unsuccessfully attempted to rally and fight several times. The brigade retreat was finally halted two and a half miles northeast of here along the Nashville-Murfreesboro Pike.

Return to your car for the drive to Stop 6

Drive west, the direction your car is pointed, 0.1 mile to Deerfield Drive, do a U-turn, and drive back to the intersection of *Braxton Bragg* Drive and Gresham Lane. Turn left on to Gresham Lane and drive north for 0.3 mile to the intersection with John R. Rice Boulevard. Just before you reach the intersection, pull off into the wide area on the left side of the road and stop. The wide area is just before the curve.

In 1862 Gresham Lane continued on interrupted for another 0.5 mile, where it intersected the Wilkinson Turnpike. Today, however, Interstate 24 divides it. The Gresham house was 300 yards in front of you on the other side of I-24. The house was used as a hospital by both armies and was also used as McCook's headquarters.

Turn left on to John R. Rice Boulevard/Gresham Lane and drive for 0.8 mile to the intersection with the Manson Pike. As you drive north you can see to your right and across I-24 where the Grisham farm was. Turn right on to the Manson Pike/Medical Center Parkway and drive for 0.3 mile to the intersection with Asbury Lane. You will cross over I-24. Be careful; don't turn on to the I-24 access ramp. Turn left on to Asbury Lane. Drive for 0.3 mile to the intersection with Cotton Mill Road. Turn right on to Cotton Mill Road, do a U-turn, and just before the intersection with Asbury Lane pull off to the side of the road and stop. Be

careful of traffic and children playing. All the land around you is
private property; do not trespass.

Stop 6—Escape of McCook's Ordnance Train

The Manson Pike, which you used to cross over I-24 and is now to
your left, in 1862 was called the Wilkinson Turnpike. The western
edge of the Stones River National Battlefield, maintained by the

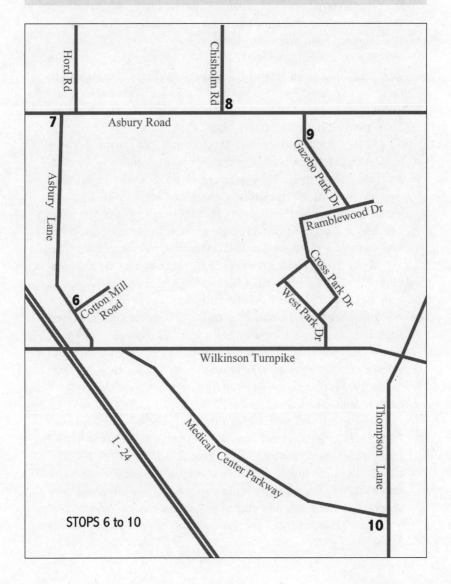

National Park Service, is 1.2 miles behind you. The ground behind you was a large cotton field, which was bordered on the north and east by a woods that went east for over a mile.

Kirk's, Willich's, Post's and Baldwin's Union brigades, who had all fought west of Gresham Lane, retreated to the area to your left and in front of you. A few regiments were able to establish defensive positions and fight for a short period of time, but many were not. Eventually all the regiments of the four Union brigades retreated to the northeast for 1.6 miles to the Nashville-Murfreesboro Pike. At that location they began to regroup, resupply ammunition, and establish defensive positions.

McCown's and *Cleburne's* Divisions halted along the Wilkinson Turnpike. They used this pause to regroup their brigades and to resupply ammunition. This pause in the attack allowed three brigades from Crittenden's Left Wing to move into position between here and the Nashville-Murfreesboro Pike.

At this point in the attack *Bragg's* enveloping maneuver was beginning to loose some of its effectiveness. As originally planned, *McCown's* three brigades would conduct the initial attack and overrun or outflank the Union right. *Cleburne* with his four brigades in the supporting line would then pass through *McCown's* Division and push the attack, pursue the retreating Union units, and capture a section of the Nashville-Murfreesboro Pike. This would effectively cut Rosecrans's army off from its base at Nashville. As *McCown* made his wheel to the right, north, dangerous gaps developed between his brigades and between his division and *Cheatham's* Division on his right. This development caused *Cleburne* to commit all four of his brigades earlier than planned. By the time the attack reached the Wilkinson Turnpike, the fresh brigades that were needed to press the pursuit all the way to the Nashville-Murfreesboro Pike and the Union rear had already been committed to the fight.

To your left and on the other side of I-24 and along the Manson Pike, the 1862 Wilkinson Turnpike, was the Right Wing's ordnance train, under the command of Captain Gates P. Thruston. The capture of this large supply of ammunition would have been of major importance to *Bragg's* army. It not only would have increased their supply of ammunition but also would have deprived Rosecrans of a valuable resource that could have had an adverse impact on his army's ability to continue the battle in its present position. As the battle came closer to him, Thruston began making preparations to move his seventy-six wagons out of harms way. Cutting across fields and through cedars, he reached Asbury Lane just north of where you are. He then moved north on Asbury Lane to the intersection with Asbury Road, one mile north of where you are now.

Captain Gates P. Thruston, USA. Massachusetts Commandery Military Order of the Loyal Legion and the U.S. Army Military History Institute.

Turn right on to Asbury Lane and drive north for 1.0 mile to the intersection with Asbury Road. Turn left on to Asbury Road and drive 0.3 mile, where you can safely turn around. Retrace your route back to the intersection. Just before the intersection with Asbury Lane, pull off to the side of the road and stop. You are facing east. You may remain in you car or get out. Be careful of traffic. The creek you crossed and recrossed is Overall Creek.

Stop 7—A Cavalry Fight

Asbury Road and this intersection were here in 1862. In front of you is the intersection of Asbury Road with Asbury Lane. Just past this intersection and on the left is the Hord Road, which goes directly north, to your left, 1.2 miles to the Nashville-Murfreesboro Pike. The Hord Road was also here in 1862. The Widow Burris House is located 0.6 mile from where you are and on the north side of Asbury Road. Another 0.7 mile past the Widow Burris House, Asbury Road intersects with the Nashville-Murfreesboro Pike. Any Confederate force reaching this point would only need to follow the Asbury Road or Hord Road for a very short distance to be in the rear of the Army of the Cumberland and to have cut its main line of supply and communication with Nashville. The ground were you are was corn and open fields.

When Thruston's ordnance train reached this intersection, it turned right, went a short distance to the east, then parked in the fields between where you are and the Widow Burris House. There, Confederate cavalry attacked it. The fight between the opposing cavalry forces was a mobile fight that covered the ground to your left and in front of you.

The Confederate cavalry operating on the west flank of the Confederate army was Brigadier General *John A. Wharton's* brigade. This brigade had begun the morning by being posted on the left of *McCown's* Division.

Widow Burris House today.

Report of Brig. Gen. *John A. Wharton,* CSA, Commanding *Wharton's* Cavalry Brigade, Army of Tennessee

I was informed that at daylight on the morning of the 31st [ultimo] our left wing would attack the enemy's right. Being drawn up on the extreme left, I was ordered to reach the enemy's rear as soon as possible, and to do

them all the damage I could. . . .
I moved the command promptly
at daylight. So vigorous was the
attack of our left upon the enemy's right, proceeding first at a
trot and then at a gallop, I had
to travel a distance of 2½ miles
before I reached the enemy's rear. I
succeeded in getting into position
near the Wilkinson pike, with the
enemy in my front; caused Colonel *Cox* to form his command for
a charge; directed Captain *White*
to open on the enemy with his
battery. After a brisk fire from the
artillery, I ordered Colonel *Cox*
to charge, which he did in gallant
style.

Brigadier General *John A. Wharton*, CSA.
Library of Congress.

The enemy's immense wagon
trains, guarded by a heavy force
of cavalry, could be seen moving
near and in the rear of the enemy in the direction of the Nashville pike.
I determined to move across the country, give the cavalry battle, and to
attempt to capture the train. Our infantry by this time had succeeded in
driving the enemy across the Wilkinson pike. In reaching a point about
three-quarters of a mile distant from the Nashville pike, I discovered the
wagon train of the enemy, together with some artillery, moving along the
pike. A heavy body of cavalry was drawn up near and parallel to the pike,
facing me, and a considerable body was drawn up nearer me to give battle.
[*OR* 20, pt.1, pp. 966–67.]

The Union cavalry brigade commanded by Colonel Lewis
Zahm met *Wharton's* attack. Prior to the Confederate attack this
brigade had been deployed on the Union west flank. As *McCown's*
Division drove back the Union extreme right and *Wharton's* Brigade moved around McCook's flank and into the Union rear area,
Zahm was forced to retreat north of the Wilkinson Turnpike and
to the general vicinity east, in front of, where you are now.

Report of Col. Lewis Zahm, USA, Commanding Second Cavalry Brigade, Cavalry Division, Army of the Cumberland

When we arrived on the open ground, General McCook's aide told me the whole of General McCook's ammunition train was close by, on a dirt road running by that point, and that I must try to save it. I soon formed my command in line, when the enemy made his appearance in a position occupying two-thirds of a circle. They prepared to charge upon us; likewise commenced throwing shells, at which the Second East Tennessee broke and ran like sheep. The Fourth [Ohio], after receiving several shells, which killed some of their men and horses, likewise retired from their line, as it became untenable. The First [Ohio] had been ordered to proceed farther on into another lot, to form and to receive a charge from another line of the enemy's cavalry. The Third [Ohio] moved to the left, in the vicinity of a white house. About the time the First was formed, the enemy charged upon the Fourth, which, being on the retreat, owing to the shells coming pretty freely, moved off at a pretty lively gait. The Third moved farther to the left, and, somewhat sheltered by the house and barns, the First charged upon the enemy; did not succeed in driving them back.

On returning from said charge the gallant Colonel Milliken and a lieutenant were killed, and another lieutenant severely wounded.

At this juncture the First and Fourth retired pretty fast, the enemy in close pursuit after them, the Second East Tennessee having the lead of them all. Matters looked pretty blue now; the ammunition train was supposed to be gone up, when the Third charged upon the enemy, driving him back, capturing several prisoners, and recapturing a good many of our men, and saved the train. I was with the three regiments that skedaddled, and among the last to leave the field. Tried hard to rally them, but the panic was so great that I could not do it. I could not get the command together again until I arrived at the north side of the creek; then I found that only about one-third of the First and Fourth Regiments were there, and nearly all of the Second East Tennessee. [*OR* 20, pt. 1, p. 637.]

In this charge and counter charge by both cavalry brigades, *Wharton's* finally gained the upper hand. Just when it appeared that he would capture Thruston's wagons, a final Union cavalry force arrived and counterattacked. This cavalry force was led by the cavalry division commander, Colonel John Kennett. Kennett had gathered together a squadron of the Third Kentucky Cavalry, six companies of the Fourth U.S. Cavalry, and the rallied Third

Ohio Cavalry and proceeded to the right rear of the army. Here his surprise attack caught part of *Wharton's* force in the right rear and drove them away from the ordnance train. After being saved from capture, Thruston moved his train east to the Nashville-Murfreesboro Pike and then north a short distance to Rosecrans's headquarters.

Return to your car for the drive to Stop 8.

Drive forward, east, on Asbury Road for 0.6 mile to the intersection with Chisholm Road. Just before you reach Chisholm Road, the Widow Burris House will be on your left. Turn left, north, on to Chisholm Road and drive for a short distance to where you can do a U-turn. Do a U-turn and drive back toward Asbury Road. Just before you reach Asbury Road, pull off to the side and stop. Get out of your car; be careful of traffic and children. Stay off of private property and stand so you can see south across the other side of Asbury Road.

Stop 8—Harker's Defense

In 1862 the ground all around you was cotton, corn, and open fields. Eight hundred yards south of you was the northern edge of the large woods that was east of Stop 6. Northeast of you and north of Asbury Lane was a cedar woods that ran along side of the Nashville-Murfreesboro Pike. Into the area directly in front of you and to your left front, three brigades were deployed to stop the Confederate attack. These brigades were from Crittenden's Left Wing and had been in position on the Union left. The pause by *McCown's* and *Cleburne's* Divisions along the Wilkinson Turnpike to resupply ammunition provided the time for these Union brigades to move to this location. Directly in front of you at a distance of 300 yards was Colonel Charles G. Harker's brigade. To Harker's left, after a gap of 250 yards, was Colonel James P. Fyffe's brigade. To that brigade's left was Colonel Samuel Beatty's brigade. Harker's brigade faced south and southwest; the other two faced south.

Harker's brigade had initially been prepared to cross Stones River as part of Rosecrans's attack against *Bragg's* right. However, because the Confederate left, *McCown* and *Cleburne,* made such rapid progress against McCook's Right Wing, this attack was called back and the units redeployed as needed.

Harker's position as seen from Stop 8.

Report of Col. Charles G. Harker, USA, Commanding Third Brigade, First Division, Left Wing, Army of the Cumberland

About 8 a.m., December 31, I received orders from General Wood, commanding division, to cross the river with my command. The movement was commenced, in obedience to General Wood's order, but was suspended for a few moments by an order emanating from Major-General Crittenden, commanding the left wing. While awaiting further orders, Major-General Rosecrans passed my command, and gave me direct instructions to proceed immediately to the support of the right wing of our army, which was yielding to the overwhelming force of the enemy at that point.

On approaching the right, much confusion was visible; troops marching in every direction; stragglers to be seen in great numbers, and teamsters in great consternation endeavoring to drive their teams they knew not whither. My progress was impeded by the confusion, while the enemy was pouring shot and shell upon us from at least three different directions, wounding several men in my command. The brigade was, however, extricated from this perilous position as soon as possible, and pressed on to a position on the extreme right of our line, Colonel Fyffe's brigade, of General Van Cleve's division, being immediately upon our left.

After reaching this last position, my brigade marched in two lines, the Fifty-first Indiana on the right, the Sixty-fifth Ohio on the left, the battery a little retired and opposite the interval between the Sixty-fifth and Fifty-first, the Sixty-fourth Ohio on the right of the second line, the

Seventy-third Indiana on the left, with the Thirteenth Michigan in rear of the caissons. We marched in this order about half a mile, when our skirmishers came up with those of the enemy, and the fire became brisk in front. About this time a battery from the enemy, situated in a cornfield, and nearly opposite my right flank, opened upon my command with canister. In order to get a commanding position for artillery, and at the same time guard well my right flank, which I was fearful the enemy would attempt to turn, I moved the command a little to the right.

While this movement was being executed, a staff officer from the command upon my left reported a strong force of the enemy in his front. I replied that my right was in danger, and that a strong force and battery was in front. No sooner had I taken a position on the crest of the hill than a most vigorous engagement commenced. The position selected for my brigade proved a most fortunate one. The enemy was completely baffled in his design to turn my right; not only were the batteries in my front silenced and the enemy there repulsed, but a most destructive fire from Bradley's [Sixth Ohio] battery played upon the heavy columns of the enemy then pressing the troops upon my left. This engagement had continued about twenty minutes, when it was reported to me that the troops on my left had given way, and that the enemy was already in rear of my left flank, and about 200 yards from it, pouring a destructive cross-fire upon my troops.

At this time my command was in a most precarious situation, with a strong foe in front, which, though repulsed, could not be followed up for want of support; my right threatened, and my left already turned. It therefore became necessary to change the disposition of my command and fall back. The commander of the Sixty-fifth Ohio anticipated my order, when he found his left turned, and fell back in good order. I directed this regiment to make a stand behind a rail fence running obliquely to the first line of battle.

During this movement this regiment was subjected to a most galling fire from the enemy, but they stood up under it nobly and fought desperately. While this movement was being executed, the Seventy-third Indiana was left in position on the second line, and the battery retired to a position about 400 yards to the rear, when it again opened. [This position was 300 yards to your left and next to the Asbury Road.] The Sixty-fourth Ohio was now ordered to change its front to the left and charge the enemy. The direction was indicated to the commanding officer, but, unfortunately, he moved too far to the right. Though this regiment handsomely repulsed the enemy in its front, it did the work of the other regiments already in position, leaving the left of the Seventy-third Indiana exposed, and permitting the enemy to advance much farther than could have been done had my design been carried out.

Bradley's battery, having taken its second position, opened again, with great effect, upon the advancing enemy, but, being in an exposed position, it was again ordered to withdraw, being badly crippled by loss of horses; two pieces were abandoned, one of which was spiked. [Bradley's third position was 700 yards northwest of where you are.]

The command was now ordered to fall back and form on a rocky eminence covered with cedars, being a very strong position. [This was Bradley's third position and was only 400 yards from the Nashville-Murfreesboro Pike.] The Thirteenth Michigan, from their position, opened upon the enemy with telling effect, and, having caused his ranks to waver, followed up the advantage with a charge, supported by the Fifty-first Illinois Volunteers, who had now come to our relief. They completely routed the enemy. The Thirteenth Michigan retook two pieces of artillery, abandoned by our battery, and captured 58 prisoners. For this act of gallantry Colonel Shoemaker and his gallant regiment are deserving of much praise. [OR 20, pt.1, pp. 502–3.]

> Captain Cullen Bradley's Sixth Ohio battery was supporting Harker's brigade. During the fighting here Bradley's six guns occupied three different firing positions and fired 162 rounds of ammunition.

Report of Capt. Cullen Bradley, USA, Commanding Sixth Ohio Battery, Third Brigade, First Division, Left Wing, Army of the Cumberland

At 10.30 a.m. engaged two four-gun batteries of the enemy, supported by two brigades of infantry, at a range of 250 yards. We received a galling fire from the infantry as well as the batteries. We held our position twenty minutes, pouring a heavy and destructive fire upon the infantry, at the same time engaging the batteries with good effect, expending 150 rounds of case-shot and canister, and sustained a loss of 1 man wounded and 2 horses killed.

Our left flank having been turned, I retired my battery and took a position 400 yards in the rear. Again opened upon the enemy (with case and canister), who were advancing in force. After an engagement of five minutes, and expending 12 rounds of ammunition, I was again compelled to retire my battery and abandon two pieces of the battery, one of which I

Colonel Charles G. Harker, USA.
Harper's Weekly.

had spiked (since removed), and sustaining a loss of 1 man killed, 2 men wounded, and 1 man missing; also 8 horses killed and 3 wounded. About this time Colonel Shoemaker charged the enemy with the Thirteenth Michigan Regiment, driving them off the field and recovering the guns, and for which Colonel Shoemaker should receive full credit. [*OR* 20, pt. 1, pp. 478–79.]

Colonel Shoemaker's regiment participated in a counterattack along with several rallied regiments from the Third Brigade of Sheridan's division. This attack succeeded in pushing the Confederates away from the Nashville-Murfreesboro Pike and back south of the Asbury Road.

In his first position south of Asbury Road, Harker's brigade was attacked frontally by part of Brigadier General *Bushrod Johnson's* brigade and on his west flank by Brigadier General *St. John Liddell's* brigade. *Johnson's* Brigade had attacked north up Grisham Lane to the Wilkinson Turnpike, where it and the rest of *Cleburne's* Division paused to resupply ammunition. From there it had moved northeast then north, where it attacked Harker's brigade.

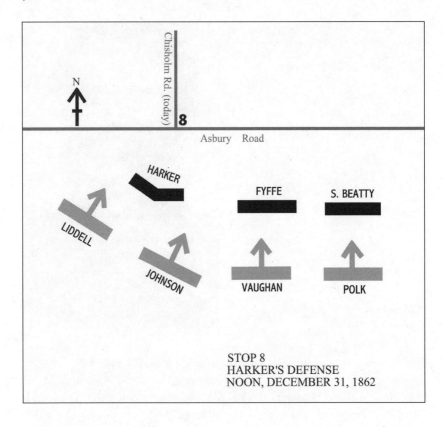

Chisholm Rd. (today)

N

8

Asbury Road

HARKER

FYFFE

S. BEATTY

LIDDELL

JOHNSON

VAUGHAN

POLK

STOP 8
HARKER'S DEFENSE
NOON, DECEMBER 31, 1862

Report of Brig. Gen. *Bushrod R. Johnson,* CSA, Commanding *Johnson's* Brigade, *Cleburne's* Division, *Hardee's* Corps, Army of Tennessee

An order now came to me from General *Cleburne* to move my brigade to support General *Liddell.* After marching some 400 yards by the left flank, we moved to our front and passed north through a long wood lot projecting into open fields. Having received a message from General *Liddell* to the effect that the aid of my brigade would rout the enemy, we came up with General *Liddell's* brigade on an ascent beyond the edge of the woods.

Before us was now an open field, declining in front. At the foot of the declivity, at the distance of about 400 yards, was a battery, strongly supported by infantry. My command steadily advanced, fighting under fire from the battery and infantry. The battery was soon silenced, and our men advanced in double-quick time to a position behind a fence and a ledge of rocks. In front, about 80 yards, was a cedar glade, in the edge of which the enemy were now seen lying close together along a ledge of rocks. Under cover of the fence and rocks our men took deliberate aim and poured upon the enemy a destructive fire, which was returned with spirit. The conflict lasted some twenty minutes, when the enemy arose to retire. At this moment a volley was discharged upon them with remarkable effect, and our men rapidly advanced to the cedars. The men of my brigade then took shelter behind the ledge of rocks at the edge of the glade, and were well covered from the enemy's fire. All concur in representing the number of dead and wounded in the edge of the cedars as very large. Many were lying side by side along the ledge in the position they assumed to await our approach, while others had fallen as they turned to retreat. [*OR* 20, pt.1, p. 879.]

After pushing Harker off the position in front of you, *Johnson's* Brigade continued its attack in a northeast direction. It almost reached the Nashville-Murfreesboro Pike before being halted and driven back by a Union counterattack.

Report of Brig. Gen. *Bushrod R. Johnson,* CSA—Continued

The fire was still being kept up on the part of our troops, when it was observed that the troops on our right, bearing colors with blue ground and red cross, were falling back, and it was reported that our right was flanked by a heavy force. A precipitate retreat immediately followed. My brigade having a strong position, held to it with tenacity, and abandoned it with reluctance, after a delay that led to considerable loss.

The retreat was made without order. The lines were broken and men of different regiments, brigades, and divisions were scattered all over the fields. The movement was to me totally unexpected, and I have yet to learn that there existed a cause commensurate with the demoralization that ensued. At the moment in which I felt the utmost confidence in the success of our arms I was almost run over by our retreating troops. Our men were in sight of the Nashville pike; some have said they were on it. The enemy's right was doubled back upon their center. Had we held this position the line of communication of the enemy would have been cut. We could have flanked them and enfiladed their whole line, which was no doubt in disorder. Had we received re-enforcements we might have returned and regained the ground. But very soon the enemy planted a formidable battery on an eminence near the railroad, sweeping all the open fields and commanding even the woods in which our lines were formed. The enemy's infantry was also brought forward and posted in great strength, so as to be protected by the side slopes of the railroad and pike, and the trees and rocks in the cedar glade. It would then have been very hazardous to assail them with any force by our former approach. [*OR* 20, pt. 1, pp. 879–80.]

Return to your car for the drive to Stop 9.

Drive forward and turn left on to Asbury Road. Drive east on Asbury Road for 0.3 mile to the intersection with Gazebo Park Drive. Turn right on to Gazebo Park Drive, drive south for 0.1 mile, pull off to the side, stop, get out of your car, and face in the direction you were driving. The land all around you is private property; do not trespass. Be alert for children playing and for school buses.

Stop 9—Fyffe's Defense

You are in the center of the position occupied by Colonel James Fyffe's brigade of Van Cleve's division. In 1862 this area was an open field with a wood lot to your right front, the north edge of the large cedar wood 400 yards to your front and a cedar thickets 450 yards to your left. The Nashville-Murfreesboro Pike and the rear of Rosecrans's army are only 1,300 yards, 0.7 mile, to your left.

At dawn on December 31 Fyffe's brigade, along with the other two brigades of the division, had been positioned to cross Stone's River and envelop the Confederate right flank. But as *Bragg* attacked first on the west flank and achieved early success, Van Cleve's movement was halted and his forces across the river were brought back. With the collapse of the Union right, McCook's Right Wing, Rosecrans ordered Van Cleve to send Fyffe's and Colonel Samuel Beatty's brigades to the west of the Nashville-Murfreesboro Pike to support Harker and build up a defensive line to stop *Hardee's* attack from reaching the pike.

When Fyffe reached this location he had four regiments and an artillery battery. He deployed into two lines. In the first line the Fifty-ninth Ohio was on the left and the Forty-fourth Indiana was on the right. The second line was composed of the Thirteenth Ohio on the left, behind the Fifth-ninth, and the Eighty-sixth Indiana on the right, behind the Forty-fourth Indiana. As the fighting progressed the Eighty-sixth was faced to the right and formed at a right angle to the Forty-fourth. The Seventh Indiana Battery was positioned between the Forty-fourth and Eighty-sixth so as to help cover the right flank.

Samuel Betty's brigade was deployed to the left of Fyffe's, and Harker's brigade was to the right. However, there was a gap between Fyffe's right and Harker's left.

Report of Col James P. Fyffe, USA, Commanding Second Brigade, Third Division, Left Wing, Army of the Cumberland

An order was received from General Van Cleve to return to the Third Division, and form on the right of the First Brigade in two lines, to support it; that Colonel Harker would support my right. The order was immediately complied with; the division began advancing down the slope of the cedar ridge south of the [Asbury] road, passing Colonel Harker's on my right, beyond the foot of the slope. After passing his brigade, which did not move, my right flank became exposed, with strong indications of a heavy force approaching in front, extending beyond my right flank. As we continued advancing, I sent three different messengers by my aides, calling Colonel Harker's attention to my exposed flank, and at length reported in person to General Van Cleve. While doing this the Sixty-fifth Ohio [of Harker's brigade], which, it appeared, had been lying down at the edge of the field, rose to their feet in the place where a force was needed. Supposing it would remain there, I passed back again to my position, to see the Sixty-fifth march by the right flank back to Colonel Harker's left. The firing in front of my first line, composed of the Fifty-ninth Ohio and Forty-fourth Indiana, was getting to be heavy, and the skirmishers, running in, reported a heavy force advancing through the woods, outflanking my right. Lieutenant Temple, of my staff, was sent at once to Lieutenant-Colonel Dick [Eighty-sixth Indiana] with orders to wheel his regiment to the right, and place it in the woods to secure my flank. Before the order reached him the enemy appeared coming through the woods.

Seeing the force would have to fall back, I galloped to the [Seventh Indiana] battery and ordered it to open fire to the right of my flank into the woods, for the purpose of checking and confusing the outflanking force, to save my brigade from the effects of the cross-fire, while falling back, as much as possible. The order to fire was complied with instantly, the whole battery opening several volleys in quick succession, and with decided effect, into the woods, while the column fell back rapidly, the front line having sustained itself gallantly until outflanked. The artillery came safely out of the field under fire, Lieutenant Buckmar, a gallant officer, being shot from his horse and badly wounded just as he was passing out of the field.

After falling back from the field, the Thirteenth Ohio, under Major Jarvis, and part of the Eighty-sixth Indiana, Lieutenant-Colonel Dick was formed near the road [Nashville-Murfreesboro Pike], the Forty-fourth being placed on duty elsewhere, and ordered to move up the road to meet the force that had followed from the field, which was represented advancing. Going in advance of the force, I found the Fifty-ninth Ohio, under

Lieutenant Colonel Howard and Major Frambes, hotly contesting the cedar ridge and hard pressed, their left flank being exposed, encouraging the men to hold on, and they should have help immediately. The force following me was hurried up. The remnant of the Thirteenth Ohio, though sadly repressed by the death of the gallant and loved Colonel Hawkins, shot dead on the field, answered the command to go forward with a cheer, and got into line on the left, opening fire just as a regiment on the right of the Fifty-ninth marched to the rear, leaving my right flank again exposed, which the enemy were not slow to perceive, and began taking advantage of. Sorely annoyed, I crossed the road and asked the officer in command, whom I do not know, what it meant. He said he had been ordered back, but on my representations he immediately marched his regiment up again, delivering a heavy fire as he reached the crest of the ridge. I then ordered the whole line to charge, which was gallantly done with a cheer, the enemy being driven from the crest of the ridge down the southern slope and back across the field. [*OR* 20, pt. 1, pp. 597–98.]

Fyffe was outflanked on his right, and he and Beatty fell back to the Nashville-Murfreesboro Pike. Here, with part of Harker's brigade and other reinforcements, they conducted a late afternoon counterattack that drove the Confederates away from the pike. As night was approaching, they settled into defensive positions to protect their supply line to Nashville.

As you have seen at Stop 8, *Liddell's* and *Johnson's* Brigades of *Cleburne's* Division attacked Harker's position. *Smith's* Brigade of *Cheatham's* Division attacked Fyffe, and *Polk's* Brigade of *Cleburne's* Division attacked Beatty.

Smith's Brigade was under the temporary command of Colonel *Alfred J. Vaughan*, who upon *Smith's* death at Chickamauga would be given permanent command of the brigade. *Smith's* Brigade began the day located just north of the Franklin Road as the left brigade of *Cheatham's* Division. From this position the brigade participated in the attack on the center of McCook's line, Davis's division, and then against the right of Sheridan's division. These actions brought the brigade to just north of the Wilkinson Turnpike and 1,700 yards, one mile, south of where you are now. From that location *Vaughan* maneuvered and fought his brigade north through the woods that were south of where you are until he encountered Fyffe's defenses.

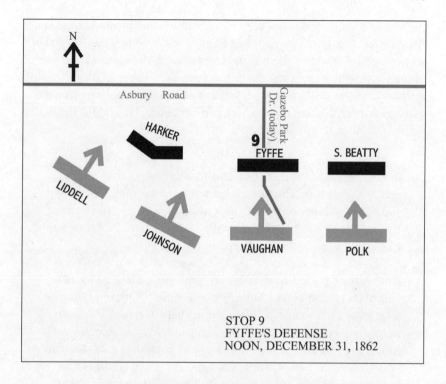

N

Asbury Road

Gazebo Park
Dr. (today)

HARKER

9
FYFFE

S. BEATTY

LIDDELL

JOHNSON

VAUGHAN

POLK

STOP 9
FYFFE'S DEFENSE
NOON, DECEMBER 31, 1862

Report of Col. *Alfred J. Vaughan, jr.*, CSA, Commanding *Smith's* Brigade, *Cheatham's* Division, *Polk's* Corps, Army of Tennessee

When about half through these woods, engaging the enemy on my right flank as I went along, I met a line of battle somewhat lapping my left, which I found to be *Wood's* brigade, engaging another force of the enemy in his front. General *Wood* desired my support to save him from being flanked on the [left]. Accordingly, I moved forward and engaged this force, driving him across the open field and dirt road into the only remaining field between us and the Nashville pike, where a large wagon train of the enemy was distinctly visible. At this point I found myself about to be flanked on my right by a strong force of the enemy posted in the woods to the right of the field. Seeing no signs of any support on my right, which I had supposed was following me to continue my alignment on the right, I concluded to rapidly continue my advance upon the enemy, which had been driven toward the pike and which had again rallied and formed in line, and, by driving him, to force the troops threatening my flank to retire. Such was the spirit and vigor with which my men pursued this object that the troops on my left did not keep up with them, and before I could effect the purpose I had in view, my right flank was so severely enfiladed that I was compelled to retire them after again driving the enemy from one of his batteries, which on that account I was unable to bring off. Withdrawing my troops to the Wilkinson pike, I there remained in line of battle on our extreme left for the remaining short portion of the day and for the entire night. [*OR* 20, pt. 1, pp. 744–45.]

In his attack against this position *Vaughan* deployed five of his six regiments on line. This placed his left flank beyond Fyffe's right and allowed him to exploit the gap between Fyffe and Harker. Having almost reached the Nashville-Murfreesboro Pike, *Vaughan* was forced back by the Union counterattack.

Dawn on December 31, 1862, saw both the Union and Confederate armies poised to conduct an enveloping maneuver and attack of each other's right flank. By the slimmest of margins, *Bragg's* attack began first and achieved immediate success. The almost immediate collapse of the Union right flank forced Rosecrans to cancel his enveloping maneuver and call back the units that had crossed Stones River. Many of the Union brigades on the left were then deployed to the right to stop the Confederate attack and protect the Nashville-Murfreesboro Pike.

Although the Confederate attack achieved immediate and stunning success, the drifting to far to the west of *McCown's* brigades opened gaps and forced the early commitment of *Cleburne's* following and supporting division. When it became necessary to reorganize units and to resupply ammunition, there was no reserve to maintain the momentum of the attack. Even though some Confederate units reached the Nashville-Murfreesboro Pike in the rear of the Union army, they had insufficient strength to hold the pike and were thrown back by counterattacks.

Although *Bragg* and his corps commanders must have lamented the absence of *Stevenson's* Division, which had departed in mid-December for Mississippi, there were several brigades that could have been used to reinforce the attack had they been positioned earlier to do so. All five of *Breckinridge's* brigades and a cavalry brigade had been positioned east of Stones River to protect the Confederate right. Brigadier General *John Pegram's* cavalry brigade was sufficient to cover the Lebanon Pike. Two, at the most three, of *Breckinridge's* brigades using Wayne's Hill to anchor the left of their line could have secured the Confederate right flank. This would have provided as a minimum two, if not three, brigades to reinforce the attack made by the Confederate left.

Military doctrine calls for the main attack, the attack designed to accomplish the commander's intent, to be given maximum combat power. *Bragg* would have been taking a calculated risk by removing part of *Breckinridge's* Division from his right, but it was the decision that needed to be made on December 30 prior to the attack. Made in a timely manner, this decision would have allowed those brigades to be in position directly behind *Cleburne's* Division prior to the attack commencing. Two or three more brigades on the Confederate left may have been enough force to cut and hold the Union line of communication and supply to Nashville.

Return to your car for the drive to Stop 10.

As you drive south from this location to the Wilkinson Turnpike, you will be traveling through an area that was a large woods in 1862.

Continue driving on Gazebo Park Drive for just over 0.1 mile to the intersection of Ramblewood Drive, turn right, and drive for 0.3 mile to the intersection with Cross Park Drive. Turn left on to Cross Park Drive and drive for 0.7 mile to the intersection with West Park Drive, then turn left and drive 0.1 mile to the intersection with the Wilkinson Turnpike. Turn left on to the Wilkinson Turnpike and drive east 0.9 mile to Thompson Lane. Turn right on to Thompson Lane and drive south for 0.4 mile to the intersection with Medical Center Parkway. Turn right on to Medical Center Parkway and make an immediate left into the parking lot. Park, get out of your car, and stand so you can look west toward the higher ground (with Medical Center Parkway to your right).

Chapter 3

THE CENTER
WEDNESDAY, DECEMBER 31, 1862

Stop 10—*Polk* Joins the Attack

In chapter 2 you followed the attack of the Confederate left from dawn until late afternoon. In this chapter you will follow the attack of the Confederate center on the right flank of the left-flank divisions. To do this, you must go back in time to just after dawn on Wednesday.

You are in the left center of Lieutenant General *Leonidas Polk's* corps. This corps was composed of Major General *Jones M. Wither's* division and Major General *Benjamin F. Cheatham's* division. *Wither's* Division, consisting of four brigades, was deployed in the first line. From left to right they were the brigades commanded by Colonel *J. Q. Loomis,* Colonel *Arthur M. Manigault,* Brigadier General *James Patton Anderson,* and Brigadier General *James R. Chalmers. Loomis's, Manigault's* and *Anderson's* Brigades were deployed between the Franklin Road and the Wilkinson Turnpike. *Chalmers's* Brigade was deployed between the Wilkinson Turnpike and the Nashville-Murfreesboro Pike.

Cheatham's four brigades were deployed in a supporting line behind *Withers.* From left to right they were the brigades commanded by Colonel *Alfred J. Vaughan,* Brigadier General *George Maney,* Brigadier General *Alexander P. Stewart,* and Brigadier General *Daniel L. Donelson. Vaughan's, Maney's,* and *Stewart's* Brigades were deployed between the Franklin Road and the Wilkinson Turnpike. *Donelson's* Brigade was deployed astride the Wilkinson Turnpike.

Because of the nature of the ground and the extended division frontages, *Cheatham* and *Withers* both realized it would be extremely difficult if not impossible for one to control the front line while another controlled the supporting line. To overcome this problem they decided that *Cheatham* would control the two attacking brigades and the two supporting brigades on the left. *Withers* would do the same for the four brigades on the right.

The grounds to your left and in front of you were corn and cotton fields. To your right, on the other side of today's road, was a wood. Three hundred yards west of here the wood ended and there was an open field. The Union position was along the higher ground 500 yards in front of you. Directly in front of you was Brigadier General Philip H. Sheridan's division. As you view the position, Brigadier General Joshua W. Sill's brigade was astride of and to the left of today's road. Colonel George W. Roberts's brigade was to the right of today's road. Colonel Frederick Schaefer's brigade was in position as a reserve behind the two forward brigades.

Brigadier General Jefferson C. Davis's division was deployed to Sheridan's right, your left. As you view the position from right to left, they were the brigades of Colonel William E. Woodruff, Colonel William P. Carlin, and Colonel P. Sidney Post. You looked at the actions of Post's brigade at Stop 3, which is 2,200 yards in a southwest direction from your location.

Polk's report gives a good overview of the fighting done by the units in the left half of his corps as they attacked Sheridan's first and two subsequent positions

Report of Lieut. Gen. *Leonidas Polk,* CSA, Commanding *Polk's* Corps, Army of Tennessee

Orders were issued by the general commanding [*Bragg*] to attack in the morning at daybreak. The attack was to be made by the extreme left, and the whole line was ordered to swing around from left to right upon my right brigade as a pivot. Major-General *Breckinridge,* on the extreme right and across the river, was to hold the enemy in observation on that flank.

At the appointed time the battle opened, evidently to the surprise of the opposing army. Major-General *McCown,* who was acting under the orders of Lieutenant-General *Hardee,* was upon them before they were prepared to receive him. He captured several batteries and one brigadier-

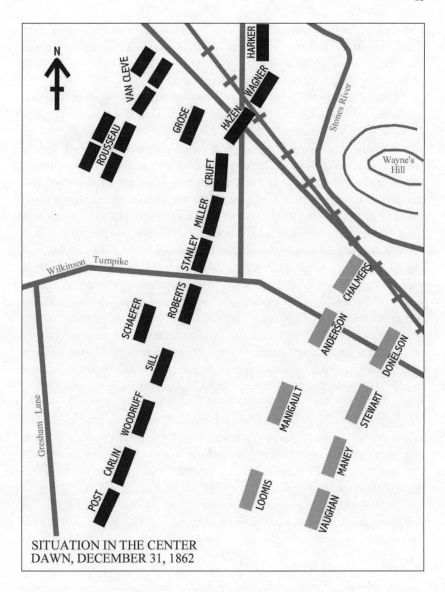

**SITUATION IN THE CENTER
DAWN, DECEMBER 31, 1862**

general, wounded another, and drove three brigades—those composing
the division of Brigadier-General Johnson—in confusion before him. He
was followed quickly by Major-General *Cleburne* as a supporting force,
who occupied the space left vacant by the forward movement of *McCown*
between the left of my front line and *McCown's* right. Opposing him in that
space was the [First] Division, of Major-General McCook's corps, under
the command of Brig. Gen. J. C. Davis, to confront which he had to wheel

to the right, as the right of General McCook's corps was slightly refused. *Cleburne's* attack, following so soon on that of *McCown,* caught the force in his front also not altogether prepared, and the vigor of the assault was so intense that they, too, yielded and were driven.

Major-General *Withers'* left was opposed to the right of General Sheridan, commanding the Third and remaining division of General McCook's corps. The enemy's right was strongly posted on a ridge of rocks, with chasms intervening, and covered with a dense growth of rough cedars. Being advised of the attack he was to expect by the fierce contest which was being waged on his right, he was fully prepared for the onset, and this notice and the strength of his position enabled him to offer a strong resistance to *Withers,* whose duty it was to move next. Colonel *Loomis,* who commanded the left brigade, moved up with energy and spirit to the attack. He was wounded and was succeeded by Colonel *Coltart.* The enemy met the advance with firmness, but was forced to yield. An accession of force aided him to recover his position, and its great strength enabled him to hold it. *Coltart,* after a gallant charge and a sharp contest, fell back, and was replaced by Colonel *Vaughan,* of Major-General *Cheatham's* division, of the rear line. *Vaughan,* notwithstanding the difficulties of the ground, charged the position with great energy; but the enemy, intrenched behind stones and covered by the thick woods, could not be moved, and *Vaughan* also was repulsed. This caused a loss of time, and *Cleburne's* division, pressing Davis, reached a point where Sheridan's batteries, still unmoved, by wheeling to the right, enfiladed it. Colonel *Vaughan* was speedily reorganized and returned to the assault, drove at the position with resistless courage and energy; and although their losses were very heavy, the enemy could not bear up against the onset. He was dislodged and driven with the rest of the fleeing [regiments] of McCook's corps.

In this charge the horses of every officer of the field and staff of *Vaughan's* brigade, except one, and the horses of all the officers of the field and staff of every regiment, except two, were killed. The brigade lost also one-third of all its force. It captured two of the enemy's field guns.

The brigade of Colonel *Manigault,* which was immediately on the right of that of Colonel *Coltart* [*Loomis*], followed the movement of the latter, according to instructions; but as *Coltart* failed in the first onset to drive Sheridan's right, *Manigault,* after dashing forward and pressing the enemy's line in his front back upon his second line, was brought under a very heavy fire of artillery from two batteries on his right, supported by a very heavy infantry force. He was, therefore, compelled to fall back.

In this charge the brigade suffered severely, sustaining a very heavy loss in officers and men, but returned to the charge a second and a third time, and, being aided by the brigade of General *Maney*, of the second line, which came to his relief with its heavy Napoleon guns and a deadly fire of musketry, the enemy gave way and joined his comrades on the right in their precipitate retreat across the Wilkinson pike. This movement dislodged and drove the residue of Sheridan's division, and completed the forcing of the whole of McCook's corps out of its line of battle and placed it in full retreat. The enemy left one of his batteries of four guns on the field, which fell into the hands of *Maney's* brigade. [*OR* 20, pt. 1, pp. 686–88.]

You are where Colonel *Arthur M. Manigault's* brigade was deployed. Five hundred yards to *Manigault's* left was Colonel *L. Q. Loomis's* brigade. Behind *Manigault* was *Maney's* Brigade, and *Vaughan's* Brigade was behind *Loomis*. *Cheatham* controlled these four brigades.

Loomis's Brigade, as *Cheatham's* left brigade, was to go forward when *McCown* began his attack. However, there was a small delay and *Loomis* did not begin his attack until 7:00. *Loomis's* three left regiments, the Twenty-sixth, Thirty-ninth, and Twenty-fifth Alabama, attacked Woodruff's position, while the right three regiments, the First Louisiana and Nineteenth and Twenty-second Alabama, struck the right of Sill's brigade where it joined with Woodruff.

Woodruff had all three of his regiments and the Eighth Wisconsin Battery on line to defend his position. From your perspective they were from right to left as follows: the Eighth Wisconsin Battery, Eighty-first Indiana, Twenty-fifth Illinois, and Thirty-fifth Illinois.

Report of Col. William E. Woodruff, USA, Commanding Third Brigade, First Division, Right Wing, Army of the Cumberland

The topography of the country in this line and in my front was a cotton-field, which we then occupied, at the farther end of which was a belt or strip of timber, ending at a corn-field on my left and front, and immediately in front of Brigadier-General Sill's right. This corn-field extended to a narrow, heavy-timbered wood, bordered by a rail fence. Beyond this timber was a corn-field, receding toward a ravine, terminated by a bluff wood bank, along the foot of which, in the ravine, was the enemy's line of battle, with its supports and artillery on the elevation.

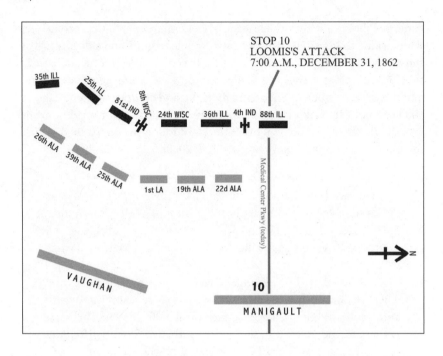

As soon as day dawned I examined the line of battle, and, as I had no supports, placed three pieces in battery on my left, and pointed out to Brigadier-General Sill the weakness of the line at this point, and requested him to order up some regiments of his brigade, held in reserve, to strengthen his right and protect my left, feeling certain that the enemy meditated an attack, and that it would be made at that place. He agreed with me, and immediately ordered up two regiments, which remained there but a short time, and then resumed their former positions as reserve. [These two regiments were from Schaefer's brigade.] Deeming the knowledge of this fact of paramount importance, I dispatched a staff officer to Brigadier-General Davis to give him the information. Afterward the general informed me that I must hold the position as best I could, for he had no supports to send me.

Almost simultaneously with the withdrawal of the reserves ordered up by Brigadier-General Sill, the enemy made their attack in five heavy lines, and we were immediately engaged. Captain Carpenter's [Eighth Wisconsin] battery opened with terrific effect with grape and canister, and they were mowed down as grass beneath the sickle, while the infantry poured in a well-directed and very destructive fire. Sheltered by the rail fence, they were partially protected, and fired with the coolness of veterans.

As soon as the battle became general, the Twenty-fourth Wisconsin [of Sill's brigade], which joined my left, gave way, leaving my battery and left flank exposed to an enfilading fire. I finally succeeded in rallying them as a reserve. At this moment the right of Brigadier-General Sill's brigade commenced to swing to the rear, and Colonel Carlin's [on Woodruff's right] was discovered falling steadily back.

I then received orders to take position to the rear, some 300 yards, in the belt of timber. I informed the staff officer who brought the order that we could maintain our position if supported. He said the order was peremptory, and I hastened to execute it, but not until I was flanked both on the right and left. The brigade moved to the rear in good order, and halted on the new line; but the right and left continuing the march, and being severely pressed, we made a vigorous charge and drove the enemy back in our front, and, strange to say, not only carried our point, but swung the enemy's lines upon right and left with it.

We regained our position occupied when the battle opened, but could hold it but a moment, when we were forced to yield to superior numbers, and steadily fell back to the ground from which the charge was first made. From this point we charged a second time, compelling the enemy to yield ground, but our ammunition beginning to fail, and no wagons to be found from which to replenish the stock, the brigade was ordered to hold its position as best it could, and, if pressed too hard, to fall steadily back until the battery could be got into position to protect their movement across the cotton-field. I placed the battery in position, and gave the officer in command (Sergeant Obadiah German) directions where to fire, pointing out to him the position of the brigade, and what he was required to do.

The ammunition of the regiments now entirely failing, and a perfect rout appearing to have taken place, the brigade fell back. At this time the whole wing was in the utmost confusion, and I used every endeavor to rally and organize them, but without avail. [*OR* 20, pt. 1, pp. 287–89.]

After *Loomis* had been repulsed, *Vaughan's* Brigade moved forward and attacked where *Loomis* had. *Vaughan's* first attack was repulsed, but he rallied his brigade and led his six regiments in a second attack that was successful.

Report of Col. *Alfred J. Vaughan*, CSA, Commanding *Smith's* Brigade, *Cheatham's* Division, *Polk's* Corps, Army of Tennessee

At daylight [Wednesday] morning the battle opened, and before sunrise I received information that the front line needed immediate support, and moved my command forward. The Ninth Texas Regiment, having been for safety rested about 100 yards in rear of its position in alignment, was unable, because of that fact and the want of room between the right of the line and the road, it being on the extreme left, to move in line with the brigade. Accordingly, Capt. *M. W. Cluskey,* assistant adjutant-general, moved it and rested it on the right of *Wood's* brigade. Moving the balance of my brigade obliquely across the open field under a tremendous artillery and infantry fire, I soon occupied the front of our line, on the left of *Manigault's* brigade, and engaged a largely superior force of the enemy in a most

Colonel *Alfred J. Vaughan*, CSA. Library of Congress.

hotly contested fight, driving him away from two of his guns, which had been prominent in contesting our advance.

About the same time my assistant adjutant-general gave Colonel *W. H. Young,* of the Ninth Texas Infantry, orders to move forward from the position in which he had placed it, on the right of *Wood's* brigade, and attack the enemy sheltered in the woods in front of him, which he did in most gallant style, and succeeded in driving him, though with great loss, through the woods and open field on the other side. On the right, after driving the enemy from the guns mentioned, *Manigault's* brigade, not being supported by its reserve, gave way, and my brigade, having none either in reserve or on my immediate left, was forced by the enemy, heavily re-enforced, to withdraw, which it did, after being commanded by me so to do, in good order, rallying on their colors on their original line. I again advanced my command, this time through the woods and to the left of my former line of advance, and reached the large open fields between the Wilkinson and Triune [Franklin Road] pikes under a heavy fire of artillery. Forming on the left of *Maney's* brigade, I placed the Ninth Texas Infantry, which had again united with my command, on my right, and rested my men, to shelter them from the severe artillery fire of the enemy, which was being unremittingly hailed upon them. [*OR* 20, pt. 1, 743–44.]

> Woodruff's brigade repulsed two attacks against their position, one by *Loomis's* Brigade and a second by *Vaughan's* Brigade. During *Vaughan's* next attack Woodruff's regiments fell back to the northwest and tried to occupy a position east, left, of Baldwin's brigade at Stop 5 and just south of the Wilkinson Turnpike. Unable to maintain that position, the brigade retreated with the rest of Davis's and Johnson's divisions to the Nashville-Murfreesboro Pike.
>
> While attacking Woodruff, *Loomis* also was attacking a portion of Sill's brigade with his three right regiments. As you view it, Sill's position was 500 yards in front of you and to the left of today's road. As you look at the position, Sill deployed, from your left to right, the Twenty-fourth Wisconsin, Thirty-sixth Illinois, and Eighty-eight Illinois. The Fourth Indiana Battery was placed between the Thirty-sixth and Eighty-eighth Illinois. The Twenty-first Michigan was held in reserve. During this fight Sill was killed and Colonel Nicholas Greusel assumed command of the brigade. The Thirty-sixth Illinois was representative of the fighting in this area.

Report of Capt. Porter C. Olson, USA, Commanding Thirty-sixth Illinois Infantry, First Brigade, Third Division, Right Wing, Army of the Cumberland

On the morning of December 31, soon after daylight, the enemy advanced in strong force from the timber from beyond the cotton-field opposite our right. They came diagonally across the field. Upon reaching the foot of the hill, they made a left half-wheel and came up directly in front of us. When the enemy had advanced up the hill sufficiently to be in sight, Colonel Greusel ordered the regiment to fire, which was promptly obeyed. We engaged the enemy at short range, the lines being not over 10 rods apart. [A rod is 5.5 yards; therefore 10 rods = 55 yards.] After a few rounds, the regiment supporting us on our right gave way. In this manner we fought for nearly half an hour, when Colonel Greusel ordered the regiment to charge. The enemy fled in great confusion across the cotton-field into the woods opposite our left, leaving many of their dead and wounded upon the field. We poured a destructive fire upon them as they retreated until they were beyond range.

The Thirty-sixth again took position upon the hill, and the support of our right came forward. At this time General Sill was killed, and Colonel Greusel took command of the brigade. A fresh brigade of the enemy advanced from the direction that the first had come, and in splendid order. We opened fire on them with terrific effect. Again the regiment on our right gave way, and we were again left without support. In this condition we fought until our ammunition was exhausted, and until the enemy had entirely flanked us on our right. At this juncture Major Miller ordered the regiment to fall back. While retreating, Major Miller was wounded, and the command devolved upon me. We moved back of the corn-field to the edge of the timber, a hundred rods [550 yards] to the right [north] of the Wilkinson pike and 2 miles from Murfreesboro, at 8 a.m. Here I met General Sheridan, and reported to him that the regiment was out of ammunition, and that I would be ready for action as soon as I could obtain it. We had suffered severely in resisting the attack of superior numbers. I had now only 140 men. [*OR* 20, pt. 1, pp. 358–59.]

Stop 10 (Continued)—*Manigault's* Attack

In 1862 there was woods to your right. In front of you and to your left were corn and cotton fields. In front of you at a distance of 500 yards was Sheridan's defensive position. Astride of and to the left of today's road was Sill's brigade. North, right as you see it, of the road was Roberts's brigade. Positioned left of where Medical Center Parkway is today was Captain Asahel K. Bush's Fourth Indiana Battery. To the right rear of Robert's brigade on a rise of ground were positioned Captain Henry Hescock's Battery G, First Missouri Artillery, and Captain Charles Houghtaling's Battery C, First Illinois Artillery. These two batteries were so positioned as to be able to bring oblique fire into the right of any Confederate force attacking Sill's position.

To your left *Loomis* and *Vaughan* attacked the right of Sill's brigade and Woodruff's brigade. You are in the center of Colonel *Arthur M. Manigault's* brigade. This five regiments brigade was a part of *Withers's* Division. *Manigault* faced west. To his right and angling off to the northeast was Brigadier General *James Patton Anderson's* brigade. In conjunction with *Loomis's* and *Vaughan's*

Brigades *Manigault* made two attacks on Sheridan's position directly to his front, and then with *Vaughan* and *Maney* he made a third attack against Sheridan's defenses after he reformed them facing south between Medical Center Parkway and the Wilkinson Turnpike.

Looking West from Stop 10. Sheridan's first position was on the higher ground.

Narrative of Col. *Arthur M. Manigault*, CSA, Commanding *Manigault's* Brigade, *Withers's* Division, *Polk's Corps*, Army of Tennessee

At four o'clock on the morning of 31st of December 1862, I received the order for battle. At seven o'clock the firing commenced on the extreme left of our line, and was taken up to the right by each brigade in succession. The first divisions engaged [*McCown's* and *Cleburne's*] taking the enemy by surprise, met with great success, and drove the Federal troops rapidly before them. But by the time our turn came, they were somewhat prepared for us. Our instructions were to attack the troops in our front, defeat and drive them back, endeavoring to swing ourselves round, so as to form a line continuous with the one to the right of our brigade, having accomplished which, the remainder of the troops beyond and to the right of the angle would in a like manner advance and attack.

Deas's brigade to our left, temporarily commanded by its senior Colonel, *Loomis,* soon became engaged, and our own immediately afterwards, the Thirty-fourth Alabama, Col. [*Julius C. B.*] *Mitchell,* [on the left of the brigade line] advancing first in line, the others following by an echelon movement, a distance of about 50 yards between them, in the following order [from left to right]: Twenty-eighth Alabama, Col. [*John C.*] *Reid;* Twenty-fourth Alabama, Col. [*William A.*] *Buck;* Nineteenth South Carolina, Col. [*Augustus J.*] *Lythgoe;* Tenth South Carolina, Lieut. Col. [*James F.*] *Pressley.* Their advance was met by a heavy fire in front, and as they cleared the woods and got well into the cotton field which lay between the two lines, the Yankee troops and two batteries to the right who, themselves not being attacked, could devote their attention to us, the formation of their line corresponding to our own, enabled them to pour into our flank a heavy fire in addition to that from the lines against which our movement was directed. Their first line was broken by each regiment in succession, but their second line, owing to the disadvantages operating against us, was to much for us. We were forced to retire, our supports, *Maney's* brigade of Tennesseans, of *Cheatham's* division, not coming to our support. [R. Lockwood Tower, ed., *A South Carolinian Goes to War: The Civil War Narrative of Arthur Middleton*

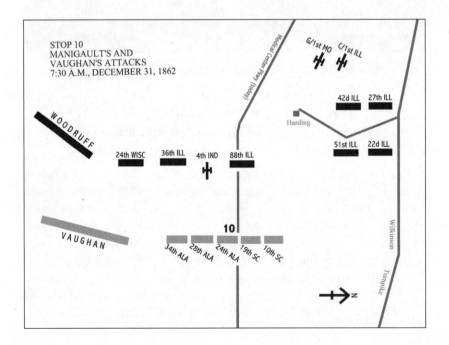

Manigault, Brigadier General, CSA (Columbia: University of South Carolina Press for the Charleston Library Society, 1983), 56–57 (hereafter cited as *Manigault Narrative*).]

Manigault's first attack was repulsed and he fell back to this location, where he rallied his troops and commenced a second attack at the same time *Vaughan's* brigade on his left began its first attack.

Narrative of Col. *Arthur M. Manigault,* CSA—Continued

Hastily reforming the brigade, and sending an officer to General *Maney* informing him of our failure of complete success, and that I was preparing for a second effort, urging him to support me promptly, I received the answer that he would do so. Again, we advanced, carrying everything before us in the first line of the enemy, suffering and losing many men from the fire to our right which we could not return, and which no other troops drew from us, the time not having arrived for them to advance and our reserves, still tardy in their movements, not appearing, reluctantly we were compelled again to withdraw. [*Manigault Narrative,* 57.]

Colonel *Arthur M. Manigault,* CSA. Charleston Library Society.

Manigault's second attack was repulsed when his right was hit by a counterattack by part of Roberts's brigade. This caused his brigade and *Vaughan's* to fall back. A third assault by *Manigault, Maney,* and *Vaughan* was successful in taking the second position that Sheridan redeployed to when Roberts made his counterattack.

Report of Brig. Gen. Philip H. Sheridan, USA, Commanding Third Division, Right Wing, Army of the Cumberland

I had taken up my position, my right resting in the timber, my left on the Wilkinson pike, and my reserve brigade, of four regiments, to the rear and opposite the center.

The enemy appeared to be in strong force in a heavy cedar wood across an open valley in my front and parallel to it, the cedar extending the whole length of the valley, the distance across the valley varying from 300 to 400 yards.

At 2 o'clock on the morning of the 31st, General Sill, who had command of my right brigade, reported great activity on the part of the enemy immediately in his front. This being the narrowest point in the valley, I was fearful that an attack might occur at that point. I therefore directed two regiments from the reserves to report to General Sill, who placed them in position in very short supporting distance of his lines.

At 4 o'clock in the morning the division was assembled under arms, and the cannoneers at their pieces. About 7.15 o'clock in the morning the enemy advanced to the attack across an open cotton-field, on Sill's front. This column was opened upon by Bush's battery, of Sill's brigade, which had a direct fire on its front; also by Hescock's and Houghtaling's batteries, which had an oblique fire on its front from a commanding position near the center of my line. The effect of this fire upon the enemy's column was terrible. The enemy, however, continued to advance until they had reached nearly the edge of the timber, when they were opened upon by Sill's infantry, at a range of not over 50 yards. The destruction to the enemy's column, which was closed in mass, being several regiments in depth, was terrible. For a short time they withstood the fire, wavered, then broke and ran, Sill directing his troops to charge, which was gallantly responded to, and the enemy driven back across the valley and behind their intrenchments.

In this charge I had the misfortune to lose General Sill, who was killed. The brigade then fell back in good order and resumed its original lines. The enemy soon rallied and advanced to the attack on my extreme right and in front of Colonel Woodruff, of Davis' division. Here, unfortunately, the brigade of Colonel Woodruff gave way; also one regiment of Sill's brigade, which was in the second line. This regiment fell back some distance into the open field and there rallied, its place being occupied by a third regiment of my reserve.

At this time the enemy, who had made an attack on the extreme right of our wing against Johnson and also on Davis' front, had been successful, and the two divisions on my right were retiring in great confusion, closely followed by the enemy, completely turning my position and exposing my line to a fire from the rear. I hastily withdrew the whole of Sill's brigade and the three regiments sent to support it, at the same time directing Colonel Roberts, of the left brigade, who had changed front and formed in column of regiments, to charge the enemy in the timber from which I had withdrawn those regiments. This was very gallantly done by Colonel Roberts, who captured one piece of the enemy's artillery, which had to be abandoned. [*OR* 20, pt. 1, p. 348.]

Brigadier General Joshua W. Sill, USA. Library of Congress.

The attack made by Roberts that Sheridan makes reference to was a counterattack into *Manigault's* right during his second attack. This counterattack forced *Manigault* to fall back to this location. To conduct this attack, Roberts faced the Fifty-first, Forty-second, and Twenty-seventh Illinois Regiments to his right and attacked in a southeasterly direction striking *Manigault's* Brigade.

Report of Col. Luther P. Bradley, USA, Commanding Third Brigade, Third Division, Right Wing, Army of the Cumberland

On the morning of the 31st, the brigade was under arms at daylight, and soon after formed line of battle. The enemy's columns opened out from the opposite woods, and Colonel Roberts ordered a skirmishing force to advance and feel the timber on our left. Companies A and B, Twenty-seventh Illinois, were thrown out under Major Schmitt, the balance of the regiment being held in reserve, its left resting on the [Wilkinson] pike.

About 8.30 a.m. Colonel Roberts ordered the Twenty-second, Forty-second, and Fifty-first to charge the enemy's columns, and gallantly led them in person. The Forty-second and Fifty-first charged in line, with the Twenty-second in rear of the Forty-second, at battalion distance. These regiments went forward at the double-quick, and cleared the wood in front of our lines, the enemy giving way before we reached him. The line was halted,

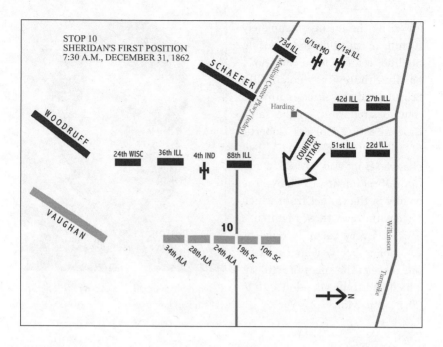

STOP 10
SHERIDAN'S FIRST POSITION
7:30 A.M., DECEMBER 31, 1862

and opened fire in the timber. After some ten minutes, the line on our right giving way, we were ordered to retire to the lane leading at nearly right angles with the pike, and take a new position. [This lane went south from the Wilkinson Turnpike to the Harding house.] [*OR* 20, pt. 1, pp. 369–70.]

While Roberts was conducting his counterattack, Sheridan pulled his right flank back to the northwest. As Roberts's brigade fell back from its counterattack, it occupied a position along the Wilkinson Turnpike. Sheridan's two other brigades went into position facing south, 400 yards south of the turnpike.

Return to your car for the drive to Stop 11.

Drive out of the parking lot; turn left on to Medical Center Parkway and drive for 1.2 miles to the Wilkinson Turnpike. Turn right on to the Wilkinson Turnpike, drive 50 yards, then turn right again and drive for 0.4 mile to a road on your left called Blanton's Pointe. Turn left on to Blanton's Pointe, do a U-turn, and drive back toward Wilkinson Turnpike. Twenty-five yards before you reach Wilkinson Turnpike pull off to the side, stop, and get out of your car. DO NOT take a bus on to Blanton's Pointe, as you will not be able to turn around. Face south toward the Wilkinson

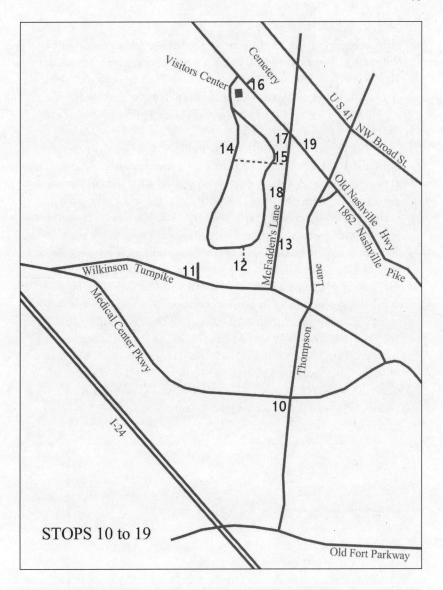

STOPS 10 to 19

Turnpike. All of the land around you is private property; do not trespass.

Stop 11—Sheridan's Second Position

The ground in front of you was a cornfield then, beyond that, open fields. To your right was a cornfield that went for 600 yards, and then there was a woods. To your immediate left was a woods, and 250 yards to your left front was a woods. It is from these woods that Roberts launched his counterattack into *Manigault's* right flank. The Harding house was 500 yards in front of you. The Medical Center Parkway and the center of Sheridan's first position were 800 yards in front of you.

Sheridan used the lull caused by Roberts's counterattack to shift his right flank back so that it now faced south. Sheridan's second position was along the rise of ground 400 yards in front of you. Two brigades occupied this position. Greusel's (Sill's) brigade formed the right of Sheridan's line with Schaefer's brigade on the left. Captain Bush moved his Fourth Indiana Battery to a position to the right front of Greusel's brigade. Captain Hescock kept Battery G, First Missouri Artillery in its initial position on the small hill but faced it to fire south and southeast. Captain Houghtaling used the protection of Roberts's counterattack to move his Battery C, First Illinois Artillery northeast off the small hill to a position just south of the Wilkinson Turnpike. As Roberts's regiments fell back from their counterattack, they regrouped to the east of Houghtaling's battery. Roberts and Houghtaling provided the left anchor for the remainder of Sheridan's division to form on when they were forced out of their second position.

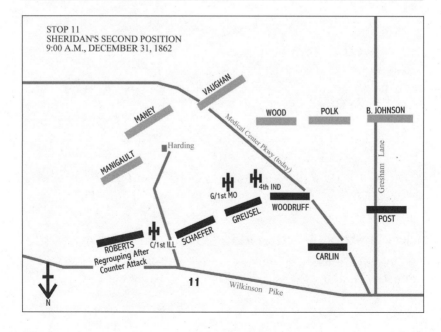

Report of Brig. Gen. Philip H. Sheridan, USA, Commanding Third Division, Right Wing, Army of the Cumberland

In the mean time I had formed Sill's [Greusel's] and Schaefer's brigades on a line at right angles to my first line, and behind the three batteries of artillery, which were placed in a fine position, directing Colonel Roberts to return and form on this new line. I then made an unavailing attempt to form the troops on my right on this line, in front of which there were open fields, through which the enemy was approaching under a heavy fire from Hescock's, Houghtaling's, and Bush's batteries. [*OR* 20, pt. 1, p. 349.]

Captain Charles Houghtaling, USA. Massachusetts Commandery Military Order of the Loyal Legion and the U.S. Army Military History Institute.

Captain Bush's report gives a good account of the artillery fight at the first and second defensive position.

Report of Capt. Asahel K. Bush, USA, Commanding Fourth Indiana Battery, Third Division, Right Wing, Army of the Cumberland

About daylight [we] were attacked by the enemy. We replied with canister at short range until General Sheridan's division was completely flanked, by General Davis' division retreating, and obliged to retire. We fixed prolongs and retired in rear of the brigade, firing canister.

Made another short stand at the [next] position and fired canister from my howitzer and 6 pounder smooth-bores into the enemy in front, and with my rifles drove two of the enemy's pieces from position, which were firing on General Davis' retreating lines; lost one caisson in reaching this position, every horse on it being shot down by the enemy's musketry.

Part of Sheridan's second position as seen from Stop 11.

Here the under-straps of one of my smoothbore 6-pounders were broken by firing double charges of canister, and I sent the piece to the rear. [*OR* 20, pt.1, p. 355.]

The collapse of Johnson's and Davis's defenses on Sheridan's right forced him to withdraw his right and establish a new position that faced south. To Sheridan's right, west, Woodruff, Carlin, and Post were also attempting to form a defensive line against the attacks by *McCown* and *Cleburne*.

Sheridan's redeployment provided the opportunity for *Vaughan* and *Manigault* to turn their brigades to the right and begin to attack north. *Maney's* Brigade joined them in this movement and attack. They lined up from your left to right as follows: *Manigault's* Brigade, *Maney's* Brigade, *Vaughan's* Brigade, and then the brigades of *S. A. M. Wood, Lucius Polk,* and *Bushrod Johnson.*

Narrative of Col. *Arthur M. Manigault,* CSA, Commanding *Manigault's* Brigade, *Withers's* Division, *Polk's* Corps, Army of Tennessee

Seeing that the enemy were much shaken and gave evidence of uneasiness, their right wing haven been driven back, and exposing the right of the troops opposite to us, in concert with General *Maney,* he moving a portion of his command still further to the left than my brigade front, a third advance was made, before which the enemy gave way. [*Manigault Narrative,* 57.]

Stop 11 (Continued)—
Sheridan's Third Defensive Position

Again outflanked on his right, Sheridan fell back to the vicinity of where you are now and established his third defensive position. Sheridan's position was in the shape of a V with the point of the V pointed south. Across the Wilkinson Turnpike and 25 yards to your left was a country lane going to the Harding house, which was 500 yards south of your present location.

Just south of the Wilkinson Turnpike, along the lane to the Harding house and facing southwest, were two guns each from the Fourth Indiana Battery and Battery G, First Missouri Artillery. Next was Battery C, First Illinois Artillery. Next to Battery C and going northeast so as to form a right angle was the Twenty-second Illinois and Forty-second Illinois of Roberts's brigade. To the left of the Forty-second was the Twenty-first Michigan of Greusel's (Sill's) brigade, which was supporting the four remaining guns of Battery G, First Missouri Artillery. To this battery's left was four guns of the Fourth Indiana Battery. Both batteries were this side of the Wilkinson Turnpike. To your left and also just this side of the turnpike were the other two regiments of Roberts's brigade, the Twenty-seventh and Fifty-first Illinois. The Fifty-first faced southeast, and the Twenty-seventh on its right formed a right angle as it faced southwest. From the right of the Twenty-seventh Illinois, Sheridan's line went northwest with the Second Missouri and then the Fifteenth Missouri of Schaefer's brigade. Schaefer's other two regiment, the Forty-fourth Illinois and Seventy-third Illinois, had earlier been sent off the line to resupply their ammunition and only rejoined the brigade in time to retreat from this position. To Schaefer's right was the Twenty-fourth Wisconsin and Eighty-eighth Illinois of Greusel's brigade. Of Greusel's other two regiments, the Twenty-first Michigan was supporting Battery G, First Missouri, and the Thirty-sixth Illinois had earlier been sent to the rear in search of ammunition.

Behind Roberts's brigade was Colonel Timothy R. Stanley's brigade of four regiments. To Stanley's left were the four regiments

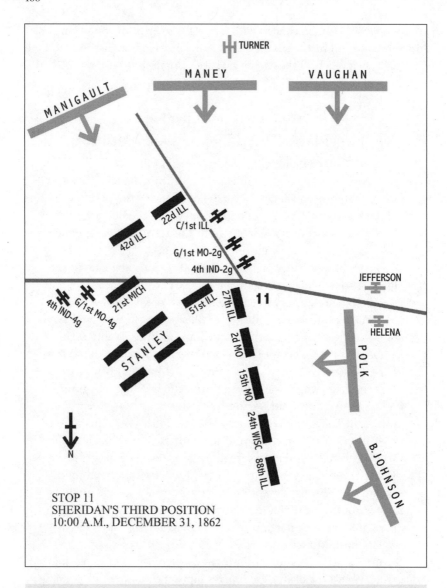

STOP 11
SHERIDAN'S THIRD POSITION
10:00 A.M., DECEMBER 31, 1862

of Colonel John F. Miller's brigade and three batteries of artillery. These two brigades and the artillery were from Brigadier General James S. Negley's division.

To the right and right rear of Greusel's brigade, three brigades of Major General Lovell H. Rousseau's division moved into the cedar woods in an attempt to extend Sheridan's line to the northwest.

Report of Brig. Gen. Philip H. Sheridan, USA, Commanding Third Division, Right Wing, Army of the Cumberland

I took position on Negley's right, Roberts' brigade having been placed in position [to the right of] Negley's line, facing to the south, the other two brigades being placed to the rear and at right angles with Roberts', and facing the west, covering the rear of Negley's lines. I then directed Houghtaling's battery [C, First Illinois] to take position at the angle of these two lines, Captain Hescock sending one section [two guns] of his battery, under Lieutenant Taliaferro, and one section of Bush's battery, to the same point. The remaining pieces of Hescock's [G, First Missouri] and Bush's [Fourth Indiana] batteries were placed on the right of Negley's line, facing toward Murfreesboro. In this position I was immediately attacked, when one of the bitterest and most sanguinary contests of the day occurred.

General *Cheatham's* division advanced on Roberts' brigade, and heavy masses of the enemy, with three batteries of artillery, advanced over the open ground which I had occupied in the previous part of the engagement, at the same time the enemy opening from their intrenchments in the direction of Murfreesboro. The contest then became terrible. The enemy made three attacks, and were three times repulsed, the artillery range of the respective batteries being not over 200 yards. In these attacks Roberts' brigade lost its gallant commander, who was killed. There was no sign of faltering with the men, the only cry being for more ammunition, which unfortunately could not be supplied.

Schaefer's brigade being entirely out of ammunition, I directed them to fix bayonets and await the enemy. Roberts' brigade, which was nearly out of ammunition, I directed to fall back, resisting the enemy. Captain Houghtaling, having exhausted all his ammunition, and nearly all the horses in his battery having been killed, attempted, with the assistance of the men, to withdraw his pieces by hand. Lieutenant Taliaferro, commanding the section of Hescock's battery, having been killed and several of his horses shot, his two pieces were brought off by his sergeant, with the assistance of the men. The difficulty of withdrawing the artillery here became very great, the ground being rocky and covered with a dense growth of cedar. Houghtaling's battery had to be abandoned; also two pieces of Bush's battery. The remaining pieces of artillery in the division were brought through the cedars with great difficulty, under a terrible fire from the enemy, on to the open space on the Murfreesboro pike, near the right of General Palmer's division.

In coming through the cedars, two regiments of Schaefer's brigade succeeded in obtaining ammunition, and were immediately put in front to resist the enemy, who appeared to be driving in our entire lines.

On arriving at the open space, I was directed by Major-General Rosecrans to take those two regiments and put them into action on the right of Palmer's division, where the enemy were pressing heavily.

The two regiments went in very gallantly, driving the enemy from the cedar timber and some distance to the front. At the same time I put four pieces of Hescock's battery into action near by and on the same front. The other two regiments of Schaefer's brigade, and the Thirty-sixth Illinois, of Sill's brigade, were directed to cross the railroad, where they could obtain ammunition. I then, by direction of Major-General McCook, withdrew the two regiments that had been placed on the right of Palmer's division; also Captain Hescock's pieces, that point having been given up to the enemy in the rearrangement of our lines.

These regiments of Schaefer's brigade, having supplied themselves with ammunition, I put into action, by direction of Major-General Rosecrans, directly to the front and right of General Wood's division, on the left-hand [east] side of the railroad. [This is the fight at the Round Forest.]

At this point I lost my third and last brigade commander, Col. Frederick Schaefer, who was killed. [These regiments], after remaining in this position until after [they] had expended [their] ammunition, [were] withdrawn to the rear of this timber, where [they were] again supplied and joined by the Thirty-sixth Illinois. I was here directed by General Rosecrans to form a close column of attack and charge the enemy, should they again come down on the open ground.

The remaining portion of the evening this gallant brigade remained in close column of regiments and under the fire of the enemy's batteries which killed about 20 of the men by round shot. In the mean time Colonel Roberts' brigade, which had come out of the cedars unbroken, was put into action by General McCook at a point a short distance to the rear, where the enemy threatened our communication on the Murfreesboro pike. The brigade, having but three or four rounds of ammunition [per soldier], cheerfully went into action, gallantly charged the enemy, routing them, recapturing two pieces of artillery, and taking 40 prisoners. The rout of the enemy at this point deserves special consideration, as they had here nearly reached the Murfreesboro pike.

The following is the total of casualties in the division: Officers killed, 15; wounded, 58; missing, 11; total of officers, 64. Enlisted men killed, 223; wounded, 943; missing, 400; total of enlisted men, 1,566. Aggregate, 1,630. Of the 11 officers and 400 enlisted men missing, many are known to be wounded and in the hands of the enemy. [OR 20, pt. 1, pp. 349–51.]

A view of the fighting from the company perspective was recorded in a letter written on January 5, 1863, by Captain John H. Phillips, Company D, Twenty-second Illinois Infantry. At dawn the Twenty-second Illinois was to your left front on the other side of the Wilkinson Turnpike. The Twenty-second Illinois began the day with 350 officers and men. At the end of the day, 199 were still with the regiment.

Narrative of Capt. John H. Phillips, USA, Commanding Company D, Twenty-second Illinois Infantry, Third Brigade, Third Division, Right Wing, Army of the Cumberland

Early on the morning of the 31st we were to arms. . . . The firing was very heavy on our right and the enemy had driven one brigade of our division out of a piece of timber when Col. Roberts rode up and ordered the brigade to charge and retake it. Which they did in gallant stile capturing one piece of artillery. It was now evident Johnson's and Davis's divisions were falling back and the rebels were flanking us, so our brigade changed position to the cedar grove where we had been the day previous and farther to the [right] Hoetling's [Houghtaling's] battery belonging to Roberts' brigade also changed position. The rebels on our front and right flank had changed front to the right. Our artillery did great service here driving the rebel columns back three times while they were coming across the cornfield. But their ammunition being exhausted and the rebels pressing us on both sides we were forced to retreat (leaving quite a number of our killed and wounded) to the opposite side of the road [Wilkinson Turnpike] where Col. Roberts ordered the Twenty-second to fix bayonets and charge which they did but were unable to drive them back—here the gallant Roberts fell and the regiment completely cut to pieces—our artillery captured and the rebels were all around us—it seemed for some time that we would all be killed or captured. Grape, shell and bullets were flying around us thick as hail and retreat was impossible. Gen. Negley rode up and said we would have to cut our way out—so we started a perfect mass of companies and came out to the Nashville Pike, which ended the fighting for the Twenty-second. [Letter of John H. Phillip, courtesy of Bob Moulder of Northglenn, Colorado.]

South of you, at a distance of 500 yards, the Confederates lined up for another attack on Sheridan. Directly in front of you was Brigadier General *George Maney's* brigade. *Maney* was taking advantage of the higher ground in front of you to protect his troops from Union fire until they were ready to attack. To *Maney's* right, your left, *Manigault* again reformed his brigade for another attack. To *Maney's* left, your right, *Vaughan* brought his brigade into position for the attack. The center of *Maney's* attack was directed toward the point of the right angle in Sheridan's line.

Report of Brig. Gen. *George Maney*, CSA, Commanding *Maney's* Brigade, *Cheatham's* Division, *Polk's* Corps, Army of Tennessee

Seeing the enemy retiring [from Sheridan's second position], the movement of my line was changed more sharply to the right, throwing a small part of it into the woods on my right and the remainder moving rapidly forward to the ridge-top he had abandoned. A short delay being necessary for Colonel *Manigault* to reform his brigade, my own got considerably in advance, and the battery in the woods opened on my right regiment. Colonel *Feild* at first took this to be our own battery, and ordered his regiment to lie down without firing, though he was within 200 yards of it; nor was this mistake discovered until one messenger to stop its fire had been killed and another narrowly escaped the same fate. His regiment was then ordered to fire, and with the aid of a portion of Colonel *Manigault's* brigade, which came up on the right, soon silenced the battery. Meantime my other two regiments, having attained the ridge-top in the open field but just abandoned by the enemy, were met with a furious shelling from a battery in plain view, about 500 yards distant, and just across the Wilkinson pike. The word coming to me from my right that we were being fired on by our own battery, led me to take the one across the road to be alluded to, that in the woods being at the moment hidden from my sight. Under these circumstances my line was ordered to lie down, and staff officers sent instantly to the right for accurate information. My battle-flag was conspicuously displayed from the ridge-top, but instead of diminishing seemed only to attract the fire of the battery across the road. Next moment suspicion became certainty as to this battery by discovering the flag of the enemy in the woods to the right of and near it. His purpose in withdrawing from the ridge was now plain. The ground between my line and the Wilkinson pike (a distance of from 400 to 500 yards) was an open field, sloping gradually to the pike, on the opposite or north side of which and directly in my front was a thick wood, affording good cover. The enemy had withdrawn from the ridge I now occupied and posted his infantry in these woods, and established his battery so as to rake the field between us with an oblique fire from my front and right. Evidently his dispositions were made in expectation of my moving directly over this field against him. Fortunately, however, the ridge he had abandoned commanded the new position he had taken, and, finding an excellent location for my battery, I got it instantly in position and opened upon him with admirable effect, my infantry line lying down the while for protection. For a short time the artillery fire was hot and spirited, but *Turner's* Napoleons and 12-pounder howitzers, being in easy range and aided by advantage of position, were more than the enemy could stand. His battery was soon silenced and his infantry in retreat under our fire. [*OR* 20, pt. 1, p. 735.]

Brigadier General *George E. Maney*, CSA. Library of Congress.

The artillery supporting *Maney* was *Smith's* Mississippi Battery.

Report of Lieut. *William B. Turner*, CSA, Commanding *Smith's* Mississippi Battery, *Maney's* Brigade, *Cheatham's* Division, *Polk's* Corps, Army of Tennessee

At this point the battery went into action a second time, firing upon one of the enemy's batteries, as well as upon their infantry. In this second engagement the battery fired about 200 rounds, and was engaged about forty minutes; succeeded in silencing the enemy's battery, as well as driving back their infantry. The enemy's battery having ceased firing, and their infantry having fallen back, I was ordered to advance farther onward and take a position near the one occupied by the enemy's battery, which had been captured during the second engagement. [*OR* 20, pt. 1, p. 742.]

On *Maney's* right *Manigault's* Brigade struck Robert's position head on.

Narrative of Col. *Arthur M. Manigault*, CSA—Continued

These two brigades [*Manigault's* and *Maney's*] now swung round [to the north] and prolonged the line, making a straight one. The enemy in our front were awaiting our attack. Their right wing [Johnson's and Davis's divisions] was in full retreat, and unfortunately, the troops who had defeated them, instead of immediately rejoining their comrades and taking a part against that portion of the Yankee army still holding their ground, followed for a considerable distance in pursuit.

Scarcely was our new line formed when I received orders to carry a battery in my front with a part of the troops under my command. [These were the four guns of Hescock's Battery G, First Missouri Artillery that was positioned on the left of Roberts's line.] This battery was near the [Wilkinson] pike, somewhat in advance of their line but supported by a brigade. The Tenth and Nineteenth [South Carolina Regiments] were ordered to carry and capture it if possible, the Tenth in advance. A partial support was given on the right by an Alabama regiment. [This was the Forty-fifth Alabama of Brigadier General *James Patton Anderson's* brigade.] The South Carolina regiments drove the gunners and supports from the battery, shot down the horses as they were endeavoring to retire the guns, and had succeeded in their undertaking, when the Yankee reserve [the Twenty-first Michigan] in turn advanced and drove them back. These regiments had barely time to reform when our entire line moved forward, and the battle, excepting on our extreme right (*Breckinridge's* Division) became general. [*Manigault Narrative,* 57.]

In addition to attacks from the south, Sheridan's position was also under attack from the west. To your right was Brigadier General *Lucius E. Polk's* brigade. *Polk* had been moving north as part of *Cleburne's* attack against Davis's division. As *Polk* reached the Wilkinson Turnpike near the Gresham house he came under fire from Sheridan's artillery positioned along the lane to the Harding house. This forced him to conduct a right wheel just north of the turnpike and attack to the east. In this attack two artillery batteries supported him: Lieutenant *Thomas J. Key's* Helena (Arkansas)

Battery, positioned north of the turnpike, and Captain *Putnam Darden's* Jefferson (Mississippi) Artillery south of the turnpike. This artillery was 400 yards west of your present position. To *Polk's* left and attacking the extreme right of Sheridan's position was Brigadier General *Bushrod Johnson's* brigade.

Report of Brig. Gen. *Lucius E. Polk,* CSA, Commanding *Polk's* Brigade, *Cleburne's* Division, *Hardee's* Corps, Army of Tennessee

I advanced in a line parallel to Wilkinson pike, General *Wood* on my right and General *Johnson* on my left *en echelon,* with the exception of the Seventeenth Tennessee Regiment (which was in advance) of his (*Johnson's*) brigade. Advancing through the pasture, the enemy were seen posted across an open field near one of their hospitals [Grisham house] and only a few hundred yards of the pike. My brigade was obliged to move across this open field with the enemy's artillery and infantry playing upon them. This they did most gallantly, causing the enemy to fall back across the pike under heavy undergrowth of cedars. Getting possession at this place of four or five ordnance wagons, which were sent to the rear, I again moved on, but did not proceed far when the enemy's batteries, posted across a corn-field on the right of the pike, commenced playing fearfully upon my ranks

The battery was so placed, by moving straight forward my line would have been enfiladed. To prevent this, my brigade was wheeled to the right. At this time, Captain *Hotchkiss* sending me word that he had three batteries that required supporting, I left two of my smallest regiments and moved the rest farther to the left, for the purpose of trying to move the enemy's batteries. The Fifth Confederate here first engaged the infantry supporting these batteries, and in a few moments (the First Arkansas arriving in position) their infantry gave way and their batteries changed their position, with the exception of four guns that fell into the hands of the Fifth Confederate and First Arkansas, and in eagerness of pursuit were passed over. [*OR* 20, pt. 1, p. 853.]

From this location *Polk's* Brigade maneuvered north and participated in the attack against Fyffe's and S. Beatty's brigades at Stop 9.

Brigadier General *Lucius E. Polk*, CSA.
Library of Congress.

At dawn on December 31 Sheridan's division had been deployed along an 1,100-yard defensive position that ran south from the Wilkinson Turnpike. By late morning, due to the collapse of the Union defenses to its right and constant attacks on its front, it had been swung back over ninety degrees on the left brigade to a final position facing south and west in the cedars north of the Wilkinson Turnpike.

The collapse of the two divisions to Sheridan's right had been a disaster. Had Sheridan's division fallen apart in the same manner, the situation easily could have been pushed passed the point of redemption. The dogged and costly defense by Sheridan's three brigades had significantly slowed down the inner turning arc of the Confederate northward right turn. This multiposition defense not only caused a significant casualty level to four of *Bragg's* brigades but also provided time for Rosecrans to redeploy forces from his left to his center and right for defense of the Nashville-Murfreesboro Pike. The cost to Sheridan had been high. Two of his three brigade commanders had been killed. The third brigade commander was killed later in the day. Sixty-four other officers and 1,566 enlisted men were killed, wounded, or missing. This was 32 percent of his division.

Return to your car for the drive to Stop 12.

Stop 12 is just 700 yards, 0.4 mile, to your left, but as it is on the other side of the fence behind the house on your left, it is under the control and protection of National Park Service. To reach Stop 12 you will have to go to the entrance of the Stones River National Battlefield and drive almost back to this area.

Drive forward then make a left turn on to the Wilkinson Turnpike. Drive east on the Wilkinson Turnpike Pike for 0.7 mile to Thompson Lane. Turn left on to Thompson Lane and drive north for 0.5 mile to the exit from Thompson Lane to the Stones River National Battlefield. The exit road goes off to the right just before Thompson Lane goes up a manmade hill. In 0.1 mile the exit road will intersect with the Old Nashville Highway. Turn left on to the Old Nashville Highway and drive northwest for 0.7 mile to the Stone River National Battlefield entrance. Turn left into the National Park Service area and follow the park road south, past the Visitor Center, for 1.0 mile. In 0.2 mile the park road will angle left, and in another 0.8 mile you will come to a parking area on your left. Park in the area that is provided. This is designated as the second stop on the National Park Service self-tour. As you drive on park roads you will see numbered tour stop signs. These are for the Park Service brochure. Some of the stops in the book are in close proximity or adjacent to the Parks Service signs, but their numbers do not correspond with the numbers designating our stops. There is a trail that goes south through the woods from the parking area. A small sign—Slaughter Pen—points the way. Leave your car and walk south on this trail for 200 yards. In 100 yards you will come to a display of damaged Union artillery. These are two damaged Wiard guns that belonged to Battery G, First Ohio Artillery, which was trying to retreat through these woods. In 1862 these guns would have been farther into the woods. They are placed here by the National Park Service to demonstrate the problems of moving artillery through the woods. Very few of these guns were made, and they are not commonly found on battlefields today. You will be close to this battery's fighting position at Stop 13. Notice the many large limestone outcroppings through out the woods. These outcroppings and the thickness of the woods made the movement of troops and artillery through this area very difficult. Continue on the trail for another 100 yards. At the fork in the trail go left and walk to the edge of an open field. You are facing south.

Stop 12—The Slaughter Pen

The Wilkinson Turnpike is 200 yards in front of you. Stop 11 is on this side of the turnpike and 700 yards to your right. In front of you was a cornfield that went to the Wilkinson Turnpike. East, to your left, of this cornfield were large open fields. South of it, on the other side of the road, was a cedar and oak woods. Where you are the tree line went from southwest to northeast. Your present location is to the left of Sheridan's last, third, position. Two brigades of Brigadier General James S. Negley's division were deployed where you are and to your left. Negley deployed Colonel Timothy R. Stanley's brigade on the right of his line and Colonel John F. Miller's brigade on his left. Sheridan's and Negley's brigades delayed the Confederate attack long enough for Rosecrans to establish a defensive position along the Nashville-Murfreesboro Pike.

Negley's report gives a good description of how this area looked and the actions of his division on December 30 and 31.

Report of Brig. Gen. James S. Negley, USA, Commanding Second Division, Center Wing, Army of the Cumberland

On Tuesday morning, December 30, 1862, [my division] composed of the [Second and Third] Brigades, Schultz's, Marshall's, and [Ellsworth's] batteries, was posted on the rolling slopes of the west bank of Stone's River, in advance, but joining the extreme right of General Crittenden's line and the left of General McCook's.

In the rear and on the right was a dense cedar woods, with a broken rocky surface. From our position several roads were cut through the woods in our rear, by which to bring up the artillery and ammunition trains. In front a heavy growth of oak timber extended toward the river, which was about a mile distant. A narrow thicket crossed our left diagonally, and skirted the base of a cultivated slope, which expanded to the width of a mile as it approached the Nashville pike. This slope afforded the enemy his most commanding position (in the center), on the crest of which his rifle-pits extended, with intervals, from the oak timber immediately in my front to the Nashville pike, with a battery of four Napoleon and two iron guns placed in position near the woods, and about 800 yards from my position. Behind this timber, on the riverbank, the enemy massed his columns for the movements of the next day.

Early the next morning [December 31], and before the heavy fog had drifted away from our front, the enemy in strong force attacked and surprised General McCook's right, commencing a general action, which increased in intensity toward his left. Sheridan's division stood its ground manfully, supported by the Second Division [Negley's], repulsing and driving the enemy at every advance. The enemy still gained ground on General McCook's right, and succeeded in placing several batteries in position, which covered my right. From these and the battery on my left, which now opened, the troops were exposed to a converging fire, which was most destructive. [Hescock's], Schultz's, Marshall's, Bush's, and Ellsworth's batteries were all ordered into action in my front, pouring destructive volleys of grape and shell into the advancing columns of the enemy, mowing him down like swaths of grain. For four hours the Second Division, with a portion of Sheridan's and Palmer's divisions, maintained their position amid a murderous storm of lead and iron, strewing the ground with their heroic dead. The enemy, maddened to desperation by the determined resistance, still pressed forward fresh troops, concentrating and forming them in a concentric line on either flank.

By 11 o'clock Sheridan's men, with their ammunition exhausted, were falling back. General Rousseau's reserve and General Palmer's division had retired in rear of the cedars to form a new line. The artillery ammunition was expended; that of the infantry reduced to a few rounds; the artillery horses were nearly all killed or wounded; my ammunition train had been sent back to avoid capture; a heavy column of the enemy was marching directly to our rear through the cedars; communication with Generals Rosecrans or Thomas was entirely cut off, and it was manifestly impossible for my command to hold the position without eventually making a hopeless, fruitless sacrifice of the whole division. To retire was but to cut our way through the ranks of the enemy. The order was given and manfully executed, driving back the enemy in front and checking his approaching column in our rear. [OR 20, pt. 1, pp. 406–8.]

You are in the center of the position occupied by Bush's Fourth Indiana Battery, Hescock's Battery G, First Missouri Artillery, and Stanley's brigade of Negley's division. Bush's and Hescock's batteries each had four guns at this position. They were directly in front of you. Stanley initially deployed his brigade in two lines. The Sixty-ninth Ohio was to your left and the Eleventh Michigan was to your right. To the left of the Sixty-ninth Ohio, and your left, was

Battery M, First Ohio Artillery. This was Stanley's first line. The Eighteenth Ohio was behind the Sixty-ninth Ohio, and the Nineteenth Illinois was behind the Eleventh Michigan. On the right of Stanley's brigade the battle line with the remnants of Schaefer's and Greusel's brigades went at a right angle to the northwest. To your right and on the other side of the Wilkinson Turnpike was the left flank of Roberts's brigade of Sheridan's division. To the left of Stanley's brigade was the rest of Negley's division: Colonel John F. Miller's brigade and two batteries of artillery.

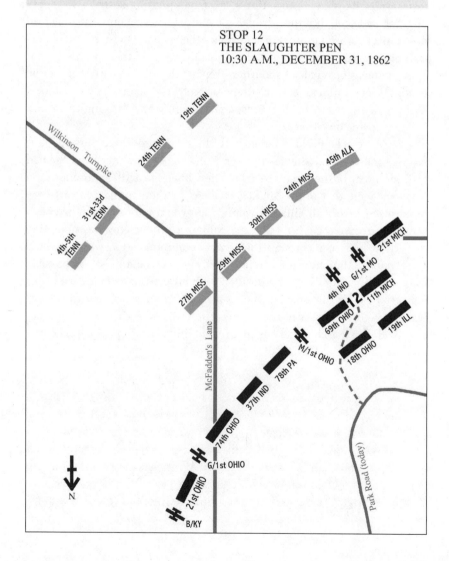

STOP 12
THE SLAUGHTER PEN
10:30 A.M., DECEMBER 31, 1862

Report of Col. Timothy R. Stanley, USA, Commanding Second Brigade, Second Division, Center Wing, Army of the Cumberland

Colonel Timothy R. Stanley, USA. Massachusetts Commandery Military Order of the Loyal Legion and the U.S. Army Military History Institute.

Early on the morning of December 31 our skirmishers advanced and drove the enemy's skirmishers partly through the woods in our front, and General McCook engaged them on our right, but eventually fell back, and then a very heavy force was precipitated on our front and right. This infantry force was supported by a battery on our front and one in intrenchments on our left, and the fire was very severe; but the brigade (as also did the Third Brigade, on my left) sustained the fire without falling back, and poured such a well-directed fire upon the enemy that they faltered, and their ranks were thin and stayed; but the troops on our right and left had fallen back so far as to bring the enemy on three sides of us and fast closing on our rear. At this time General Negley directed the division to cut its way through, to join our other troops in the rear. This we did in good order, halting at two points and checking the enemy by a well-directed fire. [*OR* 20, pt. 1, p. 421.]

Under attack by two separate Confederate brigades, Stanley was able to hold his position until he was flanked on the right. The retreat of Sheridan's division from its last position allowed Confederate forces to turn Stanley's right and at the same time move through the cedars to the rear of his brigade. This caused Stanley to abandon this position and retreat toward the Nashville-Murfreesboro Pike. Several of his regiments had to fight their way through the Confederates in their rear.

Hescock's and Bush's batteries were also forced to abandon this position as the Confederates swirled around their right and their ammunition was expended. Bush reported that two of his guns were captured as the horses had been killed. [*OR* 20, pt. 1, p. 355.]

The first sustained Confederate attack against this position was conducted by Brigadier General *James Patton Anderson's* brigade. *Anderson's* Brigade moved into a position 800 yards in front of you on Sunday, December 28. His five regiments were deployed from right to left, left to right as you view it: the Twenty-seventh Mississippi, Twenty-ninth Mississippi, Thirtieth Mississippi, Twenty-fourth Mississippi, and Forty-fifth Alabama. Captain *Overton W. Barret's* Missouri Battery was positioned on the right of *Anderson's* line. While in this position, the troops constructed rifle pits and breastworks. *Anderson's* initial position was southeast of today's intersection of the Wilkinson Turnpike and Thompson Lane.

To *Anderson's* right was Brigadier General *James R. Chalmers's* brigade, and to his left was Colonel *Arthur M. Manigault's* brigade. *Manigault's* Brigade initially faced west, and *Anderson's* Brigade faced northwest. The two brigades's positions formed a bend in the Confederate line. This bend in the line required that *Manigault* advance west and then turn north before *Anderson* could begin his attack. This caused a delay in *Anderson* moving and taking up the attack on *Manigault's* right.

Report of Brig. Gen. *James Patton Anderson,* CSA, Commanding, *Anderson's* Brigade, *Withers's* Division, *Polk's* Corps, Army of Tennessee

On the morning of the 31st, soon after daylight, a few shots on our extreme left, quickly followed by the thick roll of musketry and then by booming artillery, announced that the action had commenced. In pursuing the instructions contained in the order, it was necessary that the extreme left of our line should advance some distance, swinging around upon the right, before my command should move beyond the breastworks. The direction of Colonel *Manigault's* line on my left made it necessary for his left to describe an arc equal to the eighth of a circle, the length of his line being the radius, before reaching the point where it would be on a prolongation of my line. The enemy's right was being steadily driven back.

About 9 a.m. Colonel *Manigault* came to me and informed me that he intended to charge a battery in his front; wished me to send two regiments to his support. I consented to do so, and immediately ordered the Forty-fifth Alabama and Twenty-fourth Mississippi forward to perform that duty. They became hotly engaged soon after leaving their breastworks, the enemy being in heavy force and strongly posted, backed by many pieces of artillery, so planted as to enfilade a portion of our line. In addition to this enfilading fire, Colonel *Manigault* was exposed to a cross-fire from a battery in front of his left. In the unequal contest our line halted, staggered, and fell back in some confusion, but were easily rallied, reformed, and moved to the front. The Thirtieth, Twenty-ninth, and Twenty-seventh Mississippi were now successively ordered forward, with instructions to swing round upon and preserve the touch of elbow to the right. Captain *Barret,* commanding the battery, was directed to hold his fire, not to respond to the long-range guns of the enemy, and only to use his pieces when a favorable opportunity of playing upon the masses or lines of the enemy was presented. Immediately in front and in short range of these regiments the enemy had two batteries advantageously posted, so as to sweep an open field over which they had to pass in their advance. As often as their ranks were shattered and broken by grape and canister did they rally, reform, and renew the attack under the leadership of their gallant officers. They were ordered to take the batteries at all hazards, and they obeyed the order, not, however, without heavy loss of officers and men.

Not far from where the batteries were playing, and while cheering and encouraging his men forward, Lieut. Col. *James L. Autry,* commanding the Twenty-seventh Mississippi, fell, pierced through the head by a minie ball.

The death of this gallant officer at a critical period caused some confusion in the regiment until they were rallied and reformed by Capt. *E. R. Neilson,* the senior officer present, who subsequently was seriously wounded on another part of the field.

About the same time that Lieutenant-Colonel *Autry* fell, Colonel *Brantly,* of the Twenty-ninth Mississippi, and his adjutant (First Lieut. *John W. Campbell*) were knocked down by concussion, produced by the explosion of a shell very near them, but the regiment was soon after carried forward by Lieut. Col. *J. B. Morgan* in gallant style, capturing the battery in their front, and driving the enemy in great confusion into and through the dense cedar brake immediately beyond. On the left of this last regiment was the Thirtieth Mississippi, commanded by Lieutenant-Colonel *Scales.* In moving across the open field in short range of grape, canister, and shrapnel, 62 officers and men were killed and 139 wounded, of this regiment alone, all within a very short space of time. The Twenty-fourth Mississippi, Lieutenant-Colonel *McKelvaine* commanding, and the Forty-fifth Alabama, Colonel *Gilchrist* commanding, respectively, on the left of the Thirtieth Mississippi, also encountered a battery in their front, strongly supported by infantry on advantageous ground. For a moment these regiments appeared to reel and stagger before the weight of lead and iron that was hurled against them. They were encouraged to go forward by the example of their officers, and a battery was taken. A number of prisoners also fell into our hands. Artillerists, who felt confidently secure in the strength of their positions, were captured at their pieces, and others were taken before they knew that their guns had fallen into our hands. One company, which had been posted in a log-house near the battery in front of the Twenty-ninth Mississippi, was captured by the Twenty-seventh Mississippi, while the pieces were falling into the hands of the Twenty-ninth.

Brigadier General *James Patton Anderson*, CSA. Library of Congress.

After losing his artillery, the enemy retired through a dense cedar forest in a direction almost parallel to our original [line] and to the right. In this forest they made no obstinate stand, but, owing to the density of the growth and the exhausted condition of our troops, the pursuit was slow and cautious.

Our loss in this engagement was heavy, as the long list of killed and wounded will show. The loss of this brigade was 766, as follows: Killed, 119; wounded, 584; missing, 63. [*OR* 20, pt. 1, pp. 763–64, 767.]

The next Confederate brigade to attack this position was Brigadier General *Alexander P. Stewart's*. *Stewart's* regiments had initially been in a position 800 yards behind *Anderson*. They were deployed from right to left, left to right as you view it: the Fourth and Fifth (Combined) Tennessee, Thirty-first and Thirty-third (Combined) Tennessee, Twenty-fourth Tennessee, and Nineteenth Tennessee. When *Anderson* began his attack, *Stewart* moved his brigade up behind his and assumed a supporting role. As *Anderson's* attack began to falter and some of his regiments fell back, *Stewart* moved forward to take up the attack. Some of *Anderson's* regiments continued their attack as *Stewart* was conducting his. The attacks of these two brigades not only struck the Union line where you are but also that part of the line to your left occupied by Miller's brigade. The center of *Stewart's* line struck this position just to the left of where you are.

Report of Brig. Gen. *Alexander P. Stewart*, CSA, Commanding *Stewart's* Brigade, *Cheatham's* Division, *Polk's* Corps, Army of Tennessee

On Wednesday morning, December 31, about 8 o'clock, I was notified to move forward, gradually wheeling to the right and maintaining a distance of a few hundred yards (supporting distance) from *Anderson's* brigade, *Withers'* division. After advancing some distance directly to the front across the open field, the brigade was moved to the left by the flank, so as to place the entire line under cover of the forest from the enemy's artillery fire. The ground over which we were then moving being wet and heavy.

The line of infantry advanced through the woods, gradually wheeling to the right, and occasionally halting to readjust the line, and maintaining its supporting distance from *Anderson,* General *Withers* himself being often with us, and the movements of the brigade corresponding to his wishes. At one point he sent word that *Anderson's* two left regiments would be thrown forward, perhaps, to attack the battery that continued to play upon our advancing lines, and desired me to throw forward two regiments in a corresponding manner. Fearing this would scatter the brigade and produce confusion, it was suggested to him that the entire brigade had better be advanced, to which he assented. We shortly arrived at the stonewall built by *Anderson's* men, where they were placed in line on Sunday, the 28th. While in this position the Twenty-ninth and Thirtieth Regiments Mississippi Volunteers [of *Anderson's* brigade] fell back in disorder, leaving a large number of dead and wounded in the open ground beyond the Wilkinson pike, over which they had charged. They were rallied in our rear chiefly by Major [L. W.] *Finlay,* of my staff, and again sent forward. The Twenty-ninth ultimately formed on my left, where it remained until the close of the battle, when it moved away to join its brigade. The brigade moved on from this position to the pike, where it was faced by the left flank and marched a short distance down the road, to bring its right under cover of the woods, when it moved again to the front. It crossed the open ground intervening between the pike and the cedar forest beyond, and advanced to the relief of the front line, which was giving way, and, by a rapid fire, commencing with *Walker's* regiment (the Nineteenth) on the left, and gradually extending to the right, repulsed the enemy, who fled in confusion to the dense cedar woods, leaving many dead and wounded behind. Near the edge of the woods we came upon the battery that had previously annoyed us so much, and which the enemy were now attempting to remove. Our advance was so rapid and fire so destructive that they were compelled to abandon two pieces and one or two caissons. We left them behind, and, pressing rapidly forward, drove the enemy before us. They attempted to make a stand at several points, but, unable to endure our fire, were driven through the forest and across the open field beyond to the high ground in the vicinity of the railroad. Here they took shelter under the guns of three or four batteries, leaving a number of prisoners in our hands and many dead and wounded scattered through the woods and covering the open field over which they fled in double-quick time. These batteries opened upon us, and for some time we were exposed to a terrific fire of shell, canister, and spherical case. Having no battery of our own, and being nearly out of ammunition, it was impossible to proceed farther. Staff officers were dispatched—one to bring up *Stanford's* battery, another for ammunition. The latter was soon supplied, but word came from Lieutenant-General *Polk* that *Stanford* was employed under his own immediate orders, and could not be spared. While moving through the cedar forest the command of Brigadier-General *Jackson* came up on the right. The Fifth Georgia, immediately on the right, with the Fourth and Fifth Tennessee, advanced beyond the general line and delivered a heavy and well-sustained fire upon the retreating ranks of the enemy, doing fine execution.

About this time Colonel [*J. A.*] *Jaquess,* of the First Louisiana (Regulars), rode rapidly up to Colonel [*E. E.*] *Tansil* and delivered some order, which I did not hear. Immediately *Tansil's* regiment began to fall back without waiting for a command, and was gradually followed by the rest of the brigade, and I learned from *Tansil* that *Jaquess* brought to him an order purporting to come from Major-General *Cheatham* to "move by the right of companies to the rear." The order not having been delivered to me, not recognizing Colonel *Jaquess* as a member of General *Cheatham's* staff, and satisfied that the movement was demoralizing in a high degree, it was arrested as promptly as possible. The line was halted and reformed, and moved forward again to the edge of the woods, where we remained until dark, when, leaving a strong picket guard, the command was withdrawn a few hundred yards to the rear, to bivouac, taking along a large number of small-arms, ammunition, and equipments, which were removed next day by wagons brought out for the purpose. [*OR* 20, pt. 1, p. 724–25.]

Retrace your steps along the path to where your car is parked. At the parking area, turn right and walk along the park road for 60 yards to the edge of the woods. Turn right and walk along the edge of the wood and field for 140 yards to a road. As you walk, the woods will be on your left and the field on your right. At the road, which is McFadden's Lane, turn right and walk for 20 yards, then turn left and walk to the edge of the field. You should be able to look across the field. McFadden's Lane is behind you. This lane went from its intersection with the Wilkinson Turnpike 400 yards to your right to McFadden's Ford, which is one and a half mile north, to the left, of your present position. The Thompson Lane and Wilkinson Turnpike intersection is to your right front.

Stop 13—Miller's Defense

You are in the center of Colonel John F. Miller's defensive line. The ground in front of you looks similar to the way it was in 1862. The tree line would have been behind you, in front were large open fields, and to your right was a cornfield. The Wilkinson Turnpike is 400 yards to your right. The Nashville-Murfreesboro Pike is 800 yards to your left.

Colonel Miller deployed all four of his regiments and two batteries of artillery on his first line. The Seventy-fourth Ohio was where you are now. To that regiment's left was Battery G, First Ohio Artillery, then the Twenty-first Ohio, and then Battery B, Kentucky Artillery. To the Seventy-fourth Ohio's right were the Thirty-seventh Indiana and then the Seventy-eighth Pennsylvania. Stanley's brigade was on Miller's right, and Brigadier General Charles Cruft's brigade was on his left. The regiments in the right half of *Anderson's* and *Stewart's* attacks and perhaps the left regiment of *Chalmers's* Brigade hit this position.

Report of Col. John F. Miller, USA, Commanding
Third Brigade, Second Division, Center
Wing, Army of the Cumberland

On the morning of the 31st, skirmishing was resumed along our line, and heavy firing was heard on the right along General McCook's line. The firing on our right gradually increased and neared our position, until a

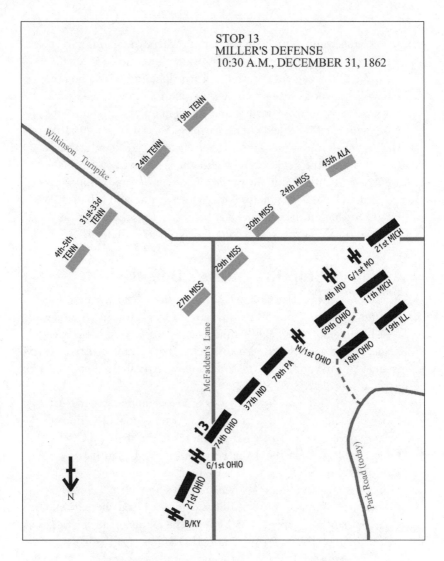

STOP 13
MILLER'S DEFENSE
10:30 A.M., DECEMBER 31, 1862

continuous roar of artillery and musketry was heard directly in our rear, and the advancing columns of the enemy were seen on our right and front.

Here I received orders from General Negley to hold my position to the last extremity. For this purpose I executed a partied change of my front, and placed my troops in the convex order, as follows: The Seventy-eighth Pennsylvania, Colonel Sirwell, on the right, at the brow of a small hill, the right resting near Schultz's battery [M, First Ohio Artillery], of Colonel Stanley's brigade; the Thirty-seventh Indiana, Colonel Hull, on the right center; the Seventy-fourth Ohio, Colonel Moody, on the left center, behind a rail fence; Marshall's battery [G, First Ohio Artillery] on a small hill in the open field, to the left of the Seventy-fourth Ohio; the Twenty-first Ohio, Lieutenant-Colonel Neibling, on the left, in a thicket fronting the enemy's works, and Ellsworth's battery [B, Kentucky Artillery] near the log-house, between Palmer's right [Cruft's brigade] and the Twenty-first Ohio. Simultaneously with the advance of the enemy from the right, a heavy force advanced from the enemy's works on my left wing.

The batteries were worked with admirable skill, and the firing along our whole line was executed with creditable precision. The enemy halted, but did not abate his fire. The roar of musketry and artillery now became almost deafening, and as the unequal contest progressed it became more terrible. Once the strong force in the open field in front of my left wing attempted a bayonet charge on the Twenty-first Ohio, but were gallantly met and repulsed with great slaughter. The battle continued with unabating fierceness on both sides until the 60 rounds of ammunition with which my men were supplied were nearly exhausted.

The Thirty-seventh Indiana was the first to report a want of ammunition, and withdrew a short distance to the rear for a supply, the Seventy-fourth Ohio and Seventy-eighth Pennsylvania filling up the interval. The teamsters of the ammunition wagons had moved to the rear, and when ammunition was being brought forward they turned and fled. Colonel Hull [Thirty-seventh Indiana] again led his regiment forward and fired the few remaining cartridges on the persons of the men, taking also such as could be had from the dead and wounded.

At this juncture the troops on our right retired, and some unauthorized person ordered Colonel Sirwell [Seventh-eighth Pennsylvania] to retire his regiment. This regiment was fighting gallantly and holding the position on the crest of the hill, but on receiving the order, retired to the cedars in the rear. Seeing this, I immediately ordered Colonel Sirwell forward to the same position. This order was obeyed promptly, and the men again took position in admirable order. Soon after this a heavy force was observed to advance on General Palmer's left, and a hard contest ensued. [This was the opening attack against the Union position in the Round Forest, just on the other side of the Nashville-Murfreesboro Pike.]

General Palmer's right brigade [Cruft's] held their ground for a short time, and then began to retire. Just at this time I received orders from General Negley to retire slowly with my command into the woods. My troops were nearly out of ammunition; the enemy was advancing on my right flank and on my left, and the fire in front was no less destructive than it had been during the engagement.

The movement was executed in good order by the infantry, but it was impossible for the artillery to obey; nearly all the horses had been killed: the ground was soft and muddy; the men had not the strength to haul away the pieces. Five guns were lost; four were saved by the men of the batteries, assisted by the infantry.

On reaching the woods, I halted the command and formed a line of battle, faced by the rear rank, and delivered several well-directed volleys into the enemy's ranks, now crossing the open field over which I had retreated. This checked the advance of the enemy for a short time, strewing the ground with his dead. Being closely pressed on both flanks, and receiving fire from three directions, I again retired my command, the men loading while

Colonel John F. Miller, USA. Massachusetts Commandery Military Order of the Loyal Legion and the U.S. Army Military History Institute.

marching, and firing to the rear as rapidly as possible In this way my command retreated for the Nashville pike, in a northeasterly direction. [*OR* 20, pt. 1, pp. 431–33.]

To your left was the position of Battery G, First Ohio Artillery. The battery commander, Lieutenant Marshall, gives a detailed and excellent account of the fighting in this area.

Report of Lieut. Alexander Marshall, USA, Commanding Battery G, First Ohio Artillery, Second Division, Center Wing, Army of the Cumberland

At daylight of the 31st, opened with the four guns stationed in the cornfield, shelling the woods to the right and the battery and rifle-pit in front, as the night before. About 8 a.m., moved the center section down to the left about 40 rods [220 yards], taking position near two log-houses in rear of the corn-field, a dense thicket across the corn-field directly in front, open country to the left and front, where the enemy was in position. Remained in this position about thirty minutes without firing; then moved this section up and took position in center of the battery; worked the battery till about 11 a.m. The enemy up to this time fired but few rounds from their batteries in our front, firing being mostly from their skirmishers in the woods, when, in obedience to Colonel Miller's order, moved to the right; partially changed front. The batteries of the enemy opened over the advancing infantry a heavy fire before we had fairly got into position. Ordered caissons under shelter a short distance in the rear, and opened upon the rapidly advancing enemy with canister. As our support advanced, we moved our pieces forward by hand and worked them as rapidly as possible. [This is where you are.]

One of our 12-pounder howitzers being disabled, the trail having been cut nearly off by a shot, ordered it to the rear. Went to work with canister, the enemy advancing in the woods close upon us. As our infantry support advanced we advanced our pieces by hand to the fence close to the woods, that we might hold an interval in their lines, and continued firing canister as fast as possible. During this time our horses were suffering severely from fire from the enemy; had them replaced by the teams from battery and forge wagon, which I had ordered up the day before, leaving the battery and forge wagon 1½ miles in the rear, in charge of artificers. All of my spare horses were soon used up and several taken from the caissons. Had 3 men killed and several wounded.

Saw the enemy moving down the open field in masses on our left flank, and firing extending far to our rear on our right flank, and one of our 12-pounder rifles having a shot wedged and but three horses remaining, I ordered Lieutenant Crable to take the two disabled pieces and caissons to the rear through the cedar swamp, and ordered the remaining four pieces to fix prolonge, to fire retiring. The enemy had already been twice repulsed, when they moved upon both our flanks and front with renewed ranks and vigor, which caused our support to give way. I ordered the battery to retire to the woods in our rear, two pieces having but three horses and two four horses each.

My own, Lieutenant Whittlesey's, and one sergeant's horse were killed; three of the guns moved off as ordered; prolonge of the left piece, 12-pounder Wiard, broken; at the same time the lead rider was shot; the gunner mounted his team, when the off wheel horse was killed and the off lead horse wounded, which prevented us from using the limber. I then ordered a limber of one of the pieces already in the woods out, to draw the remaining 12-pounder off the field into the woods.

We had no sooner started back when I found the right and center of the brigade had fallen back, and the left Twenty-first Ohio was coming in, leaving the pieces about 40 yards outside of our lines, between us and the enemy, which was fast closing in on us, with a heavy fire. Saw that it was impossible to reach the gun. I ordered the limber back and gun limbered up; moved back through the cedar swamp in rear of brigade. There being no road, I was considerably bothered to work my way through. As the brigade was moving rapidly and the enemy pressing close upon us, two more of my wheel horses were shot and one rider, when I was obliged to leave two more guns, having but one wheel and middle horse on each piece. Sergeant Farwell, to-

Lieutenant Alexander Marshall, USA. Massachusetts Commandery Military Order of the Loyal Legion and the U.S. Army Military History Institute.

gether with Sergeant Bills, took the remaining piece, passed the pieces left, and worked their way through and took position on the right of Captain Stokes' battery, where I found them and went to work, using up the balance of our ammunition—about 40 rounds. I found that our loss for December 31, 1862, summed up 43 horses, 4 guns, 3 limbers, 2 caissons and limbers; 3 men killed, 8 wounded, and 12 missing. [*OR* 20, pt. 1, pp. 413–15.]

Sheridan and Negley had a total of six artillery batteries. The fighting here and just on the other side of the Wilkinson Turnpike had taken a heavy toll on these six batteries. They had lost fourteen of their thirty-five guns, 122 men, and 253 horses.

There are no reports from any of *Anderson's* regiments that attacked in this area. However there is a report from one of *Stewart's* regimental commanders whose unit attacked this part of the Union line.

Ground crossed by *Anderson's* and *Stewart's* attacks. Union soldiers were in position in front of the far tree line.

Report of Col. *Otho F. Strahl,* CSA, Commanding Fourth and Fifth (Consolidated) Tennessee Infantry, *Stewart's* Brigade, *Cheatham's* Division, *Polk's* Corps, Army of Tennessee

About 9 o'clock in the morning of the 31st, we were ordered to advance in such a manner as to change direction gradually to the right, keeping dressed to the left. We advanced in this manner until we came to where General [*Anderson's*] men had thrown up small breastworks. At this point we were halted for a short time, and had several men wounded by grape and canister from the enemy's guns. While remaining here, a regiment from General [*Anderson's* brigade] fell back and formed immediately in my rear. We then advanced, first through a cedar thicket and then through an open field for some 400 or 500 yards, where we entered a cedar glade. All this time we were

Colonel *Otho F. Strahl*, CSA. Library of Congress.

gradually changing direction to the right. In a few minutes after passing into the cedar glade we were engaged by the enemy, but drove them before us, taking quite a number of prisoners. We continued to press the enemy, fighting as we advanced, until we had driven them entirely out of the glade. The slaughter of the enemy was very great just at the edge of the glade, as they were slow to leave the timber and our men were close upon them, and every shot did its work. Then the enemy opened a very heavy fire upon us from a battery within a few hundred yards of our lines. We soon silenced it, however, by sending out some sharpshooters, who so disabled it that the battery retired, leaving one gun and caisson behind. [*OR* 20, pt. 1, p. 727.]

Strahl's regiment's losses for this action were eight officers and men killed and sixty-eight officers and men wounded.

Retrace you route back to where your car is parked for the drive to Stop 14.

Depart the parking area and continue driving on the park road for 0.8 mile to the parking area on the left. Park in this area and get out of your car.

Stop 14—Battle in the Cedars

The wood you just drove through, except for the road, looks much as it did in 1862. You can see how difficult it would have been to move through this area, much less effectively deploy and fight a regiment or a brigade. Where you are now, in 1862 the area to the left, west of the road, was a cedar forest just as it is today. To the right of the road, for 500 yards to the Nashville-Murfreesboro Pike, there was a cotton field.

As Stanley's and Miller's brigades were fighting at Stops 12 and 13, Sheridan's decimated regiments were withdrawing from their third and final defensive position. The right portion of Sheridan's last line had been 150 yards to your left as you drove to where you are now. As these regiments withdrew, many of them crossed the area you just drove through. To replace them, Major General Lovell H. Rousseau was ordered to send two brigades from his division into the cedars to the left, west, of the park road. Rousseau deployed Colonel John Beatty's Second Brigade on the left and Lieutenant Colonel Oliver L. Shepherd's Fourth Brigade on the right. Colonel Benjamin F. Scribner's First Brigade was placed in a supporting position in the open field and to the rear of Beatty's and Shepherd's brigades.

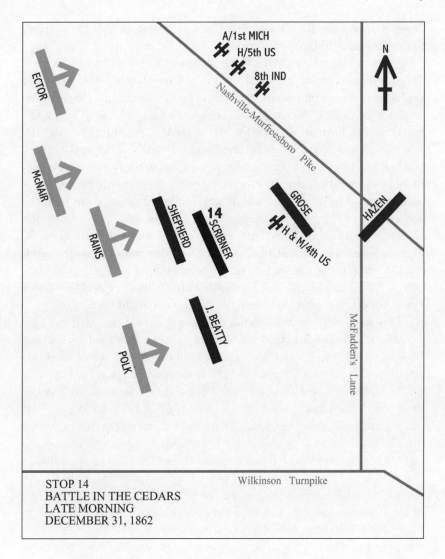

STOP 14
BATTLE IN THE CEDARS
LATE MORNING
DECEMBER 31, 1862

Report of Maj. Gen. Lovell H. Rousseau, USA, Commanding First Division, Center Wing, Army of the Cumberland

At about 9 a.m. on the 31st, the report of artillery and heavy firing of small-arms on our right announced that the battle had begun, by an attack on the right wing, commanded by Major-General McCook. It was not long before the direction from which the firing came indicated that General McCook's command had given way and was yielding ground to the enemy. His forces seemed to swing around toward our right and rear. At this time

General Thomas ordered me to advance my division quickly to the front, to the assistance of General McCook.

On reaching the right of General Negley's line of battle, General Thomas there directed me to let my left rest on his [Negley's] right, and deploy my division off toward the right as far as I could, so as to resist the pressure on General McCook. We consulted and agreed as to where the line should be formed. This was in a dense cedar brake, through which my troops marched in double-quick time, to get into position before the enemy reached us. He was then but a few hundred yards to the front, sweeping up in immense numbers, driving everything before him. This ground was new and unknown to us all. The woods were almost impassable to infantry, and artillery was perfectly useless, but the line was promptly formed; the [Second] Brigade, Col. John Beatty commanding, on the left; the [Fourth] brigade of regulars, Lieut. Col. O. L. Shepherd commanding, on the right; the [Third] Brigade, Col. B. F. Scribner commanding, was placed perhaps 100 yards in rear and opposite the center of the front line, so as to support either or both of the brigades in front, as occasion might require.

Our lines were hardly formed before a dropping fire of the enemy announced his approach. General McCook's troops, in a good deal of confusion, retired through our lines and around our right under a most terrific fire. The enemy, in pursuit, furiously assailed our front, and, greatly outflanking us, passed around to our right and rear. By General Thomas' direction, I had already ordered the artillery [Van Pelt's Battery A, First Michigan Artillery and Guenther's Battery H, Fifth U.S. Artillery] to the open field in the rear. Seeing that my command was outflanked on the right, I sent orders to the brigade commanders to retire at once also to this field, and, riding back myself, I posted the batteries on a ridge [where today's National Cemetery is] in the open ground, parallel with our line of battle, and as my men emerged from the woods they were ordered to take position on the right and left, and in support of these batteries, which was promptly done. We had, perhaps, 400 or 500 yards of open ground in our front. While the batteries were unlimbering, seeing General Van Cleve close by, I rode up and asked him if he would move his command to the right and aid in checking up the enemy, by forming on my right, and thus giving us a more extended line in that direction in the new position taken. In the promptest manner possible his command was put in motion, and in double-quick time reached the desired point in good season. As the enemy emerged from the woods in great force, shouting and cheering, the batteries of Guenther and [Van Pelt], double-shotted with canister, opened upon

From Stop 14 looking across fields to the National Cemetery, where Rosecrans's final defensive position was located.

them. They moved straight ahead for a while, but were finally driven back with immense loss.

In a little while they rallied again, and, as it seemed, with fresh troops, and assailed our position, and were again, after a fierce struggle, driven back. Four deliberate and fiercely sustained assaults were made upon our position and repulsed. [*OR* 20, pt. 1, pp. 377–78.]

The open field that Rousseau refers to is the cotton field, which is to the right, east, of the park road. The ridge where he placed the artillery is the rise of ground where today the National Cemetery is (on the other side of the Nashville-Murfreesboro Pike). The units from Van Cleve's division that he makes reference to were the brigades of Colonel Samuel Beatty and Colonel James Fyffe, whose actions you studied at Stop 9.

The actions of the First Battalion, Sixteenth U.S. Infantry were typical of the other units of Shepherd's brigade and of the confusion of fighting in the cedars.

Report of Capt. Robert E. A. Crofton, USA, Commanding First Battalion, Sixteenth U.S. Infantry, Fourth Brigade, First Division, Center Wing, Army of the Cumberland

At 7 o'clock on the morning of December 31, 1862, this command (then under Maj. A. J. Slemmer, Sixteenth Infantry) was ordered to move to the front from the bivouac where we had rested the night previous. We marched about a mile in the direction of Murfreesboro, and were then marched into line of battle on the right [west side] of the turnpike, the First Battalion Fifteenth Infantry being on our right, and the First Battalion Eighteenth Infantry on our left. Here we stacked arms and rested for some time.

About 9.15 o'clock we were ordered into a thicket of cedars. We moved into line of battle, changing our front to the right, to oppose the advancing columns of the enemy. Company B, First Battalion, under command of First Lieutenant Bartholomew, was thrown to the front in skirmishing order, to cover the front of our line. In about five minutes these skirmishers were driven in, and formed on the right of the battalion. The enemy was now seen advancing in line, and at the same moment opened a deadly fire on our ranks. The command, however, succeeded in checking their advance, the men behaving with the greatest possible coolness, and aiming with accuracy. The battalion on our right having moved to the rear, it became necessary to fall back, which we did, by the right of companies, to the rear.

Having fallen back about 100 paces, we came into line, faced to the front, and returned the enemy's fire. Again, for want of support, we were obliged to retire, and did so, as before, for about another 100 yards. Maintaining this position for some minutes, we found it necessary to make a retreat to where we could be supported, as the enemy was moving his line on our right and left, and threatening to surround us.

We then moved, by the right of companies, to the rear, out of the woods and across a cotton-field, where the enemy poured musketry and round shot upon us, but without doing much injury. We continued our retreat across the turnpike to the railroad, where we joined the remainder of the brigade, and were ordered to support Battery H, Fifth Artillery.

We remained in this position till about 11.30 a.m., when we were again ordered into the cedars. We advanced this time about 30 yards from the edge of the woods, when we became engaged, and a most terrific conflict ensued. Almost at the commencement of this action Maj. A. J. Slemmer was so seriously wounded as to be obliged to fall to the rear. About the same time Adjt. John Power was dangerously wounded.

After remaining in this position for about twenty-five minutes, and seeing the right of the brigade retire in order, we were compelled reluctantly to fall back, as the enemy out-flanked us on our right and left. The men moved out of the woods by the right of companies with great regularity, notwithstanding the fearful fire to which they were exposed. As we crossed the open [cotton] field between the woods and railroad, the fire was terrible, and the men fell before it in great numbers, until the enemy were driven back by the fire from Battery H, Fifth Artillery. Arriving at the railroad, we again formed and remained with the rest of the brigade in support of the above battery.

Captain Robert E. A. Crofton, USA. Massachusetts Commandery Military Order of the Loyal Legion and the U.S. Army Military History Institute.

Fifteen officers and 293 enlisted men went into action. [Casualties: 16 killed, 133 wounded, and 16 captured, for a total of 165.] [*OR* 20, pt. 1, pp. 401–2.]

Major General *John McCown*, whose division had been on the left of the Confederate envelopment of the Union right, had paused for ammunition resupply along the Wilkinson Turnpike west of Gresham house. From that location he maneuvered his division in a northeast direction toward the Nashville-Murfreesboro Pike. When he struck Union resistance in the cedars, he sent *Raines's* Brigade directly against Shepherd's brigade and maneuvered *Ector's* Brigade and *McNair's* Brigade (now commanded by Colonel *Robert W. Harper*) in an attempt to pass around Shepherd's right and gain the pike. *Rains's* Brigade made two attacks against Shepherd's brigade and succeeded in pushing it out of the cedars and across the cotton field. However, as *Rains's* Brigade came out of the cedars,

Brigadier General *James Rains*, CSA.
Library of Congress.

about where you are now, and charged unsupported across the cotton field, it came under withering artillery fire from the twenty-six guns of four batteries and rifle fire from at least four and at times seven infantry regiments. Many of these Union regiments were located near the railroad, which you can see across the open field. *Rains* was killed in the cotton field, and his brigade was forced back into the cedars.

Report of Col. *Robert B. Vance*, CSA, Commanding *Rains's* Brigade, *McCown's* Division, *Hardee's* Corps, Army of Tennessee

Colonel *Stovall,* Third Georgia [Battalion], was placed on right; Major *J. T. Smith,* Ninth Georgia, next then Colonel *Vance,* Twenty-ninth North Carolina, leaving Colonel *G. W. Gordon,* Eleventh Tennessee, on left. In this manner we advanced, encountering the enemy in force in a few moments. The enemy formed again on a slight elevation in our front, from which they were soon driven into a cedar thicket, and from thence finally into a large field under cover of their guns, a heavy battery of which opened on us at once with shell, grape, and canister, while the enemy's infantry rallied and opened fire from two or three heavy lines of battle. Here was the struggle for the day, and a hard one it was. Almost immediately after this hard contest began our gallant and noble brigadier-general (*James E. Rains*) was shot through the heart, falling dead from his horse. Still, the troops fought on, though the fall of so daring a leader necessarily produced considerable confusion. Owing to the dense cedar thicket through which we were charging, the Third and Ninth Georgia Battalions got separated from the Twenty-ninth North Carolina and Eleventh Tennessee. From the reports of Colonel *Stovall* and Major *Smith,* I learn that these gallant commands were hotly engaged in front and on the right flank, being subjected to an enfilading fire. [*OR* 20, pt. 1, p. 939.]

Colonel *Robert B. Vance*, CSA. Library of Congress.

At the same time that *Rains's* Brigade was engaged with Shepard's, *Polk's* Brigade moved forward and made contact with Beatty's brigade while *Maney's* Brigade crossed the Wilkinson Turnpike and moved on Beatty's left flank. Beatty did not receive the order to fall back out of the cedars and continued to fight until he was almost cut off.

Realizing his precarious position, Beatty order his regiments to fall back and regroup on the other side of the Nashville-Murfreesboro Pike. Major General *Patrick Cleburne* stopped *Polk's* attack into the cedars, and his brigade was withdrawn and moved north in an attempt to move around the northern part of the Union flank. *Polk's* Brigade joined up with *Vaughan's, Johnson's,* and *Liddell's* Brigades for the attack on Samuel Beatty's, Fyffe's, and Harker's Union brigades at Stops 8 and 9.

You can walk or drive to Stop 15. If you walk, follow the directions in the next paragraph. If you drive, skip the next paragraph and go to the driving instructions.

TO WALK: As you drove to Stop 14, you were headed north. Walk back south on the park road for 90 yards, where there is a walking trail in the woods going east, your left, as you walk south. Once you enter the woods, if the trail branches off, stay next to the fence and the open field. Follow this trail for 300 yards to where you will cross the park road you drove on en route to Stop 12. The trail continues on the other side of the road. Continue to follow this trail east for another 60 yards to where the artillery pieces are located. Walk to the third gun and face in the direction it is pointed. You are looking southeast.

TO DRIVE: Depart Stop 14 and drive 0.1 mile to where the park road goes straight and to the right. Turn right and drive for 0.3 mile to the parking area on your left. Park in this area, get out of your car, and follow the walking path east for 60 yards to where the artillery pieces are. Walk to the third gun and face in the direction it is pointed. You are looking southeast.

Stop 15—Parsons's Battery

These guns represent the position of Lieutenant Charles C. Parsons's combined Batteries H and M, Fourth U.S. Artillery. Parsons's actual position was approximately 75 yards behind you in the open field where the sinkhole is today. Also deployed here was Colonel William Grose's Third Brigade of Brigadier General John M. Palmer's Second Division of the Left Wing.

Today the ground looks very much as it did in 1862. Thirty yards directly in front of you is McFadden's Lane. Miller's brigade of Negley's division, Stop 13, was located 800 yards to your right. To your left you can see the Nashville-Murfreesboro Pike. Just across the pike and to your left front is the Hazen Brigade Monument. It marks the center of the Round Forest.

The next division in the Union defensive line was Palmer's Second Division. This three-brigade division went into position on the left of Negley's division with two brigades in the front line and one brigade in reserve. Palmer's right brigade was Brigadier General Charles Cruft's First Brigade. Cruft initially deployed his brigade to your right front so that it faced east and southeast. To your left front was deployed Colonel William B. Hazen's Second Brigade. The right of Hazen's brigade was just this side of the Nashville-Murfreesboro Pike. From there his line went east across the pike and into the Round Forest. You will study the actions of Cruft's and Hazen's brigades at later stops.

Grose's brigade and Parsons's battery were placed in a reserve position in the vicinity of your location. Initially they were facing southeast; however, as the Confederate attack began to roll up the Union right and the sound of gunfire was heard on their right and rear, Grose redeployed his brigade and Parsons's guns so that they faced west. Their line now formed a right angle with Hazen's line.

Walk back to the first gun and face back toward where you just walked or drove from and look across the cotton field. You should be looking in the opposite direction the guns are pointed.

After Grose repositioned his brigade, his infantry and Parson's battery faced west and northwest with fields of fire across the cotton-field. Grose had five regiments in his brigade. As *Rains's* attack developed against Shepherd's brigade, the Thirty-sixth Indiana and Sixth Ohio were sent forward into the cedars. Having proceeded a short distance, these two regiments were also caught up in the confused fighting in the thick wood.

Report of Colonel William Grose, USA, Commanding Third Brigade Second Division, Left Wing, Army of the Cumberland

Thus, on Wednesday morning, December 31, the division, under command of its general, at early day was in battle line. The brigade of General Cruft on the right, that of Colonel Hazen on the left, with my brigade in reserve in rear of the center, in supporting distance, with the batteries of Cockerill and Parsons in position to support the lines. While we were perfecting our lines in the morning, the divisions of Generals Negley and Rousseau filed by my rear through a heavy cedar grove, which lay in rear of General Cruft's brigade, and immediately up to the right of my brigade

The engagement had been raging fiercely some distance to our right during the early morning, and at near 8 o'clock the clash of arms to our right had so far changed position that I saw the rear of my brigade would soon be endangered. Hence I set to work changing my front to rear, which was done in quick time, with the left, when changed, a little retired, to support the right of Colonel Hazen's brigade, then closely engaged with the enemy, our two brigades forming a V. My brigade was not more than thus formed to the rear before the enemy appeared in heavy lines, pressing the forces of ours that had been engaged to the right of our division on our front in fearful confusion. In this new formation the Sixth Ohio and Thirty-sixth Indiana were in the front lines, the latter on the right, supported in the second line by the Eighty-fourth Illinois and Twenty-third Kentucky, with the Twenty-fourth Ohio in an oblique form, a little to the right of the rear line. In this shape the Thirty-sixth Indiana and Sixth Ohio advanced into the woodland about 250 yards, and there met the enemy in overwhelming numbers. [*OR* 20, pt. 1, p. 560.]

Colonel William Grose, USA. Massachusetts Commandery Military Order of the Loyal Legion and the U.S. Army Military History Institute.

Lieutenant Parsons's combined Batteries H and M, Fourth U.S. Artillery were armed with four 12-pound smoothbore Howitzers and four 3-inch Ordnance Rifles. This combination of guns made this battery ideal for engagement of long-range and short-range targets. An 1861 graduate of West Point, Parsons was in his third major battle. His experience and the superior training of his battery would show during the fighting on Wednesday and Friday.

Report of Lieut. Charles C. Parsons, USA, Commanding Batteries H and M, Fourth U.S. Artillery, Second Division, Left Wing, Army of the Cumberland

On the morning of the 31st I thought it most in accordance with my instructions from General Palmer to remain in the position where I then was, in order to check the advance of the enemy, should he turn our

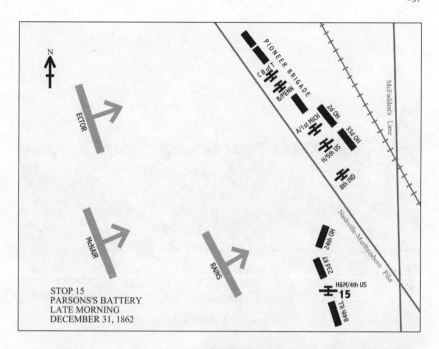

STOP 15
PARSONS'S BATTERY
LATE MORNING
DECEMBER 31, 1862

right. Our infantry came falling back from the pine wood in this direction, when our batteries were swung around and brought at once into action. The approach of the enemy was parallel, instead of perpendicular, to our front, and when he had arrived within about 300 yards we opened upon his first line and column of reserves an enfilade fire of canister. The attempt to advance was continued for a few moments; then an effort to change front was followed by a feeble charge upon the batteries, when, upon being repulsed, the enemy fell back beyond our view. He reappeared shortly afterward to our left; but again, upon receiving our fire, fell back. [*OR* 20, pt. 1, p. 524.]

Lieutenant Charles C. Parsons, USA. Massachusetts Commandery Military Order of the Loyal Legion and the U.S. Army Military History Institute.

The cotton field as seen from Parsons's battery at Stop 15.

Parsons's battery would not only fight facing west but also, later in the day, face again back to the southeast and assist in the defense of the Round Forest. On January 2, 1863, his battery also participated in the action at McFadden's Ford. During these two days of fighting an incredible 2,299 rounds were fired by this battery, 11 percent of all Union artillery ammunition expended at Stones River and 600 more rounds than any other battery.

To Parsons's left was the Eighty-fourth Illinois, and to his right was the Twenty-third Kentucky. The Twenty-fourth Ohio was to the right of the Twenty-third Kentucky. These infantry regiments also added their fire to that of the artillery as *Rains's* Brigade came out of the cedars.

Report of Capt. Armistead T. M. Cockerill, USA, Commanding Twenty-fourth Ohio Infantry, Third Brigade, Second Division, Left Wing, Army of the Cumberland

Early in the morning of the 31st ultimo heavy artillery and musketry firing was distinctly heard on our right, and as the sound neared our position it was evident that our forces were falling back, and our position in danger of being flanked, when our front was immediately changed to the right and rear: immediately in rear of the Sixth Ohio, which had now become earnestly engaged with the enemy, who was under cover of thick woods. We immediately moved forward to support the Sixth, and were ordered to lie down in the open space, about 50 paces in their rear, being much exposed to a galling fire of rebel infantry.

The deadly fire of the enemy in superior numbers was mowing down the ranks of the gallant Sixth, and they were compelled to fall back. Colonel Jones now ordered the regiment to fall back, which was done in good order. We halted at about 150 paces, and lay down to await the enemy's approach from the cover of the woods into the open space that separated us. On they came like a tornado that would destroy everything in its path. Encouraged by their success in driving the forces upon our right, they charged upon a battery lying upon our right, belonging to General Rousseau's command, when almost simultaneously our forces lying in their front opened upon them with a tremendous fire from our infantry and artillery, mowing them down almost by ranks, causing dismay and confusion, when they broke and fled in disorder to the cover of woods from which they had but just emerged. [*OR* 20, pt. 1, pp. 571–72]

In addition to the fire from this position, *Rains's* Brigade was subjected to the fire of several infantry regiments and three batteries of artillery. This force was located where the National Cemetery is today, 500 yards north of your location.

Return to your car for the drive to Stop 16.

If you walked, retrace your path along the walking trail. If you drove, depart the parking lot and drive on the park road for 1.3 miles to the parking area for Stop 14. The park road is one way; do not reverse your driving direction on the road. When you reach the parking area for Stop 14, continue with the instructions below.

Continue to follow the park road for 0.3 mile to where it intersects with the Nashville-Murfreesboro Pike—today's Old Nashville Road. Two-tenths of a mile after you leave the parking area you will see some artillery on your left. This is one of the positions of the Chicago Board of Trade Artillery. You will look at this battery later and see how they got here. At the intersection with the Nashville-Murfreesboro Pike turn right and drive for 0.1 mile to the entrance of the National Cemetery. Turn left into the cemetery and immediately park on the right in the area provided. Leave your car and walk back to the wall that parallels the Nashville-Murfreesboro Pike. Take a position so that you can look southwest across the open fields

Stop 16—Final Defensive Line

This location is part of Rosecrans's final defensive line. This area between the pike and the railroad is a slightly raised plateau with open fields, which made it an ideal artillery position. The ground on the other side of the pike was a cotton field with the cedar woods beyond.

The defensive position here and to your left and right was the last position that had to be held to stop the Confederate attacks from cutting the Nashville-Murfreesboro Pike. If the pike could be captured and held at any point, those Union units north of that point would be cut off from the rest of the army and the direct supply and communication route for units south of that point would be disrupted. Such a situation would leave Rosecrans no choice but

From Stop 16 looking south. The road is Nashville-Murfreesboro Pike. The position of Parsons's battery and Stop 15 are directly in line with the telephone pole in the center of the photo and next to the far wood line.

to retreat back to Nashville with whatever units he could salvage from that disaster. Even worse, a breakthrough on the Nashville-Murfreesboro Pike defensive position may have pinned a large part of Rosecrans's army against Stones River. This would have been the first truly decisive battle of the war, resulting in the destruction of an army. For *Bragg* either scenario would be nothing less than total victory and would ensure the Confederacy began 1863 in control of northern Middle Tennessee. In conjunction with other victories in the last months of 1862 this would politically and militarily give the Confederacy the appearance of being unconquerable.

At this position were two batteries of artillery, both from Rousseau's division. They were Battery A, First Michigan Artillery and Battery H, Fifth U.S. Artillery. These batteries initially had been on the other side of the pike. When Rousseau's infantry was sent into the cedars, these batteries were held back and then deployed to this location. A gun 90 yards behind you marks the center of Guenther's Battery H. Van Pelt's Battery A was to Guenther's right. One hundred and seventy-five yards to your left, on the other side of the south cemetery wall, two guns mark the position of Lieutenant George Estep's Eighth Indiana Battery from

The cotton field from Stop 16, looking southwest. Stop 14 is in the center of the wood line.

Brigadier General Thomas J. Wood's First Division. From these position all three batteries, eighteen guns, had a commanding field of fire across the cotton field to your front. Deployed to support these batteries were the Second and Thirty-third Ohio Infantry Regiments from Scribner's brigade. Joining Scribner's two regiments was part of Shepherd's brigade, which rallied on this line after being driven from the cedars.

Seven hundred yards to your left Hazen's brigade occupied a southeast-facing defensive position in the Round Forest. Five hundred yards to your left front were Parsons's Batteries H and M, Fourth U.S. Artillery and the center of Grose's brigade, Stop 15. Stop 14 is across the field in front you and to the right of Parsons's battery. The three batteries here and Parsons's battery provided a cross-fire across the cotton field.

As *Rains's* Brigade came out of the cedars, the artillery where you are joined in the fight.

Report of Lieut. Francis L. Guenther, USA, Commanding Battery H, Fifth U.S. Artillery, First Division, Center Wing, Army of the Cumberland

On the morning of December 31 [the battery] was moved forward with the brigade, and, after a short halt, preceded through a dense grove of cedars to take a position. Finding it impossible to operate with the battery in so dense a wood, I reported to General Rousseau, who, after seeing the impossibility of taking up a proper position, ordered the battery into action in the open field, which it had previously left. The battery was formed in time to check the advance of the enemy from the cedars, and was then moved to a position on a rise of ground on the opposite side of the pike. A heavy column of the enemy advanced from the cedars, but was finally driven back in disorder by the fire of canister from the battery.

On the afternoon of the 31st the enemy again moved forward in heavy force from a position to our left and front, but were unable to advance under the fire of the different batteries which was concentrated upon them. Though the battery changed positions several times, in order to follow up the movements of the troops, its main position was on the rise of ground already spoken of [just behind you], and on which it camped at night.

I have the honor to append the following list of casualties in my command: Wounded: Corpl. Charles Allitzon and Privates Thomas Burns,

James F. Mohr, Michael McGrath, and Benjamin F. Burgess; total wounded, 5; total of horses killed, 10; total of horses wounded, 5; rounds of ammunition expended, 558. [*OR* 20, pt. 1, pp. 381–82.]

As Guenther's and Van Pelt's batteries went into action they were joined by Lieutenant Estep's Eighth Indiana Battery, which was 175 yards to your left.

Report of Lieut. George Estep, USA, Commanding Eighth Indiana Battery, First Division, Left Wing, Army of the Cumberland

I put my battery in position on Wednesday morning about 9 o'clock, by order of General Rosecrans, on the west side of the railroad, supported on the right by two batteries, and on the left by the Nineteenth Infantry (regulars); fired 114 rounds (at a range of 800 yards) at the enemy, who were driving back our infantry advance. I then advanced the battery 75 or 80 yards, supported, as in the first position, by the two batteries on my right and the Nineteenth Infantry on my left.

At this position the enemy in three lines made three desperate charges, and were as often repulsed by my battery. I expended 70 rounds of canister, and was compelled four or five times to double-charge the pieces in order to drive the enemy; this beginning at a range of 90 yards, and increasing as the enemy became confused and retired. I also fired from this position 106 rounds of shrapnel and solid shot, at a range of about 800 yards, at the lines of the enemy advancing on our right. [*OR* 20, pt. 1, pp. 475–76.]

As the Confederate assault came closer to the pike the supporting infantry regiments added their fire to that of the artillery.

Report of Maj. Anson G. McCook, USA, Commanding Second Ohio Infantry, First Brigade, First Division, Center Wing, Army of the Cumberland

On the morning of the 31st, after being ordered into the woods on our right center, with the balance of the brigade, and before being engaged, Lieutenant-Colonel Kell, then in command of the regiment, was ordered by Captain McDowell, assistant adjutant-general on Major-General Rousseau's staff, in person, to leave the position assigned us in the woods, and move to the support of Captain Guenther's battery (H), [Fifth] United States Artillery, then stationed on the left of the main Murfreesboro turnpike. The regiment was formed on the flank of the battery, and, in conjunction with it, successfully repulsed the efforts of a brigade to capture it, killing and wounding many of the enemy, and capturing about 30 prisoners and a stand of colors belonging to the Thirtieth Regiment Arkansas Volunteer Infantry.

Our loss was 11 officers and men killed and 34 officers and men wounded; among the former, Lieut. Col. John Kell, commanding the regiment. [*OR* 20, pt.1, p. 387.]

Major Anson G. McCook, USA. Massachusetts Commandery Military Order of the Loyal Legion and the U.S. Army Military History Institute.

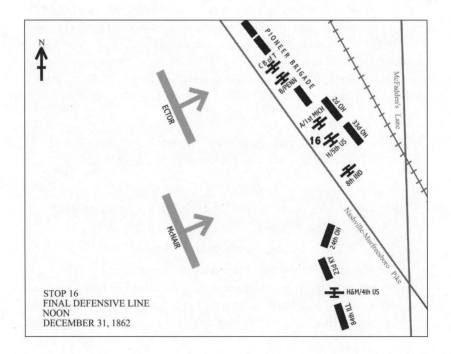

STOP 16
FINAL DEFENSIVE LINE
NOON
DECEMBER 31, 1862

McCown had halted his division along the Wilkinson Turnpike west of the Gresham house to be resupplied with ammunition. It was from this location that his brigades moved in an attempt to capture and cut a section of the Nashville-Murfreesboro Pike. As *Rains's* Brigade was attacking across the cotton field, the other two brigades of *McCown's* Division were moving north and then east to outflank the Union defenses and gain the pike. By the time *McNair's* Brigade and *Ector's* Brigade were in position to attack, *Rains's* Brigade had been stopped and driven back to the cedars. Both Confederate brigades had difficulty in keeping formation on each other, and they became separated and attacked individually. As *McNair's* and *Ector's* Brigades moved forward, they ran into that part of the final defensive position where you are and to your right.

Report of Brig. Gen. *Matthew D. Ector,* CSA, Commanding *Ector's* Brigade, *McCown's* Division, *Hardee's* Corps, Army of Tennessee

As most of my men had nearly exhausted their 40 rounds, they were also halted [along the Wilkinson Turnpike] and ordered to supply themselves with ammunition. General *Rains* thought his men were pretty well supplied, and, after making a short halt, he was ordered to the right of the other two brigades in a northeast direction until he came up with the enemy. He had gone, I would say from the firing in this direction, but little over half a mile before he engaged them. We were ordered forward, and I was told to cause the left of my brigade to oblique to the right. General *Rains* in the mean time was driving back the enemy, when unfortunately, he fell, mortally wounded. He had driven them through a dense cedar forest and into a field. Their left wing had either been routed or driven back upon their center; the right of their center had also been driven back some distance, and their forces were thus massed in a very formidable position in a field not far from the Nashville pike. I had thought for some time the left of my command was obliquing too much, and so informed the division commander. He sent me word that General *Hardee,* who was in command of that corps of our army, desired I should continue to move in this way. The enemy were in ambuscade in [a] cedar brake on the left of my command. They had a very formidable battery planted about 250 yards in a northeast direction from us; one nearly in a north direction about the same distance off, and the third one in a field a quarter of a mile northwest of us. All these batteries turned loose upon us. About the same time their infantry, whose position had been ascertained by my skirmishers, unmasked themselves and opened fire. The Fourteenth and Fifteenth Texas Regiments were soon in a desperate struggle; the regiments on the right of them were equally exposed to their artillery. Immediately sent Major *F. M. Spencer* to Colonel *Harper,* who was in command of [*McNair's*] brigade on my right (General *McNair* having become too unwell), to move his brigade up to my assistance. I hastened to the left of my command. My men had driven back one line of their infantry upon the second line; still behind them was a third line The cedars were falling and being trimmed by bombs, canister,

Brigadier General *Matthew D. Ector,* CSA. Library of Congress.

and iron hail, which seemed to fill the air. My men had not yielded an inch, but, sheltering themselves behind the rocks, would lie down and load, rise to their knees, fire into the closed blue line not over 60 yards from them. Believing it to be impossible to bring my entire brigade to bear with full force, and that an attempt to do it would be attended with great sacrifice of life, I ordered them to fall back. [*OR* 20, pt. 1, pp. 927–28.]

Ector found his brigade under fire from two directions. To his left, northwest, was Colonel Samuel Beatty's brigade, which was in the process of extending the Union line to the west. While deploying at that position, Beatty took the opportunity to fire into the flank of *Ector's* attack. Shortly there after Beatty's brigade, along with Fyffe's and Harker's was attacked by part of *Cleburne's* Division, Stops 8 and 9. Directly in front of *Ector's* Brigade was the Army of the Cumberland's Pioneer Brigade.

Shortly after assuming command of the army, Rosecrans had ordered that each infantry regiment provide twenty men with an officer and two sergeants. These troops, 1,700 in number at Stones

River, were organized into three pioneer battalions and grouped together as a brigade. They were trained to do road repair, fortification construction, and bridge building. In an emergency they could also perform as infantry. They were the modern-day equal of combat engineers. In addition, the brigade had attached Captain James H. Stokes's Chicago Board of Trade Artillery Battery.

On the morning of December 31 the Pioneer Brigade had been busy improving McFadden's Ford and doing road construction work. As the Confederate attack began to collapse the right of Rosecrans's defensive line, the three pioneer battalions with their artillery battery were ordered to take up a position between the pike and the railroad 400 yards to your right. There Lieutenant Alanson J. Stevens's Battery B, Pennsylvania Artillery of Van Cleve's division joined them.

The Pioneer Brigade and the two artillery batteries engaged the attacking Confederate from this side of the pike. After the Confederate attack was stopped, they counterattacked and occupied the position just on the other side of the Visitor's Center that is marked with artillery representing the Board of Trade Battery. You passed these guns as you drove to this stop.

Report of Capt. James St. Clair Morton, USA, Commanding Pioneer Brigade, Army of the Cumberland

On the morning of the 31st, the brigade was engaged in improving the fords of Stone's River, in which the right battalion sustained the fire of some rebel cavalry, when I was ordered to take position in the line of battle, and formed my brigade, by the orders of the commanding general in person, fronting toward the right, where the enemy appeared on a rise of ground in front of us, from which they had driven one of our batteries. I immediately opened fire with canister from Stokes' battery and drove them back. I then, by order of the commanding general in person, advanced to the said rise, and held it under the fire of three rebel batteries. I supported the battery by the First Battalion of Pioneers on the left, posted in a thicket, and by the Third Battalion on the right. The Second Battalion was placed in a wood still farther to the right.

Shortly after I had formed my line, the enemy appeared across the field, preparing to charge upon some of our troops, who were retiring, but had been rallied by the commanding general. I opened fire upon these from

Stokes' battery, which played over the head of the commanding general and our troops, and arrested their advance. My right battalion was soon after attacked, the object of the enemy being to penetrate through the line under cover of the woods. Said battalion changed front so as to obtain a flanking fire, and by a single volley repulsed the enemy, composed of the Eleventh and Fourteenth Texas Regiments. In this the battalion was aided by the Seventy-ninth Indiana, which had rallied on its right. [*OR* 20, pt.1, p. 243.]

Fighting with the Pioneer Brigade was Lieutenant Stevens's Battery B, Pennsylvania Artillery. This battery had originally been with Colonel Samuel Beatty's brigade as it moved from a position on the Union left to the far right in an attempt to stop the Confederate attack south of Asbury Road, Stop 9. Unable to keep up because of the stragglers and confusion on the roads, Stevens was given permission to go into action wherever he could.

Report of Lieut. Alanson J. Stevens, USA, Commanding, Battery B, Pennsylvania Artillery, Third Division, Left Wing, Army of the Cumberland

I took position on the rising ground on the left of the old block-house, along the line of the railroad, and opened fire on the enemy, who were advancing through the woods on the right of the pike and in our front. We fired as rapidly as possible with spherical case from our smooth-bores and Schenkl shells from our rifles, when, finding the enemy checked and our infantry advancing, we limbered to the front, advanced a short distance across the pike, where we came in position and fired a few rounds, when the Board of Trade Battery advanced and took position on our [right], covering all the intermediate ground in our front.

We changed position by moving by the left flank, and occupied the rising ground in the corn-field to the right of the pike, and covering the woods, out of which General Rousseau's and Negley's troops were retiring. We reserved our fire until our own troops were clear of the woods, and the enemy's lines, with banners flying, came in sight on the verge of the timber, within 500 yards of our battery. We opened upon them with spherical case, shell, and canister, and fired briskly for about fifteen minutes, when, seeing no more of the enemy, we ceased firing; some of the enemy's advance fell within 15 or 20 yards of our guns. By General Rousseau's advice, we then fell back on the rising ground between that and the railroad, firing a few shots at the enemy. [*OR* 20, pt. 1, p. 580.]

Stevens's battery also participated in the action at McFadden's Ford. Although not equaling Parsons's battery, in two days of action Stevens's gunners fired a respectable 1,650 rounds.

Sergeant Henry V. Freeman of the Second Battalion wrote the best account of the actions of the Pioneer Brigade from the individual soldier's view. Commissioned an officer in 1863 with the Twelfth U.S. Colored Troops, he saw action in Alabama and Tennessee, including the Battle of Nashville.

Narrative of Sgt. Henry V. Freeman, USA, Second Battalion, Pioneer Brigade, Army of the Cumberland

At early dawn the sound of cannon had come booming over from the right. The morning sun shot his rays through the thickets of cedar, and illuminated the smoke of battle rising over the distant right. The sounds of battle were unmistakably coming nearer with omens of disaster. Rumors of trouble began to run through the lines. A few minutes later apparently, the woods were suddenly filled with stragglers, riderless horses, and ambulances driven with frantic speed. An aid dashed up to Morton, the brigade commander. A moment afterwards the battalion was moving out of the cedar thicket into the open ground through which ran the railroad and Nashville Pike, and was passed behind the center and toward the right. Not until then did we begin to comprehend the full extent of the disaster. Moving at the double-quick, as the brigade emerged from the cedars, which had shut off a clear view of that part of the field, the rear of the center and a part of the right of the army became more plainly visible. . . . The Confederate advance was already within eighty rods [440 yards] of us.

From the woods to the right [west] of the Nashville Pike issued a stream of stragglers. The debris was drifting back rapidly. It is impossible to describe the scene adequately. Cannon and caissons, and the remnants of batteries, the horses of which had been killed, were being hurriedly dragged off by hand. There were men retiring with guns, and men without guns; men limping, others holding up blood-stained arms and hands; men carrying off wounded comrades; and faces blackened with powder, and in some cases stained with blood. Two or three riderless horses dashed out of the woods, which still partly hid the combat, ran for a distance, and stopped and stared back at the tumult. And all the steady crackling of musketry, approaching nearer and nearer, sounded as if some mighty power was breaking and crashing to the ground every tree in the forest.

General Rosecrans, looking every inch a soldier, passed us with a part of his staff riding to the front and center. He himself planted Stokes' battery on a rising ground [to your right], and placed the Pioneer Brigade in position for its support, the First Battalion on the left and the others on the right of the battery. Shells were bursting over and missiles of all kind hailed around. Crossing the railroad to the open space between it and the Nashville Pike we filed down to the right and formed line of battle. "Battalion, lie down!" was ordered and the line lay prostrate, each man keenly peering into the thicket in front for the retreating "blue-coats" and "gray-backs" following hard after, of whom the approaching musketry told. Bullets zipped over and about, and threw dirt in the faces of the prostrate men. On came the sounds of battle nearer and nearer. Then at length the battle line of struggling blue-coats slowly falling back came into view through the trees. They were loading and firing as they retired. But their ammunition was about exhausted, and they passed over our prostrate line and laid down behind it. The order "Battalion, rise up!" came like an electric shock.

The brigade was by some mischance short of ammunition; some companies had not more than twenty rounds [per soldier]. [Morton] rode to the front saying: "Men, you haven't got much ammunition, but give them

Sergeant Henry V. Freeman, USA. Massachusetts Commandery Military Order of the Loyal Legion and the U.S. Army Military History Institute.

what you have, and then wade in on them with the bayonets." He then gave the order, "Fix, bayonets!" "Confound it," said a lieutenant, "that will interfere with loading." The order was obeyed for the time being, though the men soon removed them as the firing began. The battery was [now] stationed at the left of our battalion. It was Stokes' Chicago Board of Trade Battery. The Confederates were near at hand. Suddenly their line seemed to burst through the thicket just in front. "Commence firing!" and our volleys were fired into them. Men were dropping here and there, and others filled the vacant places. The rebel flag, seen dimly through the smoke and trees, started forward, and then surged back. "Pour in the shot, boys!" "Give them hell!" were some of the exultant exclamations. The immediate danger was over. The Confederates gave way rapidly, and the line pressed forward after them.

But it was not prudent to push ahead too far. The advance was stopped, the line formed anew and then pushed forward again. The rocky surface in the cedar woods was uneven and the progress in line of battle was comparatively slow. Dead and wounded lay everywhere.

Very soon the Board of Trade Battery again opened with renewed vigor. Its shot and shell went crashing into the woods in front. Then through the cedars came dense Confederate columns, flushed with previous success, and rolling forward to anticipated victory. "Battalion, rise up!" and again came the shock battle. But the fire of the battery demoralized them, and they did not stand long. "Forward!" came the command; and our line steadily advance, but only for a short distance. [*Military Order of the Loyal Legion of the United States* (Chicago: Dial Press, 1899), 3:232–27.]

Return to your car for the drive to Stop 17.

Drive out the Cemetery gate, turn left on the Nashville-Murfreesboro Pike, and drive 0.4 mile to the parking area for the Hazen Brigade Monument. Turn left into the parking area, park, and get out of your car. Be careful of traffic and cross the Nashville-Murfreesboro Pike. Turn right and walk northwest for 200 yards to McFadden's Lane. Stay well off the road. Turn left at McFadden's Lane, walk a few yards, stop, and face left so that you are looking back in the direction you just came from. Look at the area on both sides of the pike.

Stop 17—Palmer's Division

You are now standing at the intersection of the Nashville-Murfreesboro Pike and McFadden's Lane. Both were here in 1862. Today the Nashville-Murfreesboro Pike is called the Old Nashville Highway. The railroad to your left was also here in 1862. To your left rear McFadden's Lane goes north for one mile to McFadden's Ford at Stones River. To your right front McFadden's Lane goes south across the field and next to the woods for eight-tenths of a mile, 1,400 yards, where it intersects with the Wilkinson Turnpike. This is in the vicinity of Stops 12 and 13. Looking directly southeast along the Nashville-Murfreesboro Pike at a distance of 425 yards, you can see the overpass for Thompson Lane. Neither

Thompson Lane nor the overpass was there in 1862. Just beyond the overpass and to the right of the road was the Cowan house. This brick structure was the home of Varner and Susan Cowan. Accidentally burnt just before the battle, the house and its out-buildings were an obstacle to Confederate forces attacking the Round Forest defenses. The Cowan house is referred to in many reports, usually as the burnt brick house. There is nothing there to mark where the house was. The ground to your right and in front of you was a mixture of cotton fields and open fields. The ground to your left beyond the forest was a cornfield.

You are standing just behind the center of the defensive line occupied by Brigadier General John M. Palmer's Second Division of the Left Wing. This division consisted of three infantry brigades and three batteries of artillery. The area to your left front and on the other side of the pike (where you parked) was a four-acre wood called the Round Forest. Colonel William B. Hazen's Second Brigade defended this position. To Hazen's left was Colonel George D. Wagner's Second Brigade of Wood's division. To Hazen's right (your right front) on this side of the pike was Brigadier General Charles Cruft's First Brigade. To Cruft's right were Negley's and Sheridan's divisions, Stops 11, 12, and 13.

Hazen and Cruft did not initially occupy the positions just described. Hazen's brigade was initially deployed in the field in front of you. Earlier in the morning both brigades were ordered forward to occupy the small but tactically significant rise of ground where the Cowan house was. However, before they had moved forward more than 100 yards they were ordered to halt and then fall back and occupy the positions as previously indicated on either side of the Nashville-Murfreesboro Pike.

To the rear and centered between these two brigades was Colonel William Grose's Third Brigade and Lieutenant Charles C. Parsons's battery. You looked at the action of this brigade and the artillery at Stop 15. To your right you can see the artillery representing Parsons's guns. They are pointed to the southeast, which was their initial orientation, but were later turned west to cover the cotton field. As the fighting progressed in this area, Parsons's guns were again pointed southeast.

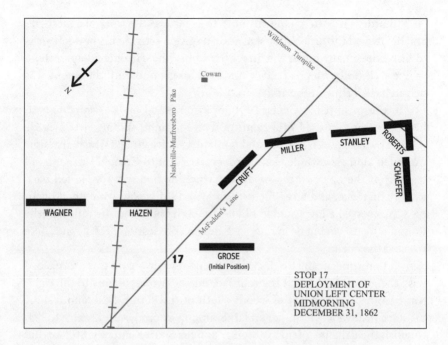

Cowan

Nashville-Murfreesboro Pike

Wilkinson Turnpike

McFadden's Lane

MILLER STANLEY ROBERTS SCHAEFER

CRUFT

WAGNER HAZEN

17 GROSE
(Initial Position)

STOP 17
DEPLOYMENT OF
UNION LEFT CENTER
MIDMORNING
DECEMBER 31, 1862

Report of Brig. Gen. John M. Palmer, USA, Commanding
Second Division, Left Wing, Army of the Cumberland

Early in the morning I rode to the right of my own command, and then
the battle had commenced on the extreme right of the line. Soon afterward General Negley, through one of his staff, informed me he was about
to advance, and requested me to advance to cover his left. I gave notice of
this to the general commanding, and a few minutes later received orders
to move forward. I at once ordered General Cruft to advance, keeping
closed up well toward Negley; Colonel Hazen to go forward, observing the
movements of Wood's right, and Grose to steadily advance, supporting the
advance brigades and all to use their artillery freely.

My line had advanced hardly 100 yards, when, upon reaching my own
right, I found that General Negley had, instead of advancing, thrown back
his right [Stanley's brigade at Stop 12] . . . and it was also apparent that the
enemy were driving General McCook back, and were rapidly approaching
our rear.

Cruft's line was halted by my order. I rode to the left to make some
disposition to meet the coming storm, and by the time I reached the open
ground to the [west] of the pike, the heads of the enemy's column had
forced their way into the open ground to my rear.

To order Grose to change front to the rear was the work of a moment, and he obeyed the order almost as soon as given, retiring his new left so as to bring the enemy under the direct fire of his line. He opened upon them in fine style and with great effect, and held his ground until the enemy was driven back. [This is Stop 15.]

In the mean time General Negley's command had, to some extent, become compromised by the confusion on the right, and my First Brigade [Cruft's] was exposed in front and flank to a severe attack, which also now extended along my whole front. Orders were sent to Colonel Hazen to fall back from the open cotton-field into which he had moved. He fell back a short distance, and a regiment from Wood's division, which had occupied the crest of a low wooded hill between the pike and the railroad [the Round Forest], having been removed, he took possession of that, and there resisted the enemy.

At that time, near 11 o'clock, as I think, my command was all engaged with the enemy; Hazen on the railroad; one or two regiments to the right; some troops in the point of woods south of the cotton-field, and a short distance in advance of the general line, among whom I was only able to distinguish the gallant Colonel Whitaker and his Sixth Kentucky. Still farther to the right Cruft was fighting, aided by Standart's guns, and to the rear Grose was fighting, with apparently great odds against him. [*OR* 20, pt. 1, pp. 516–17]

McFadden's Lane as seen from Stop 17, looking north. Stop 15 is to the right of the lane. Stop 18 is in the far distance to the left of the lane.

Follow McFadden's Lane to your right and walk south for 240 yards. In 140 yards you will walk past Parsons's battery and Stop 15. Keep walking for another 100 yards. Stop, face left, and look across the field.

Stop 18—Cruft Defends, *Chalmers* and *Donelson* Attack

You are in the center of Cruft's brigade. Seven hundred yards in front of you was the Cowan house. This site is just on the other side of today's Thompson Lane. Three hundred yards to your left, where the Hazen Brigade Monument is, was the Round Forest and Hazen's brigade. Five hundred yards to your right was the center of Miller's brigade of Negley's division, Stop 13. Miller's brigade was the left brigade of Negley's division. To Miller's right was Negley's other brigade, Stanley's. One hundred yards to your left rear was Grose's brigade and Parsons's battery, Stop 15. Initially they faced in this direction but were redeployed to face west as the Confederate attack came through the woods behind you.

Cruft's brigade was composed of four infantry regiments and one artillery battery. He deployed it in two lines. The Thirty-first Indiana to your right and the Second Kentucky to your left occupied the first line. These regiments were positioned along the edge of the woods, which in 1862 was where you are now. In the second line the First Kentucky was behind the Thirty-first Indiana and the Ninetieth Ohio was behind the Second Kentucky. Captain William E. Standart divided his Battery B, First Ohio Artillery into two sections. One section was positioned on the right of the brigade and the other on the left.

Cruft had initially been ordered to advance and occupy the ground where the Cowan house was. This order was soon countermanded, but not before his first line made contact with an attacking Confederate force.

Cruft's brigade had just begun its forward movement when it made contact with Brigadier General *James R. Chalmers's* brigade of *Withers's* Division. This six-regiment brigade had moved forward from a temporary defensive position 800 yards in front of where you are. As the brigades on Cruft's left and right did not maintain contact with his flanks when he made contact with *Chalmers's*

Brigade, Cruft was forced to halt his movement and assume a hasty defensive position. The center of *Chalmers's* six-regiment brigade went by the Cowan house and outbuildings. This disrupted the brigade's battle line, and three regiments moved past the southwest side of the buildings while the other two went to the northeast side. During this attack *Chalmers* was wounded. Soon after this his brigade fell back away from the Union fire.

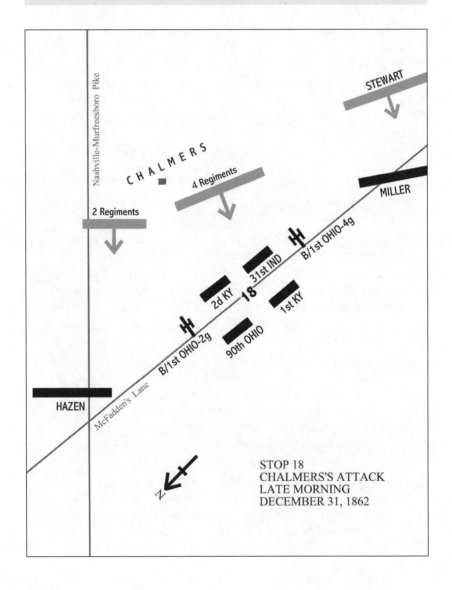

STOP 18
CHALMERS'S ATTACK
LATE MORNING
DECEMBER 31, 1862

Report of Brig. Gen. Charles Cruft, USA, Commanding First Brigade, Second Division, Left Wing, Army of the Cumberland

The brigade was formed in two lines, as follows: The Second Kentucky and Thirty-first Indiana (under general charge of Colonel Sedgewick as ranking officer) constituting the front line, and Ninetieth Ohio and First Kentucky (under general charge of Colonel Enyart as ranking officer) forming the second line; Captain Standart's artillery was formed on each flank of the front line. The brigade, by this formation, exhibited a front of, say, 600 men, or less than a full regiment. Colonel Hazen's brigade was in position on my left, and brigades of General Negley's division on the right. Upon giving the orders to advance, my skirmishers ran rapidly forward from the wood and engaged those of the enemy in the open field. They drove them, and my front line advanced promptly up to the rail fence in the margin of the woods. The enemy pushed toward us rapidly, and charged my line in great force and in solid rank.

After the first repulse, and before my line could be advanced, the enemy made a second charge (reserving fire until a close approach was had), which was more furious than before. The Second Kentucky and Thirty-first Indiana nobly held their ground, and, after some thirty minutes' well-directed fire, drove him back again for a short distance. [*OR* 20, pt. 2, p. 527.]

> The next attack against Cruft's position was by Brigadier General *Daniel S. Donelson's* brigade of *Cheatham's* Division.

Report of Brig. Gen. Charles Cruft, USA—Continued

A respite of a few minutes in active firing enabled me to execute a passage of lines to the front, to relieve the first line, the ammunition of which was nearly exhausted. This maneuver was well executed, considering that it was done under a brisk fire of the enemy's skirmishers, the cross-fire of flanking parties that had already passed to the right and left of the line, and in face of two of the enemy's batteries.

The rear line (now front) was soon actively engaged. I attempted with it to assail the enemy, and ordered an advance. The First Kentucky, Colonel Enyart, on the right of the line, made a gallant charge, and drove the enemy before it, rushing forward to the crest of the hill, clear beyond and to the right of the burnt house. The fire was so severe from the enemy's force at the burnt house, on the left, that the order to move up the Ninetieth Ohio was countermanded; not, however, until many of the officers and men of this gallant regiment had pressed forward over the fence in line with the old First Kentucky.

Standart, with his gallant gunners, was throwing in grape and canister from the flanks as my men ran forward to the charge, and thinning the enemy's ranks. He was too strong for us, however, and soon my gallant advance was beaten back to the point of woods. This point was still held. The brigade on the left was never pressed up to my front, and left me exposed from this quarter. General Negley's [division], on the right, first advanced with me, but, yielding to the impulsive charge of the enemy, broke up, and a portion of it drifted in disorder immediately to my rear, and left me exposed to the cross-fire of the enemy from the woods on the right. We were now completely flanked. Our own troops impeded my retreat. Cannon, caissons, artillery wagons, and bodies of men in wild retreat filled the road and woods to my rear, precluding everything like proper and orderly retreat. Captain Standart's artillery ammunition was failing rapidly. He was shifting front constantly to keep off the enemy. The cartridges of my men were becoming short. Messages were sent to the rear for re-enforcements and for the reserve brigade of the division. The enemy's fire was upon three sides of my position, and apparently exactly to the rear, in the woods. It was impossible to get ammunition up, to communicate with the general commanding the division, or to obtain re-enforcements.

Brigadier General Charles Cruft, USA. Massachusetts Commandery Military Order of the Loyal Legion and the U.S. Army Military History Institute.

In this condition the ground was still held for some forty minutes longer than seemed right or proper. My command had some cover in the edge of the woods from the enemy's bullets, and still kept up a fire sufficiently strong to keep them from rushing into the woods. Seeing my little brigade failing rapidly, and many of its best men carried wounded to the rear, without hope of support, or further ability to hold on, I withdrew it in as good order as practicable. The enemy pressed closely, firing constantly into the retreating mass. We faced to rear, and covered the retreat of General Negley's men as well as could be done. The Second Kentucky Regiment brought off three pieces [of artillery] and the Ninetieth Ohio Volunteers one piece of abandoned artillery by hand which the enemy were rushing upon and about to capture.

I met Major-General Thomas and reported to him, and, with his consent, continued to fall back across the open ground to the turnpike with my shattered forces, now numbering about 500. After forming in line along the turnpike (about 12 m.), the brigade was ordered, by a member of General Rosecrans' staff, to the left, to support a battery on the railroad. [*OR* 20, pt. 1, pp. 527–28.]

Battery B, First Ohio Artillery was divided into two sections. A section was placed on either end of Cruft's infantry line. Lieutenant Eben P. Sturges commanded one of the sections and provided an excellent account of the artillery fight.

Narrative of Lieut. Eben P. Sturgis, Battery B, First Ohio Artillery, Second Division, Left Wing, Army of the Cumberland

Heard heavy fighting on our right. We were on the edge of a cedar grove, the trees of which would once in a while be shattered by the enemy's artillery. They seemed to be driving us on the right. I was ordered by Lieutenant Wright of Cruft's staff to take my section around to the left of the angle we were fighting. Found hot fighting going on there. Unlimbered and ran my pieces down almost to the line of the infantry by hand. The enemy [was] about 300 yards distant on a ridge under cover of cornfields and bushes. Gave them for about three quarters of an hour shrapnel and Schenkl shell. By that time the action was very hot and I advanced my pieces a few rods and changed shrapnel for canister. By this time also their batteries had answered and rattled their projectiles of all kinds through the cedars around us. Sam Earl my rifled pieces gunner put his shells right into their battery. The canister I could not see the effect of for the smoke and cover. Our right seemed to be being driven. We saw the enemy being reinforced by solid columns of infantry prominently bearing the stars and bars. I directed my fire at the later and they went down. The ammunition for my rifled piece was all gone and I sent it to the rear. My smooth bore I had previously ordered to get out of a shower of canister. All this time the right of our line had been driven and we were in sort of a horseshoe and as our reserves had gone to keep the right we had to retire before the largely superior forces of the rebels. I found my smooth bore with but one man with it. The rest however were near. I rallied them and helped them to limber up and sent them out. A careless driver (a new man) ran the [limber cart's] pole up against a tree and broke it. We saved the piece, back by hand and started it off again. I followed up on foot. I lingered some to look back. Our infantry were beginning to rally. Old Rosey [Rosecrans] was here on the ground and I heard him say something to encourage the men. I saw him several times afterward on the field giving directions and encouragement. [Diary of Lieutenant Eben P. Sturgis, Stones River Battlefield National Park Service Archives, Ohio folder.]

Elements of two Confederate brigades attacked this position. The first attack was by *Chalmers's* Brigade and the second was by *Donelson's* Brigade. *Donelson's* Brigade had five regiments, four of which were used in the attack. The brigade initially had been in a position one mile southeast of where you are to support *Chalmers's* Brigade.

Report of Brig. Gen. *Daniel S. Donelson,* CSA, Commanding *Donelson's* Brigade, *Cheatham's* Division, *Polk's* Corps, Army of Tennessee

During the night a general order from General *Bragg* was received directing a vigorous and persistent attack at daylight by our left wing on the right of the enemy, the whole of both lines conforming to the movements of the left wing, gradually wheeling and attacking the enemy as soon as the advance of the left wing should justify it. Orders were received from Lieutenant-General *Polk* directing me to conform the movements of my brigade to those of General *Chalmers'* brigade, always keeping in close supporting distance—about 2,000 feet in rear—and to support it promptly when ordered. Orders also came from Major-General *Cheatham* directing me to obey any orders, which I might receive from Major-General *Withers,* who gave me orders similar to those received from Lieutenant-General *Polk.*

In obedience to the foregoing orders, I moved my brigade, except *Stanton's* [Eighty-fourth Tennessee] regiment, forward at 10 o'clock Wednesday morning, December 31 (the right being the directing regiment and the railroad the line of direction), until it reached the front line, from which

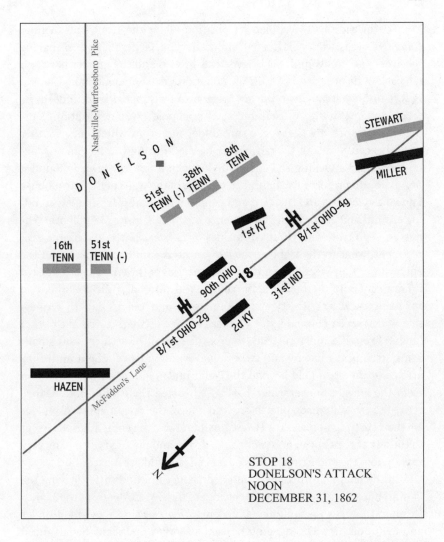

STOP 18
DONELSON'S ATTACK
NOON
DECEMBER 31, 1862

General *Chalmers'* brigade had started, where it was halted until orders should be received to advance to the support of General *Chalmers.* From the moment I moved from my first position in the morning until dark that night my brigade was constantly under the fire of shot and shell from the enemy's batteries, and it sustained more or less loss in killed and wounded on every part of the field to which it was assigned for duty. This accounts to some extent for the heavy loss it sustained.

Colonel *Stanton's* regiment, being a new and small one, and having received its arms only the day before, I deemed it best to leave it in the rear, in support of Captain *Carnes'* battery.

The brigade had occupied its position along the front line (behind *Chalmers'* breastworks) only a few minutes, when, General *Chalmers* having received a severe wound, his brigade was broken and the greater part of it fell back in disorder and confusion. Under orders from Lieutenant-General *Polk*, I immediately advanced my brigade to its support, and, indeed, its relief, under a shower of shot and shell of almost every description. During this advance my horse was shot under me, from which, and another wound received at the Cowan house, he died during the day. In advancing upon and attacking the enemy under such a fire, my brigade found it impossible to preserve its alignment, because of the walls of the burnt house known as Cowan's and the yard and garden fence and picketing left standing around and about it; in consequence of which, *Savage's* [Sixteenth Tennessee] regiment, with three companies of *Chester's* [Fifty-first Tennessee] regiment, went to the right of the Cowan house, and advanced upon the enemy until they were checked by three batteries of the enemy, with a heavy infantry support, on the hill to the right of the railroad, while the other two regiments—*Carter's* [Thirty-eighth Tennessee] and *Moore's* [Eighth Tennessee]—with seven companies of *Chester's* regiment, went to the left of that house through a most destructive cross-fire, both of artillery and small-arms, driving the enemy and sweeping everything before them until they arrived at the open field beyond the cedar brake, in a northwest direction from the Cowan house, when, having exhausted their ammunition, they retired to the Wilkinson pike in order to reform their regiments and replenish their cartridge-boxes. The two regiments and seven companies that went to the left of the Cowan house charged, drove, and pursued the enemy very rapidly, loading and firing as they advanced, and did great execution.

In the charge immediately upon entering the woods after leaving the Cowan house, we had to deplore the loss of Col. *W. L. Moore*, of the Eighth Regiment Tennessee Volunteers. Colonel *Moore's* horse was killed under and fell upon him. Disengaging himself as soon as possible, he advanced on foot with his regiment only a short distance when he was shot through the heart and instantly killed.

Colonel *Savage's* regiment, with three companies of Colonel *Chester's*, held, in my judgment, the critical position of that part of the field. Unable to advance, and determined not to retire, having received a message from Lieutenant-General *Polk* that I should in a short time be re-enforced and properly supported, I ordered Colonel *Savage* to hold his position at all hazards, and I felt it to be my duty to remain with that part of the brigade, holding so important and hazardous a position as that occupied by him. Colonel *Savage*, finding the line he had to defend entirely too long for the number of men under his command, and that there was danger of his being flanked, either to the right or left, as the one or the other wing presented the weaker front, finally threw out the greater part of his command as skirmishers, as well to deceive the enemy as to our strength in his rear as to protect his long line, and held his position, with characteristic and most commendable tenacity, for over three hours. *Jackson's* brigade came up to my support, but instead of going to the right of the Cowan house and to the support of Colonel *Savage,* it went to the left of the house and over the ground which the two left regiments and seven companies of my brigade had already gone over. General *Adams'* brigade came up to the support of Colonel *Savage,*

Brigadier General *Daniel S. Donelson,* CSA. Library of Congress.

when, the latter withdrawing his regiment to make way for it, it attacked the enemy with spirit for a short time, but it was soon driven back in disorder and confusion, Colonel *Savage's* regiment retiring with it. Subsequently, *Preston's* brigade came up to the same position. [*OR* 20, pt. 1, pp. 710–12.]

Although Cruft's brigade was struck hard by *Chalmers's* and *Donelson's* attacks, it was able to maintain its position. Cruft was forced to retreat from this position by a ripple cause and effect on his right flank. As Sheridan's last defensive positioned collapsed, Negley's division found it was outflanked and was forced to retreat. Negley's retreat exposed Cruft's right flank and right rear to attacks from *Stewart's* and *Maney's* Brigades. Cruft's brigade fell back in a northerly direction, crossed the pike, reformed, and went into position between the pike and railroad tracks 600 yards northwest of where the cemetery is today.

Depart this location and return to where your car is parked by retracing your route on McFadden's Lane to the Nashville-

Murfreesboro Pike. Be careful of traffic, cross the pike, turn right, and walk to the parking area for the Hazen Brigade Monument. Stand in the parking area and look southeast along the pike. The pike will be to your right and the Hazen Brigade Monument will be to your left. If you walk anywhere near the railroad tracks, be extremely careful. Trains use the tracks today.

Stop 19—The Round Forest

You are on the western edge of an 1862 four-acre wood called the Round Forest. This slightly elevated piece of ground provided a tactical advantage to the defenders and was the pivot point of the Union line as the right fell back under Confederate attack. The forest extended from where you are to the other side of the railroad tracks, to your left. The ground in front of you and to your right was a mixture of open fields and cotton fields. To your left at the eastern edge of the Round Forest was a cornfield. The open ground around this forest provided the defenders with excellent fields of fire. Six hundred and fifty yards in front of you Stones River makes an almost right angle bend. The river flows northwest to this bend and then turns north and flows to McFadden's Ford. The northwest portion of the river is next to and parallels the Nashville-Murfreesboro Pike. This section of the river limits the area in which the right flank of any Confederate attacks against this position can deploy. Essentially it prevents the Union position from being flanked on its left and forces the Confederates into frontal attacks.

At dawn on December 31, 1862, the Union line went from this location to your right, southwest, for 2.5 miles (4,400 yards) to the vicinity of the intersection of Gresham Lane with the Franklin Road, Stop 2. To your left, the line extended 600 yards northeast and east until it touched Stones River. Although every Union unit to your right, except for Parsons's battery and a few infantry regiments, were pushed back by the Confederate attack, the units at this position and to your left were able to hold their positions. After the collapse of the Union right this position became the critical point of the defense.

By early afternoon Rosecrans's position resembled an inverted L. The long part of the L went from this location northwest along the Nashville-Murfreesboro Pike. The short part of the L went to your left, through the woods and across the railroad tracks to Stones River.

From midmorning to late afternoon elements of six Confederate brigades attacked the defenses in this location. Had *Bragg's* attacks been successful in capturing or turning the defenders from the Round Forest, the Army of the Cumberland would have been faced with a disaster of major proportions. Confederate success here would have collapsed the center part of the defenses and rolled up the defensive line that had been reestablished along the pike.

Colonel William B. Hazen's brigade was the initial unit to defend here. Earlier his brigade had been positioned in the open field to your right. From that location, along with Cruft's brigade, it had been ordered forward to occupy the slightly higher ground around the Cowan house. Both brigades had just commenced to move forward when they were halted. Cruft's brigade was left along McFadden's Lane, Stop 18, while Hazen's brigade was pulled back and deployed into the Round Forest. To Hazen's right rear were the five regiments of Grose's brigade and Parsons's Batteries H and M, Fourth U.S. Artillery, Stop 15. During the fighting Grose's regiments and the artillery would alternate between facing southeast and west, depending on where the most threatening attacks came from. To Hazen's left were Colonel George D. Wagner's four-regiment Second Brigade of Brigadier General Thomas J. Wood's First Division of the Left Wing and four guns of Captain Jerome B. Cox's Tenth Indiana Battery. Cox's two other guns were in position with Hazen's brigade. Brigadier General Milo S. Hascall's First Brigade of Wood's division was in position directly behind Hazen. Hazen deployed all four of his regiments and Captain Daniel T. Cockerill's Battery F, First Ohio Artillery in the front line. To your right and on the other side of the road was the Ninth Indiana. During the fighting this regiment was moved to the other side of the railroad tracks. Where you are was the Sixth Kentucky, to that regiment's left was the One hundred and tenth Illinois, and farther left on the other side of the railroad tracks was the Forty-first Ohio. Cockerill's six guns were deployed between the Sixth Kentucky and the One hundred and tenth Illinois, with Cox's two guns farther to the left.

The defense of this position was dynamic, with the defenses constantly in motion. As regiments ran low on ammunition they were pulled back to resupply and then moved forward again. Other regiments from supporting positions were moved forward to take the place of resupplying regiments until they also fell back for ammunition and other regiments took their place.

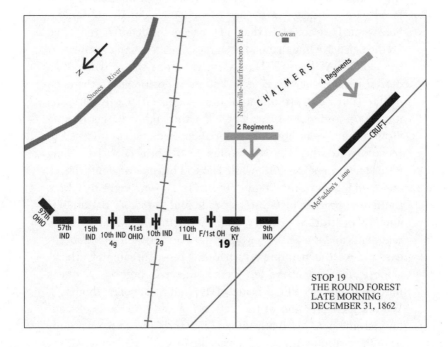

STOP 19
THE ROUND FOREST
LATE MORNING
DECEMBER 31, 1862

Report of Col. William B. Hazen, USA, Commanding Second Brigade, Second Division, Left Wing, Army of the Cumberland

A fierce battle had commenced at daylight on our right, and progressed with ominous changes of position until about 8.30 a.m., when it could no longer be doubted that our entire right was being driven around in rear to a position nearly at right angles to its proper line. At this moment authority was given to move forward to seize the commanding positions in front, and the burnt house of Mr. Cowan. The line advanced about 20 yards, when orders were given to face to the rear, the necessity of which was apparent, the enemy having by this time pushed forward quite to our rear. He at the same moment broke cover over the crest in front, at double quick in two lines. I faced my two right regiments to the rear, and, moving them into the skirt of woods. My two left regiments were retired some 50 yards, and moved to the left of the pike to take cover of a slight crest, and engaged to the front.

The enemy had by this time taken position about the burnt house, and the action became at my position terrific. The efforts of the enemy to force back my front and cross the cotton-field, out of which my troops had moved, were persistent. Upon this point, as a pivot, the entire army oscillated from front to rear the entire day. The ammunition of the Forty-first Ohio Volunteers was by this time nearly exhausted, and my efforts to replenish were up to this time fruitless. I dispatched word to the rear that assistance must be given, or we must be sacrificed, as

Colonel William B. Hazen, USA. Massachusetts Commandery Military Order of the Loyal Legion and the U.S. Army Military History Institute.

the position I held could not be given up, and gave orders to Lieutenant-Colonel Wiley to fix his bayonets and to Colonel Casey (without bayonets) to club his guns and hold the ground at all hazards, as it was the key of the whole left. The responses satisfied me that my orders would be obeyed so long as any of those regiments were left to obey them. I now brought over the Ninth Indiana from the right, and immediately posted it to relieve the Forty-first Ohio Volunteers.

It is proper to state here that, in advancing to this position under a galling fire, a cannon-shot passed through the ranks of the Ninth Indiana, carrying death with it, and the ranks were closed without checking a step. The Forty-first Ohio Volunteers retired with its thin ranks in as perfect order as on parade, cheering for the cause and crying for ammunition.

A few discharges from the fresh regiment sufficed to check the foe, who drew out of our range, and rest came acceptably to our troops.

Another assault was made by the enemy, in several lines, furiously upon our front, succeeding in pushing a strong column past the burnt house, covered by the palisading, to the wood occupied by the First Brigade

[Cruft's] and the Sixth Kentucky. All of our troops occupying these woods now fell back, exposing my right flank, and threatening an assault from this point that would sweep away our entire left. General Palmer seeing this danger, and knowing the importance of this position, sent the Twenty-fourth Ohio Volunteers, Colonel Jones, and a fragment of the Thirty-sixth Indiana, under Captain Woodward, to my support. It was a place of great danger, and our losses were here heavy, including the gallant Colonel Jones, of the Twenty-fourth Ohio Volunteers; but with the timely assistance of Parsons' battery the enemy was checked, and the left again preserved from what appeared certain annihilation. [*OR* 20, pt. 1, pp. 544–45.]

> The first attack against this position came about 10:00 a.m. The attacking units were the right of *Chalmers's* Brigade. This was the same brigade that also attacked Cruft's brigade at Stop 18. The attack was divided into two parts as it passed the Cowan house. *Chalmers's* two right regiments, the Forty-fourth Mississippi and Ninth Mississippi, attacked Hazen's position while the rest of the brigade struck Cruft's defenses. To support *Chalmers's* attack there were all or part of four batteries, with fourteen guns on Wayne's Hill, which is 1,050 yards east of where you are now. In addition, two batteries with a total of eight guns were in position 1,000 yards southeast of your location.
>
> The second attack was a repeat of the first. *Donelson's* Brigade conducted this attack. The Confederate artillery southeast of you having been reinforced by eight guns from two more batteries, there were thirty guns available to support the attack. Again the Cowan house split the brigade battle line. *Donelson's* right regiment, the Sixteenth Tennessee, and part of the Fifty-first Tennessee went to one side of the house and attacked this location. The left part of the brigade went to the other side of the house and attacked Cruft.

Report of Col. *John H. Savage,* CSA, Commanding Sixteenth Tennessee Infantry, *Donelson's* Brigade, *Cheatham's* Division, *Polk's* Corps, Army of Tennessee

When the advance was ordered, my regiment being the right of *Cheatham's* division, I was directed by General *Donelson* (through his aide, Captain [*John*] *Bradford*) to move along the railroad, two companies to its

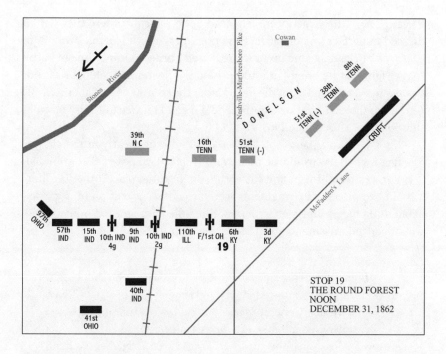

STOP 19
THE ROUND FOREST
NOON
DECEMBER 31, 1862

right and eight on its left, taking the guide to the right. The advance was made under a heavy cannonade, and the line of battle and direction maintained, although serious obstructions impeded the march. The eight left companies advanced between the railroad and the turnpike in front of the Cowan house without the slightest protection, engaging a battery and the enemy's infantry in the woods at a distance of less than 150 yards. The right companies advanced through a stalk-field to the edge of a cotton-patch. Here the enemy opened a heavy fire at short range from a line extending to the right as far as I could see. This killed Captain *Spurlock,* who fell while leading his men in the most gallant manner. At this moment it seemed to me that I was without the expected support on my left, and that the line had divided and gone off in that direction. My men shot the horses and gunners of the battery in front, but I could not advance without being outflanked by the enemy on my right; I therefore ordered them to halt and fire. In a few moments my acting lieutenant-colonel (*L. N. Savage*) fell by my side, supposed mortally wounded, and my acting major (Captain *Womack*) had his right arm badly broken. There were batteries to the right and left of the railroad, which literally swept the ground. The men maintained the fight against superior numbers with great spirit and obstinacy. The left companies, being very near and without any protection, sustained a heavy loss. Thirty men were left dead upon the spot where they halted dressed in perfect line of battle. Here the Thirty-ninth North Carolina [of *Anderson's* Brigade] came up in my rear, and I ordered it into line of battle to my right, but before it got into position the lieutenant-colonel was shot down and was carried from the field. Under the command of Captain [*A. W. Bell*] it continued under my control and did good service until driven from this position, after which I lost sight of it.

My flag-bearer (Sergeant *Marberry*) was disabled early in the charge. The flag was afterward borne by Private *Womack,* who was also wounded. The flagstaff was broken and hit with balls in three places; the flag literally shot to pieces. The fragments were brought to me at night. I carried about 400 officers and men in action. The killed amount to 36; the killed, wounded, and missing to 208. [*OR* 20, pt. 1, pp. 717–18.]

When *Bragg* deployed his army for the attack on the Union right on December 31, he moved all of it to the west side of Stones River, except for Major General *John C. Breckinridge's* infantry division and Brigadier General *John Pegram's* cavalry brigade. *Breckinridge's* four brigades, plus the attached brigade of Brigadier General *John K. Jackson,* remained east of the river to secure *Bragg's* right flank.

Breckinridge's left was anchored on Wayne's Hill. From there his division line went east for two miles to the Lebanon Road. *Pegram's* two-regiment cavalry brigade was positioned to cover *Breckinridge's* right front.

As mentioned in chapter 2, when *Bragg* formulated his plan of attack he should have brought at least three of *Breckinridge's* brigades to the west side of the river. A risk for *Bragg,* but a necessary one if his attack was to be successful. These brigades would have provided additional weight to his enveloping maneuver and perhaps the additional reinforcements needed to capture and hold the Nashville-Murfreesboro Pike. However, *Bragg* did not do this, and *Breckinridge's* five brigades remained on the east side of the river as the envelopment began.

The morning of the thirty-first was a period of confusion as to what would be done with *Breckinridge's* Division. At midmorning *Bragg* called upon *Breckinridge* to send one brigade to the west side of the river to reinforce *Hardee's* attack. Before this could be done *Breckinridge* received a report, which was passed on to *Bragg,* of a Union force on the Lebanon Pike. The order was cancelled and

Breckinridge was order to move forward and attack this Union force. Before this attack could begin, it was discovered the report was incorrect and the attack was cancelled. It is interesting to speculate what might have been the effect on Rosecrans's defensive line had *Breckinridge* moved forward and crossed Stones River at McFadden's Ford, or even farther north, and hit Rosecrans's left as the enveloping maneuver was forcing back the Union right. Even a demonstration threatening to cross the river would have complicated Rosecrans's decisions on what units to shift from his left to his right.

Bragg then ordered *Breckinridge* to immediately send two brigades, *Adams's* and *Jackson's,* to the west side of the river and to follow with two more, *Palmer's* and *Preston's.* Using Wayne's Hill, which is 1,050 yards east of you (0.6 mile), to cover their movements, these brigades crossed the river one mile southeast of your location. As each moved across the river they were positioned in succession astride or just west of the Nashville-Murfreesboro Pike.

By the time the first of these brigades arrived, *Bragg* and *Polk* had become fixated on the Union defenses centered on the Round Forest. Rather than wait and concentrate these four brigades into a strong attack, they were committed as they arrived in piecemeal attacks against the Round Forest position.

After *Donelson's* attack was repulsed, Hazen's brigade and Wagner's, to Hazen's left, began to receive reinforcement. The first reinforcements were from Brigadier General Milo S. Hascall's First Brigade of Wood's First Division. Wood's and Van Cleve's divisions initially had been positioned on the left of the Union line as part of Rosecrans's planned attack across McFadden's Ford to envelop the right of *Bragg's* army. This attack was cancelled when *Bragg's* attack on Rosecrans's right achieved immediate success. As the Confederate attack swept around his right and threatened the Nashville-Murfreesboro Pike, Rosecrans ordered these two divisions to reinforce the right of his defenses. Van Cleve's two brigades, Samuel Beatty's and Fyffe's, successfully made the move and went into action south of Asbury Lane, Stop 9. Wood ordered Wagner to keep his brigade in position facing the river, while Harker and Hascall were order to the Union right. Harker successfully made the move and went into action on the Union far right, Stop 8. Because of the confusion and blocked roads, Hascall was unable to comply with the order. As the Confederate attacks began to develop against the Round Forest and the area west of it, Hascall placed his brigade in a reserve position behind Hazen. As the senior officer present, Hascall assumed responsibility for directing the defense in this area.

About 1:00 p.m. the Union defenses in this vicinity were as follows. Hazen's Sixth Kentucky and Ninth Indiana were to your left. Hascall's One hundredth Illinois was to the left of the Sixth Kentucky, and next to the left was Hazen's One hundred and tenth Illinois (this regiment's left was swung forward so as to almost form a right angle to the front). Next were Wagner's Fifty-seventh Indiana and Fifteenth Indiana. To your right, Hascall's Third Kentucky straddled the pike and his Twenty-sixth Ohio was to the right of the Third Kentucky. Battery F, First Ohio Artillery was deployed between the Sixth and Third Kentucky Regiments. Two guns of the Tenth Indiana Battery were just on the other side of the railroad track with the Ninth Indiana. The remaining four guns of the Tenth Indiana Battery were farther to the left. Having succeeded in helping repulse the Confederate attack across the cotton field, Grose began turning his regiments to face south and had two regiments, the Thirty-sixth Indiana and Twenty-fourth Ohio, behind the Third Kentucky and Twenty-sixth Ohio. Lieutenant Parsons also turned the guns of his battery to face southeast. Behind the center of this Union line two regiments, the Fifty-eighth Indiana and Twenty-third Kentucky, were positioned in the vicinity of the pike. Two more regiments, the Fortieth Indiana and Forty-first Ohio, were near the railroad tracks. In addition, as some of Sheridan's regiments began to recover and resupply with ammunition, they were moved toward the Round Forest. Five of Sheridan's regiments participated in the fighting here.

About 2:00 p.m. *Adams's* Brigade made the next attack against this position. This brigade was composed of one regiment, two combined regiments, and one battalion. Artillery in position to support this attack and succeeding attacks now numbered forty-six guns from nine batteries deployed on both sides of the river.

Report of Brig. Gen. *Daniel W. Adams*, CSA, Commanding *Adams's* Brigade, *Breckinridge's* Division, *Hardee's* Corps, Army of Tennessee

I crossed the river at the ford above the Nashville pike, and finding Lieutenant-General *Polk*, reported to him in person, and received from

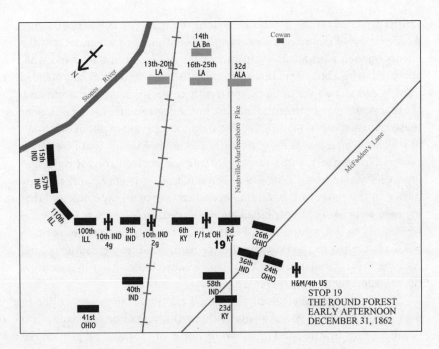

STOP 19
THE ROUND FOREST
EARLY AFTERNOON
DECEMBER 31, 1862

him an order to take a battery of the enemy [either Battery F, First Ohio or Tenth Indiana Battery], which was some 700 or 800 yards in advance of the ford where I had crossed the river, and on an eminence between the Nashville pike and the river. I immediately formed the infantry of my brigade in line of battle in the open plain near the river, and advanced until reaching a place known as Cowan's house, on the pike, where I found the burnt ruins of a large brick house, a close picket fence, and a deep cut in the railroad, which ran parallel with the pike, and the rough and broken ground on the river bank, presented such serious obstacles as prevented my continuing to advance in line of battle. I therefore moved Colonel *Gibson's* [Thirteenth and Twentieth Louisiana, combined] right flank through a gateway in the direction of the river, and formed it in line of battle, with its right resting on the river. I then moved Colonel *Fisk's* [Sixteenth and Twenty-fifth Louisiana, combined] in column of companies up the pike until clear of the obstacles, where I had it formed in line of battle, with its right resting on the railroad. The Thirty-second Alabama, having moved by the left flank so as to avoid the burnt buildings, was again formed in line on the left of Colonel *Fisk.* [The] line being again formed, I gave the command to charge the battery, which was promptly executed.

As the men approached the brow of the hill, they came fully in view and range of the enemy's guns, and were checked by a terrible fire from his artillery, posted on the second elevation, about 150 or 200 yards distant. At my repeated command, however, they continued to advance until the enemy opened with a battery from a cedar thicket on my left, and what appeared to be a brigade of infantry, and at the same time they commenced moving down the river in force, apparently to get in rear of my command. [This was Wagner's Fifteenth Indiana and Fifty-seventh Indiana.] Under these circumstances, I continued the fight for a period of about one hour, in which my men fought most gallantly and nobly. Finding that I was over-powered in numbers, with a force of infantry on my front, on my right, and on my left, supporting a battery of some fifteen or twenty guns, strongly posted in the cedar thicket on the second eminence on my front, and that my men were being rapidly killed and wounded, and the effort to turn my right likely to prove successful, I had reluctantly to give the command to fall back. Owing to the obstacles before mentioned, some confusion and disorder was created in falling back, which caused some delay in reforming the brigade, much to my regret.

At one time during the engagement a portion of the enemy's line in my front faltered and gave way under the well-directed fire and continued advance of my brigade, and I had strong hopes of success, and pressed the command forward, but the enemy was promptly re-enforced; and, finding it wholly impracticable to take this battery, supported, as it was, on the right and left by heavy forces of infantry. I was convinced it was more than any brigade could accomplish, and [was] full work for a division, well directed. [*OR* 20, pt. 1, pp. 793–94.]

One of the batteries that *Adams* was attacking was Battery F, First Ohio Artillery, which was positioned where you are. The battery fought in this position through out the day.

Report of Lieut. Norval Osburn, USA, Commanding Battery F, First Ohio Artillery, Second Division, Left Wing, Army of the Cumberland

We then took up position between the railroad and turnpike. The enemy opened a destructive fire of shot and shell from two batteries before we got into position. Captain Cockerill [wounded during the fighting], deeming it prudent, ordered the caissons to the rear under cover, but the drivers, misunderstanding the order, did not go where ordered, excepting one. Five of them got entirely separated from the battery, and could not be found until 12 m. We opened upon the enemy and maintained our position, with the support of the gallant Second Brigade, which suffered terribly from an enfilading fire of the enemy's artillery, until our ammunition was exhausted.

In the mean time we had 1 man killed and 6 wounded; we had 16 horses killed and disabled, Captain Cockerill having a horse shot under him. One limber was blown up by a shell from the enemy's artillery, killing and disabling the team, so as to render it impossible for us to bring the piece off the field, but was saved from falling into the enemy's hands by the unflinching courage of our supporting infantry. Two of our other pieces, upon examination, were found to be unfit for service, the axles being badly shivered.

After finding our caissons, replenishing our limbers, and repairing one of the disabled pieces, we were then ordered by Captain Mendenhall [the Left Wing's chief of artillery] to take position, [again to the right] of the railroad, supported by the Second Brigade on our left, and the Third Brigade, Colonel Grose commanding, on our right.

No sooner had we taken our position than the enemy opened upon us with two batteries, one in front, and the other on our left. Our fire for a short time was directed at the enemy's advancing columns of infantry with marked effect, but our attention was soon drawn to the enemy's artillery, which was doing much damage. Our fire was now directed at their batteries. We soon succeeded in silencing the battery on our left, but the one in our front kept up a destructive fire. [*OR* 20, pt. 1, p. 522.]

Brigadier General *John K. Jackson's* brigade conducted the next attack against the Round Forest. His brigade was composed of three infantry regiments and one infantry battalion. This brigade had crossed Stones River at the same ford used by the preceding two brigades. Once over the river *Jackson* deployed his regiments in the vicinity of the pike and, moving up on *Adams's* left, launched his attack.

Report of Brig. Gen. *John K. Jackson*, CSA, Commanding *Jackson's* Brigade, attached to *Breckinridge's* Division, *Hardee's* Corps, Army of Tennessee

I received an order to cross Stone's River at the ford and support Brigadier-General *Donelson's* brigade, reporting for this purpose to Lieutenant-General *Polk.* Upon doing so, I was directed to push forward with my infantry to a point indicated beyond the ruins of a house (Cowan's), where the battle was raging fiercely. I advanced, passing Brigadier-General *Donelson's* brigade, a part of Brigadier-General *Chalmers'* brigade, and a part of the brigade commanded by Colonel *Coltart.* My command became immediately engaged, and so continued for about three hours. Twice I ordered a charge upon the enemy's strong position, but for the want of support from others, and the smallness of my own numbers, was forced to take the cover of a thick cedar wood. Both times my men fell back in good order and were reformed in line, until they were ordered to retire from the want of ammunition. My command was not afterward brought into action, although frequently under fire, and most of the time in the front line of battle. [*OR* 20, pt. 1, pp. 838–39.]

Jackson's Brigade carried 874 officers and men into the attack; 307 were killed or wounded.

Just prior to *Jackson's* attack there was a change in units on the Union defensive line where you are and to your right. The Second Missouri, Fifty-eighth Indiana, Thirty-sixth Indiana, and Twenty-fourth Ohio moved to the front line, while the Third Kentucky and Twenty-sixth Ohio fell back. In addition, the Fifteenth Missouri was deployed as skirmishers to the left of the pike. The two Missouri regiments were from Sheridan's division. These regiments, along with others from Sheridan's division, after retreating through the cedars to your right rear, had been rallied and resupplied with ammunition and were being redeployed to assist in defending the Round Forest. Lieutenant Estep's Eighth Indiana Battery, which had helped repulse the Confederate attack across the cotton field, was moved to a position between the pike and Parsons's guns. After firing a few rounds it was then again moved to the left of the Union line between the Fifty-seventh Indiana and One hundred and tenth Illinois.

Report of Maj. Francis Ehrler, USA, Commanding Second Missouri Infantry, Second Brigade, Third Division, Right Wing, Army of the Cumberland

The regiment marched down to the pike, and at the same time advancing toward Murfreesboro, we were ordered to make a stand on the left of the pike, in an oblique line, on a rather rocky ground, which offered excel-

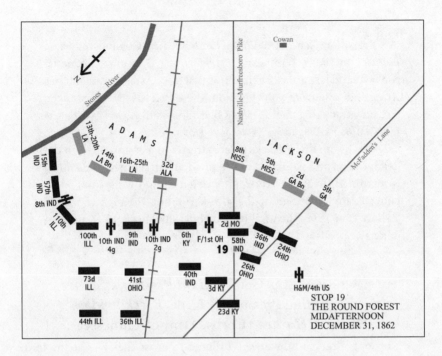

STOP 19
THE ROUND FOREST
MIDAFTERNOON
DECEMBER 31, 1862

lent natural breastworks for all our fighting men. They received the advancing rebels with a steady and murderous fire, accompanied by the batteries from the hill in the rear of our line. Here we remained, and kept the enemy in check until we were out of ammunition, when another regiment relieved us, and we retired to the cedar woods in our rear. For nearly two painful hours we remained in this dreadful position; then we were marched out into the open air to provide our men with ammunition. After a short rest, we received orders to proceed forward, and to take position [near] the embankment of the Chattanooga Railroad, from where we poured a very effective and steady fire upon the desperate enemy.

In this position our worthy and gallant Col. Frederick Schaefer was killed in the execution of his duties as our brigade commander. He fell, a hero, and his fellow officers and his brave soldiers mourn about this heavy loss for the country as well as for ourselves. [This was the third of the original brigade commanders from Sheridan's division to be killed.]

For the second time we were out of ammunition, and Lieut. Col. B. Laiboldt, of the Second Missouri Volunteers, now in command of the Second Brigade, Third Division, ordered the Second Missouri Volunteers to fall back into a reserve and get ammunition. [*OR* 20, pt. 1, pp. 368–69.]

Brigadier General *William Preston's* and Colonel *Joseph B. Palmer's* brigades, both from *Breckinridge's* Division, conducted the next and last attack against this position. After fording Stones River one mile from your location, these brigades were arranged so as to attack together. *Preston's* Brigade was deployed astride the pike. *Palmer's* Brigade was deployed on *Preston's* left. These two brigades began their attacks in late afternoon. Passing through the dead, dying, and wounded of the previous attacks they advanced to within 200 yards of the Union defenses and were stopped by concentrated rifle and artillery fire. Holding their positions for a short time, they then fell back a short distance and assumed a defensive position.

Report of Brig. Gen *William Preston*, CSA, Commanding *Preston's* Brigade, *Breckinridge's* Division, *Hardee's* Corps, Army of Tennessee

Not long after noon, we were ordered to cross the river at the ford, and, under the supervision of Major-General *Breckinridge,* my brigade, on the right, and that of *Palmer* on my left, were formed in line of battle on the ground originally occupied by Lieutenant-General *Polk's* command. The right of my brigade rested near the intersection of the Nashville Railroad and turnpike, and extended nearly at right angles westward, about half a mile south of Cowan's, or the burnt house.

These dispositions made, the order was given to advance in the direction of the burnt house toward a cedar forest beyond. Wide and open fields intervened, through which the command passed with great animation, in fine order. As we came near the farm-house, heavy batteries of the enemy, supported by strong lines of infantry near a railroad embankment, forming a strong defense, were visible obliquely to the right, on the northeast of the Nashville turnpike. The brigade advanced rapidly and steadily under a destructive fire from the artillery. The Twentieth Tennessee, passing to the right of the house, engaged the enemy with vigor on the right in some woods near the river, capturing some 25 prisoners and clearing the wood. The First and Third Florida, on the extreme left, pressed forward to the cedar forest with but little loss. The two central regiments (the Sixtieth North Carolina and Fourth Florida) found great difficulty in pressing through the ruins and strong inclosures of the farm-house, and, retarded by these obstacles and by a fire from the enemy's sharpshooters in front, and a very fierce cannonade,

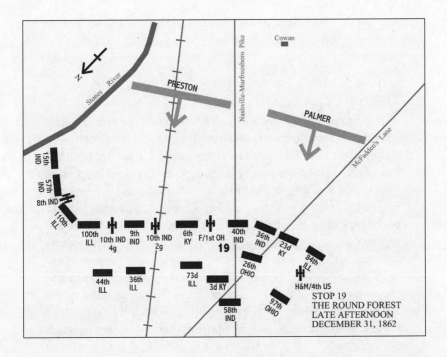

N

Stones River

PRESTON

Nashville-Murfreesboro Pike

Cowan

PALMER

McFadden's Lane

15th IND

57th IND

8th IND

110th ILL

100th ILL

10th IND 4g

9th IND

10th IND 2g

6th KY

F/1st OH

40th IND

36th IND

23d KY

84th ILL

26th OHIO

H&M/4th US

19

44th ILL

36th ILL

73d ILL

3d KY

58th IND

97th OHIO

STOP 19
THE ROUND FOREST
LATE AFTERNOON
DECEMBER 31, 1862

partially enfilading their lines, were for a moment thrown into confusion at the verge of the wood. They halted and commenced firing, but, being urged forward, they responded with loud shouts and gained the cedars. The enemy turned upon the wood a heavy fire from many pieces of artillery, across a field 400 or 500 yards distant, and, though we lost some valuable lives, the brigade maintained its position with firmness in the edge of the wood.

Having met Lieutenant-General *Hardee*, he ordered me, with *Adams'* brigade (under Colonel *Gibson*) added to my command, to hold the wood. We bivouacked for the night, establishing our pickets far in the field and very near the enemy.

Brigadier General *William E. Preston*, CSA. Library of Congress.

THE CENTER

At roll-call, about dark, it was ascertained that the loss suffered by my command was 155 killed and wounded. [*OR* 20, pt. 1, pp. 811–12.]

The termination of *Palmer's* and *Preston's* attacks brought the fighting to an end on the thirty-first.

Bragg and *Polk* both developed a fixation on the Round Forest position. As a result, six brigades, equal to a division and a half, were committed to frontal assaults against a strong defensive position. Two of the six brigades were part *of Bragg's* original and supporting lines of attack and through the normal course of events were committed to the attack of this position. However, the combat power of the four brigades of *Breckinridge's* Division was squandered in repeated attacks against a defensive position that only became stronger as the afternoon went on. As previously discussed, these brigades should have been positioned to support the early morning envelopment of the Union right or to assist in breaking up the defenses by attacking or threatening to attack across McFadden's Ford on the Union left. Neither of these alternatives was pursued. No matter what was done with these brigades, it should have been as a coordinated action. This would have maximized the combat power of this force rather than weaken it with separate, uncoordinated actions. Eight months and twenty days later, *Bragg and Polk* made the same mistake at Chickamauga. There, on September 20, they massed eight brigades to turn the Union left flank in Kelly Field and cut one of Rosecrans's lines of communication to Chattanooga. On this day also they lost the striking power of this force by piecemeal commitment of brigades. Ironically, several of them were the same brigades that had attacked the Round Forest.

In addition to the piecemeal attacks of the infantry, the Confederate artillery on this part of the field was mishandled. Beginning with *Adams's* attack there were forty-six artillery pieces, rifled and smoothbore, that were available on the Confederate right to support the infantry attacks. Fourteen of these guns were east of Stones River on Wayne's Hill. Thirty-two guns were just west of the river. None of this artillery was concentrated and coordinated so as to bring maximum firepower against the Round Forest defensive position. Part of the problem was the lack of a centralized command and control for *Bragg's* artillery. The rest of the problem was a failure of senior commanders to take the initiative or appoint someone to coordinate artillery operations above division level.

As the winter sky began to darken, the fighting came to a halt. Rosecrans's army had survived the day and was now deployed in an almost two-mile-long defensive position. His left flank was

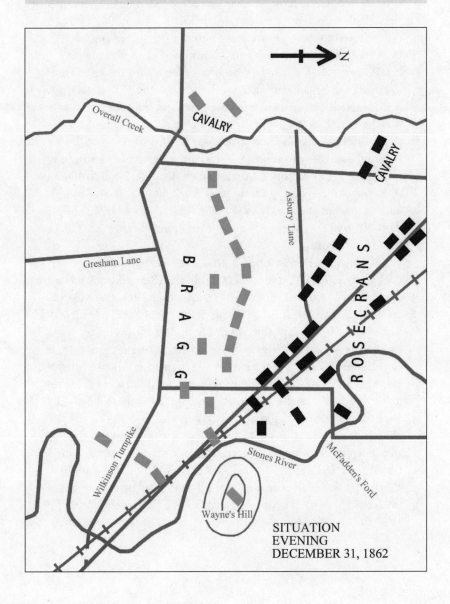

SITUATION
EVENING
DECEMBER 31, 1862

anchored 700 yards (0.4 mile) to your left on Stones River. From there the line came southwest to where you are. From this position it turned ninety degrees and went northwest along the Nashville-Murfreesboro Pike for 1,300 yards (.75 mile) to the intersection with Asbury Lane. Three hundred yards west of the Asbury Lane and Nashville-Murfreesboro Pike intersection Rosecrans's line continued northwest for another 900 yards (0.5 mile). Rosecrans's right flank was cover by cavalry. McFadden's Ford, 1,300 yards (.75 mile) north of where you are and a potential avenue of approach to the Union rear, was cover by an infantry brigade and artillery.

As *Bragg's* attacks were repulsed, especially in the left half of his army, he began pulling units back from the Union defenses and establishing his own defensive line. The right of *Bragg's* line was anchored on Wayne's Hill on the east side of Stones River by an infantry brigade and guns from four artillery batteries. The line continued on the west side of the river 500 yards (0.3 mile) directly in front of your location, southeast down the pike. From that location *Bragg's* line went directly west for 2,600 yards (1.5 miles), almost to where Interstate 24 is today. Cavalry covered *Bragg's* left flank. *Pegram's* small cavalry brigade maintained observation over McFadden's Ford.

At dawn on December 31 both armies were preparing to conduct an envelopment of the others right flank. *Bragg's* attack started first and achieved immediate success. This forced Rosecrans to cancel his attack and shift to the defense. The success of *Bragg's* attack was reduced by the gaps that opened in his left division. These gaps caused the supporting line to be committed to action earlier than expected. Subsequently, the enveloping maneuver lacked a reserve at the critical time to carry the attack into the Union rear to cut and hold the vital Nashville-Murfreesboro Pike. The superb defense by Sheridan's division in the Union center provided Rosecrans the necessary time to shift forces from his left to his right in time to stop *Bragg's* envelopment. Rosecrans's strong defense of the Round Forest provided a much-needed anchor for his final defensive line. *Bragg's* fixation with attacking that position used up four brigades that could have been better employed on the Confederate left.

Dark came just after 5:00 p.m., and both armies settled into defensive positions and began to gather up their dead and wounded and resupply with ammunition. They had been fighting for almost eleven hours and the casualties had been high. The fighting, however, was not over.

Return to your car for the drive to Stop 20.

Chapter 4

THE EAST FLANK
FRIDAY, JANUARY 2, 1863

Sunset on New Year's Eve 1862 was at 4:42 p.m. Thirty minutes later it was dark. However, with the darkness activity did not cease. Throughout the night solders on both sides improved their defensive positions in anticipation of a renewal of the battle the next day. Darkness found parties, Blue and Gray, roaming the battlefield searching for their killed and wounded. Many of these groups, by mutual consent, allowed one another to proceed unmolested. On other parts of the field no consent was established and there were efforts to capture these roving parties.

One of the most pressing problems for Rosecrans's soldiers was food. Many had not eaten all day, and with the coming of dark they were searching for rations. Their problem was increased by the absence of supply trains. At midnight on December 29 Brigadier General *Joseph Wheeler* led his cavalry brigade from its position on the right of the Army of Tennessee on a raid into the rear of Rosecrans's army. The raid lasted throughout the next day. *Wheeler's* cavalry cut across the major Union supply lines from Nashville, disrupting the forward movement of logistics by destroying wagons and supplies. As a result, rations were short among Rosecrans's army. In addition, Rosecrans estimated that there was only sufficient ammunition for one more day of combat.

That night Rosecrans met with his commanders to decide what course the army would follow in the coming days. There are numerous accounts of this meeting, with minor conflicts as to who actually made what recommendation. Regardless of version you read, however, the results of the meeting were the same. Rosecrans left the meeting to conduct a reconnaissance, and when he returned announced that the army would hold its position. In addition, rations, ammunition, and several additional infantry brigades were ordered forward. Orders were also issued to shorten and adjust the defensive line by falling back from the Round Forest.

Bragg did not have a meeting with his commanders to discuss the situation and possible future courses of action. He was sure his army had won a significant victory and that Rosecrans was in the process of retreating back toward Nashville. These thoughts may have been reinforced by reports of the sound of moving wagons behind the Union lines. But what was heard were wagons carrying wounded away from the battlefield and the movement of artillery and infantry as Rosecrans tightened up his defensive line. *Bragg* also ordered Colonel *Joseph B. Palmer* to march his brigade back across Stones River and occupy a position near *Hanson's* Brigade on Wayne's Hill.

That night *Bragg* sent an optimistic telegram to the Adjutant General, General *Samuel Cooper,* in Richmond.

MURFREESBORO, TENN.
December 31, 1862.

We assailed the enemy at 7 o'clock this morning, and after ten hours hard fighting have driven him from every position except his extreme left, [where] he has successfully resisted us. With the exception of this point, we occupy the whole field. We captured 4,000 prisoners, including 2 brigadier-generals, 31 pieces of artillery, and some 200 wagons and teams. Our loss is heavy; that of the enemy much greater.

BRAXTON BRAGG,
General,
Commanding

[*OR* 20, pt.1, p. 662.]

Over the next several days he would receive telegrams congratulating him on his victory.

The next day, Thursday, brought in the new year of 1863. That day Lincoln's Emancipation Proclamation went into effect. From that day forward the political goals of the war would be modified from those first established in 1861. Of more immediate concern to *Bragg*, Rosecrans had not retreated.

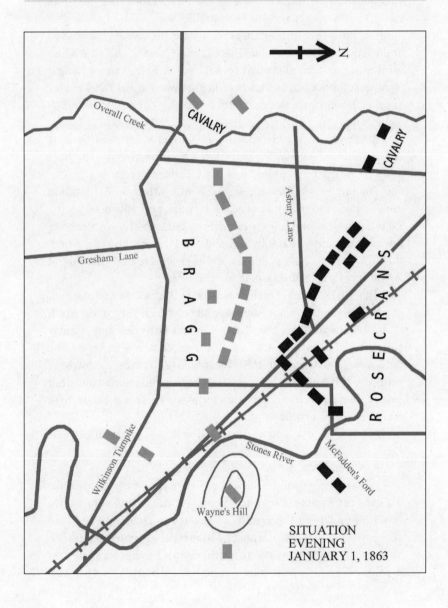

SITUATION
EVENING
JANUARY 1, 1863

Rosecrans began adjusting his lines by withdrawing the units at the Round Forest 250 yards so that this part of the line was tied in with the left flank, which rested upon Stones River in the vicinity of McFadden's Ford. When this was complete, the Union left rested on the high ground 1,400 yards (0.8 mile) north of your location on the west side of the river. From there the line came southwest, crossed the Nashville-Murfreesboro Pike 250 yards behind you, just southeast of where the cemetery is today, and went into the open field. There it made a right angle turn and went northwest for 800 yards to Asbury Lane. At Asbury Lane it went west for 400 yards then turned northwest again and went for another 1,400 yards, where it ended. Cavalry covered Rosecrans's right flank.

Rosecrans then ordered Colonel Samuel Beatty, temporarily commanding the wounded Van Cleve's division, to cross the river and occupy the high ground east of McFadden's Ford.

On January 1 Captain *West's* Ninth Mississippi Battalion of *Chalmers's* Brigade was ordered forward and advanced to the Round Forest. Later they were driven back to the Confederate lines by a counterattack by elements of Harker's brigade, which then fell back to their positions on the defensive line. The Round Forest remained a no-man's-land on Friday.

The battle resumed on Friday January 2, 1863. At midmorning an artillery duel developed between the eighteen guns of the Sixth Ohio, Eighth Indiana, and Tenth Indiana Batteries and twenty-two guns of *Stanford's, Carnes's, Turner's, Scott's,* and *Robertson's* Batteries. The Union batteries were located 250 yards northwest of your position, and the Confederate guns were positioned on either side of the pike 800 yards to the southeast. There was no decisive result from this artillery fight.

Later in the day the last major attack took place on the east flank.

Return to your car for the drive to Stop 20.

Depart the parking area and drive southeast on the pike for 0.2 mile to the access road to Thompson Lane. This is just after you drive under the Thompson Lane overpass. Turn right on to the access road and follow it a short distance to its intersection with Thompson Lane. Turn right, north, on to Thompson Lane and drive for 0.2 mile to the intersection with U.S. 41. U.S. 41 is also

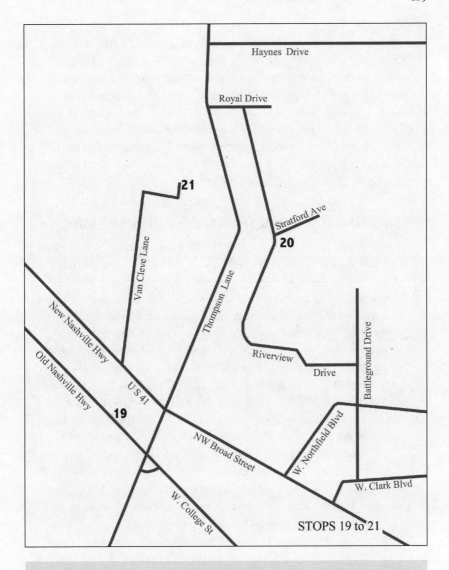

Haynes Drive

Royal Drive

Stratford Ave

21

20

Van Cleve Lane

Thompson Lane

Battleground Drive

New Nashville Hwy

Old Nashville Hwy

U S 41

Riverview

Drive

19

NW Broad Street

W. Northfield Blvd

W. Clark Blvd

W. College St

STOPS 19 to 21

called NW Broad Street. Turn right onto U.S. 41/NW Broad Street and drive for 0.7 mile to the intersection with West Northfield Boulevard. Turn left on to West Northfield Boulevard and drive for 0.6 mile to Battleground Drive. Turn left on to Battleground Drive, drive for 0.1 mile to Riverview Drive. Turn left on to Riverview Drive and drive for 1.0 mile to just before the intersection with Stratford Avenue. Pull off to the side of the road and stop. As you turn left and begin to drive on Riverview Drive, Wayne's Hill,

THE EAST FLANK

now the Stones River Country Club, is to your left. After you have traveled on Riverview Drive for 0.6 mile it will turn to the right and go north. In another 0.2 mile you will be in the location of the left of the Confederate battle line that made the attack on Friday. From here you will be following the attack until it made contact with the Union defenses. The ground will start to rise up, and in another 0.3 mile you will reach Stratford Avenue. Pull of to the side of the road, get out of your car, and face back the direction you just came from. Be careful of traffic.

Stop 20—*Breckinridge* Attacks, Beatty Defends

You are facing southeast. In 1862 the ground in front of you was an open field for 400 yards and then there was a woods. On the other side of these woods was another open field. *Breckinridge's* attack formed in the open field on the other side of the woods and then moved through the woods into the field that was in front of this position. Two hundred yards to your left a thin strip of woods went northeast. The Union regiments to your left were positioned along this woods. Behind you and behind the strip of woods was a cornfield. To your right the ground drops down to Stones River. McFadden's Ford is 700 yards (0.4) mile to your right rear, northwest. One hundred and fifty yards past the ford is the high ground that was the positioned that anchored the left of Rosecrans's line. The Round Forest is 1,500 yards southwest of you. Wayne's Hill is 1,300 yards south of you. During the fighting on December 31 Wayne's Hill was occupied by Confederate artillery and Brigadier General *Rodger W. Hanson's* brigade of *Breckinridge's* Division.

When Rosecrans adjusted his line on January 1, he ordered Colonel Samuel Beatty to move Van Cleve's division across the river and occupy the high ground east of McFadden's Ford.

Occupying the ground on both sides of McFadden's Ford provided Rosecrans with a tactical advantage, if he chose to use it. Occupation of this ground gave Rosecrans a departure point from which to attack south and possibly envelop *Bragg's* right flank. This high ground could also be use as an artillery position from which Union artillery could place enfilading fire upon the right of *Bragg's* line just to the west of the Nashville-Murfreesboro Pike. Conversely, occupation of the high ground east of the ford would provide *Bragg's* artillery the ability to enfilade a portion of Rosecrans's defenses. The focus of the battle was about to shift.

After crossing the river Beatty deployed on the high ground where you are now. He placed two brigades forward and held one in reserve. You are at the location of Colonel Samuel Price's Third Brigade. This brigade had five regiments. Price deployed three in his first line and two in the second line. To Price's left was Colonel James P. Fyffe's four-regiment Second Brigade. This defensive line was anchored on the river, to your right. From there it went 600 yards to your left and faced in a southeast direction. In position to the rear of these two brigades was Beatty's own First Brigade. Colonel Benjamin C. Grinder commanded this four-regiment brigade, while Beatty commanded the division.

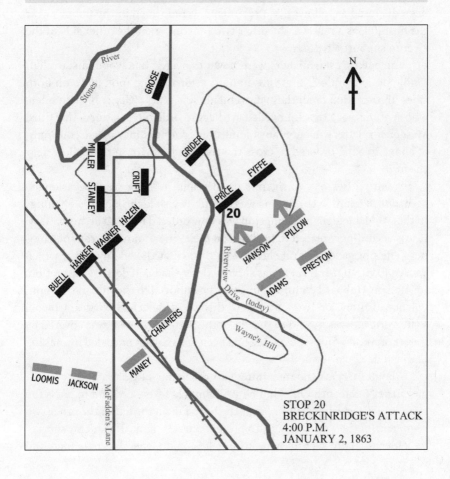

STOP 20
BRECKINRIDGE'S ATTACK
4:00 P.M.
JANUARY 2, 1863

Report of Colonel Samuel Beatty, USA, Commanding
Third Division, Left Wing, Army of the Cumberland

I was called to the command of the division on the morning of January 1, by General Van Cleve's disability, from the wound received in the battle of the preceding day. At 3 a.m. on that day I received orders to cross Stone's River with my command at the upper ford [McFadden's Ford], and hold the hill overlooking the river, near the ford. Accordingly, at daybreak, the Third Brigade, Colonel Price commanding, crossed the river at the place indicated, throwing out skirmishers and flankers. Colonel Price was quickly followed by Colonel Fyffe's [Second] brigade, the forces being formed in two lines, the right resting on the high ground near the river and east of the ford, and the left thrown forward so that the direction of the line should be nearly perpendicular to the river.

In the mean time the First Brigade, Colonel Grider commanding, had been disposed as follows: Two regiments were formed in the hollow, near the hospital, as a reserve, the other two remaining on the other side of the river to support a battery.

The enemy's skirmishers were now discovered in a wood, distant half a mile or so from our first line, and occasional firing took place on both sides. Information of all these movements was sent to General Crittenden, who sent me word that if I needed artillery to order up a battery. The Third Wisconsin Battery, Lieutenant Livingston commanding, was accordingly, at about 10 a.m., ordered to cross the river and remain in the hollow near the ford.

Small parties of the enemy's cavalry and infantry were occasionally seen, and at length a strong line was distinctly visible through the openings in the wood. Lieutenant Livingston was now ordered to bring up his battery. It was accordingly placed in position on the rising ground in front of Colonel Fyffe's brigade. Several shells were thrown at the enemy's line, which caused its disappearance. It was supposed they had laid down. One section, Lieutenant Hubbard commanding, was now moved to the hill on the right, whence also one or two shells were thrown at detached parties. Colonel Fyffe's brigade was moved to the left of the battery, where it was covered by a skirt of woods. Our whole force had been constantly concealed by making the men lie down.

About 1 o'clock the remaining two regiments of Colonel Grider's brigade (the Nineteenth Ohio and Ninth Kentucky) were ordered to cross the river, which they did, forming near the hospital, on the left of the other two regiments of the same brigade, to protect our left flank. The enemy's forces were occasionally seen moving to our left, and Generals Crittenden and

Palmer were advised of that fact. Colonel Grose was, consequently, ordered to support me, his brigade formed so as to protect our left, relieving the Nineteenth Ohio and Ninth Kentucky. These two regiments then formed in rear of the right of the second line as a reserve, being posted in the hollow near the ford. No other disturbance occurred during the day, except the occasional firing of the skirmishers, so Colonel Grose's brigade and Livingston's battery re-crossed the river.

About midnight we were alarmed by sharp firing from the skirmishers. They reported that it was caused by the enemy's skirmishers advancing and firing upon us. One of our men was killed and one wounded. Nothing else occurred during the night.

Colonel Samuel Beatty, USA. Massachusetts Commandery Military Order of the Loyal Legion and the U.S. Army Military History Institute.

On the morning of Friday, January 2, Livingston's battery came across the river again and was posted as before. There was light skirmishing during the earlier part of the day. The Seventy-ninth Indiana Regiment, Colonel Knefler, was ordered to take place in the first line, to close the gap between Colonel Fyffe's brigade and the others. [*OR* 20, pt. 1, pp. 575–76.]

The force attacking this position was *Breckinridge's* Division. On December 31 *Hanson's* Brigade had been left on Wayne's Hill when *Breckinridge's* other brigades were moved across the river to attack the Round Forest. The next day *Palmer's* Brigade moved back across the river to reinforce *Hanson*. On Friday, January 2, *Breckinridge's* two other brigades, *Adams's* and *Preston's*, and additional artillery were brought across the river. There were now four brigade and thirty-four guns from eight batteries of artillery available east of the river to conduct the attack against the Union position on the high ground where you are. Late in the afternoon, when it was to late to be of help, *Anderson's* Brigade of *Withers's* Division was moved to the east side of the river. *Breckinridge* had his four brigades positioned for the attack by 4:00 p.m. He placed two brigades in the first line and two in the supporting second line. The first line was composed of *Hanson's* Brigade and *Palmer's* Brigade, now commanded by Brigade General *Gideon J. Pillow*. *Hanson's* Brigade was on the left of the line and was 600 yards directly in front of you. *Adams's* Brigade, commanded by Colonel *Randall L. Gibson*, was positioned behind *Hanson*, and *Preston's* Brigade was behind *Pillow's*.

Report of Maj. Gen. *John C. Breckinridge,* CSA, Commanding *Breckinridge's* Division, *Hardee's* Corps, Army of Tennessee

On Friday, January 2, being desirous to ascertain if the enemy was establishing himself on the east bank of the river. . . . I proceeded toward the left of our line of skirmishers, which passed through a thick wood about 500 yards in front of *Hanson's* position and extended to the river. Directing Captain [*Chris*] *Bosche*, of the Ninth, and Captain [*Thomas*] *Steele*, of the Fourth Kentucky, to drive back the enemy's skirmishers, we were enabled to see that he was occupying with infantry and artillery the crest of a gentle slope on the east bank of the river. The course of the crest formed a little less than a right angle with *Hanson's* line, from which the center of the position I was afterward ordered to attack was distant about 1,600 yards. It extended along ground part open and part woodland. While we were endeavoring to ascertain the force of the enemy and the relation of the ground on the east bank to that on the west bank of the river, I received an order from the commanding general to report to him in person. I found him on the west bank, near the ford below the bridge, and received from him an order to form my division in two lines and take the crest I have just described with the infantry. After doing this I was to bring up the artillery and establish it on the crest, so as at once to hold it and enfilade the enemy's lines on the other side of the river.

It was now 2.30 p.m. Brigadier-General *Pillow*, having reported for duty, was assigned by the commanding general to *Palmer's* brigade. The Ninth Kentucky and *Cobb's* battery, under the command of Colonel *Hunt*, were left to hold the hill [Wayne's Hill] so often referred to. The division, after deducting the losses of Wednesday, the troops left on the hill, and companies on special service, consisted of some 4,500 men. It was drawn up in two lines—the first in a narrow skirt of woods, the second 200 yards in rear. *Pillow* and *Hanson* formed the first line, *Pillow* on the right. *Preston* supported *Pillow,* and *Adams's* brigade (commanded by Colonel *Gibson*) supported *Hanson.* The artillery was placed in rear of the second line, under orders to move with it and occupy the summit of the slope as soon as the infantry should rout the enemy. There was nothing to prevent the enemy from observing nearly all of our movements and preparations. To reach him it was necessary to cross an open space 600 or 700 yards in width, with a gentle ascent. The river was several hundred yards in rear of his position, but departed from it considerably as it flowed toward his left.

I had informed the commanding general that we would be ready to advance at 4 o'clock, and precisely at that hour the signal gun was heard from our center. Instantly the troops moved forward at a quick step and in admirable order. The front line had bayonets fixed, with orders to deliver one volley, and then use the bayonet. The fire of the enemy's artillery on both sides of the river commenced as soon as the troops entered the open ground. When less than half the distance across the field the quick eye of Colonel *O'Hara* [*Breckinridge's* acting adjutant general] discovered a force extending considerably beyond our right. I immediately ordered Major *Graves* [division Chief of Artillery] to move a battery to our right and open on them. He at once advanced *Wright's* battery and effectually checked their movements. Before our line reached the enemy's position his artillery fire had become heavy, accurate and destructive. Many officers and men fell before we closed with their infantry, yet our brave fellows rushed forward with the utmost determination, and, after a brief but bloody conflict, routed both the opposing lines, took 400 prisoners and several flags, and drove their artillery and the great body of their infantry across the river. [*OR* 20, pt. 1, pp. 784–86.]

Hanson's Brigade made the attack against the Union position where you are located. During this attack, *Hanson* was mortally wounded and Colonel *Robert P. Trabue* assumed command of the brigade.

Brigadier General *Robert W. Hanson*, CSA.
Library of Congress.

Report of Col. *Robert P. Trabue,* CSA, Commanding *Hanson's* Brigade, *Breckinridge's* Division, *Hardee's* Corps, Army of Tennessee

The two lines of the division having been formed, the signal for attack was sounded at 4 p.m., when this brigade in line moved steadily forward to the attack, with arms loaded and bayonets fixed, instructed to fire once and then charge with the bayonet. The peculiar nature of the ground and direction of the river and the eagerness of the troops caused the lines of General *Pillow's* (formerly *Palmer's*) brigade and this brigade to lap on the crest of the hill, but the fury of the charge and the effective fire of the lines put the enemy at once to flight. All in front of us that were not killed or captured ran across the river at the ford and out of range of our fire, as did a battery [the Third Wisconsin's] which had been posted off to our right, and many of the infantry mentioned before as being on the right likewise fled across this ford. A part, however, of this force [elements of Fyffe's brigade], double-quicking toward the ford from their position, finding they would be cut off, formed in line to our right on a ridge, and, not being assailed, held this ground. Meanwhile, and from the moment of beginning the attack, the enemy's artillery from the opposite side of the river directed on us a most destructive fire. Very soon, too, the crests of the opposite side of the river swarmed with infantry, whose fire was terrible. Thus exposed to the fire, seemingly, of all his artillery and a large portion of his infantry from unassailable positions, as well as to the flanking fire from the right, it was deemed prudent to withdraw. [*OR* 20, pt. 1, p. 827.]

Colonel Samuel W. Price commanded the Union brigade defending at this position.

Report of Col. Samuel W. Price, USA, Commanding Third Brigade, Third Division, Left Wing, Army of the Cumberland

January 1, I was ordered by Colonel Beatty (who, by reason of General Van Cleve having been disabled by a shell in the action of the day previous, assumed command of the division) to station the brigade again on the east side of the river, which I accordingly did, placing it half a mile up and perpendicular to the river, in two lines, Fifty-first Ohio on the right of the front line, Eighth Kentucky in the center, and Thirty-fifth Indiana on the left; also the Third Wisconsin Battery was in the front line, between the Eighth Kentucky and Thirty-fifth Indiana Regiments, the Twenty-first Kentucky and Ninety-ninth Ohio forming the rear line, the Twenty-first Kentucky on the right and Ninety-ninth Ohio on the left. During the day there was heavy skirmishing in our front, and occasionally bodies of cavalry appeared in the distance in front of my command. Our artillery opened on them at different times and dispersed them; but after the firing ceased they reappeared. At sundown our artillery was ordered back to the rear, to the west side of the river.

On the morning of January 2, the Third Wisconsin Battery was ordered up and occupied its former position. Through the day our skirmishers reported at different times the appearance of rebel artillery in our front, and also of fifteen rebel infantry regiments that seemed to pass toward our left, which was promptly reported to the commander of the Third Division, Colonel Beatty. The rebel artillery frequently shelled the woods we occupied.

At [4:00 p.m.] the rebels advanced in force through the corn-field in our front, supposed to be a division. As they advanced to our skirmish line, Captain Banton, of the Eighth Kentucky, who was in command of the skirmishers of the Eighth Kentucky Regiment, was shot and instantly killed. When they had advanced to within gun-shot of our line, the Fifty-first Ohio Regiment, commanded by Lieut. Col. R. W. McClain; the Eighth Kentucky Regiment, commanded by Lieut. Col. R. May, and the Thirty-fifth Indiana Regiment, commanded by Col. B. F. Mullen, poured into their ranks a deadly and effective fire, which seemed, for a while, to stop their advancing column, but again they advanced slowly, and here the battle raged desperately.

After these three regiments had contended with the enemy, far superior in numbers to my command, for ten or twelve minutes, and under a severe fire of three batteries of the enemy, and seeing that to oppose them further would only end in the slaughter of my men, I ordered the front line to fall back in order, which it did, as far as possible, and for the second or rear line, composed of the Twenty-first [Kentucky] Regiment, commanded by Lieut. Col. J. C. Evans, and Ninety-ninth Ohio Regiment, commanded by Col. P. T. Swaine, to fire on the enemy as they advanced. Their line being broken and confused by the front line retiring, also was compelled, after a few volleys, to fall back.

After crossing to the west side of the river, by the perseverance of

Colonel Samuel W. Price, USA. Massachusetts Commandery Military Order of the Loyal Legion and the U.S. Army Military History Institute.

the officers a great number of the men were rallied and again returned to the scene of action, and aided in the ultimate defeat of the enemy. [*OR* 20, pt. 1, pp. 608–9.]

Price's brigade was pushed off this commanding ground and fell back across the river. As *Hanson's* Brigade and the supporting regiments from *Adams's* Brigade moved onto this position they came under increased artillery fire from the guns on the high ground on the other side of the river.

Return to your car for the drive to Stop 21

Continue driving north on Riverview Drive for 0.4 mile to the intersection with Royal Drive. Turn left on to Royal Drive and drive for 50 yards. Just prior to reaching the intersection with Thompson Lane, pull off to the side and stop. Stay in your car.

This is the area that the right of *Breckinridge's* attack came to as it slowly turned from going northeast to east. By the time *Breckinridge's* attack had completed its left wheel, it had become necessary to move *Preston's* Brigade forward to extend the line to *Pillow's* right. The attacking Confederate line went from here to the south, your left, for 600 yards in the order of *Preston's*, *Pillow's*, and *Hanson's* Brigades.

Report of Brig. Gen. *William Preston*, CSA, Commanding *Preston's* Brigade, *Breckinridge's* Division, *Hardee's* Corps, Army of Tennessee

As soon as the field was entered the engagement commenced, and our men, pressing forward with great ardor, drove the enemy over the crest of the hill and beyond the river. *Wright's* battery was advanced to the crest of the hill, and was soon hotly engaged. On our right the enemy far out-flanked us, and the Twentieth Tennessee suffered severely, but dashed forward into the woods and drove the enemy down the hill, capturing some 200 prisoners. A division of the enemy, said to be that of Van Cleve, was driven down the hill-side in utter rout by our division. The enemy then rapidly concentrated large numbers of fresh troops on the other side of the river, and poured upon our dense ranks a withering fire of musketry and artillery. Our lines, originally very close in the order of advance, were commingled near the river, and this new fire from an overwhelming force from the opposite banks of the stream threw them into disorder. [*OR* 20, pt. 1, pp. 812–13.]

Having captured the high ground south of the river, many Confederate units continued to press forward toward the river. Here they came under increasing Union artillery and rifle fire. The right of the attack was also threatened by a Union brigade on its flank. This was Colonel William Grose's Third Brigade of Palmer's division. This brigade had fought on Wednesday on the edge of the cotton field then had retreated north of where the cemetery is today. On Thursday it was redeployed to the Union left, and at the time of the attack occupied a position 600 yards to your right front.

Drive forward to Thompson Lane. Turn left on to Thompson Lane and drive for 1.1 miles to the intersection with U.S. Highway 41/NW Broad Street. After you turn on to Thompson Lane and drive for 0.2 mile you will drive over a bridge that goes over Stones River. McFadden's Ford is under this bridge. The Union artillery position is on the high ground 175 yards to your right.

When you reach U.S. 41/NW Broad Street, turn right and drive 0.4 mile to Van Cleve Lane, turn right again, and drive for 0.5 mile to the parking area and a tall monument. In 0.4 mile the road will make a right then left turn. Park, get out of your car, and, as you face the river, stand to the right of the two guns behind the parking lot. You are facing east.

Stop 21—Mendenhall's Artillery Line

In 1862 Van Cleve Lane was called McFadden's Lane. This is the same McFadden's Lane in the vicinity of Stops 13, 15, 17, and 18.

At the time of the battle this flat plateau, which extends north to south for 800 yards, was composed of corn and open fields. Any guns placed here had an open field of fire to and across the river. The plateau had sufficient depth to allow guns to move forward, back, and laterally as required. The length of the position allowed many guns to be brought into action without over crowding. All of these factors made this an ideal location to concentrate artillery.

Stones River and McFadden's Ford is 150 yards in front of you at the bottom of the plateau. The road to the ford is 50 yards to your right. Thompson Lane and the bridge over Stones River, neither of which was there in 1863, are 175 yards directly in front of you. You drove on Thompson Lane, from left to right as you view it, when you drove to this stop. The high ground that *Breckinridge's* attack was to capture is 800 yards in front of you.

This is the area where Van Cleve's and Wood's divisions where to cross the river on December 31 and envelop *Bragg's* right flank. However, the immediate success of *Bragg's* envelopment of Rosecrans's right cancelled this Union attack. Part of Wood's division remained near what would be the Round Forest defensive position. Two of Van Cleve's brigades were order to reinforce the Union right. Colonel Samuel W. Price's brigade and Lieutenant Cortland Livingston's Third Wisconsin Battery were left in position here to guard the ford.

On January 1 the rest of Van Cleve's division, under command of Colonel Samuel Beatty, returned to this position. When they were ordered on to the high ground across the river, Price's brigade and Third Wisconsin Battery went with them. You have already visited Price's defensive position at Stop 20.

The location where you are became a key position with the initial success of *Breckinridge's* attack and the retreat of the Union forces back across the river.

When Van Cleve's division crossed the river on January 1, one complete battery and the remains of three batteries of artillery for a total of twelve guns were brought to this position. Where you are was the Seventh Indiana Battery with six guns. To that battery's left was Battery G, First Ohio Artillery with two guns. Next to the left was Battery M, First Ohio Artillery with three guns, then Battery B, First Kentucky Artillery with one gun. The last three batteries were from Negley's division, and because of the severe fighting on December 31, were not up to full strength. In addition, Negley's two brigades, Stanley's and Miller's, were moved to this location.

As a result of the observed movements of Confederate forces back across Stones River on January 2, Captain John Mendenhall, the chief of artillery for Crittenden's Left Wing, began shifting additional artillery to this position. Prior to *Breckinridge's* attack two more batteries with twelve guns arrived here. Batteries H and M, Fourth U.S. Artillery with eight guns went into position to the right of the Seventh Indiana Battery, where you are. On Battery H and M's right, Battery F, First Ohio Artillery with four guns, went into a firing position. After these batteries arrived, and just prior to *Breckinridge's* attack, there were a total of twenty-four guns covering the ford. During the attack an additional four batteries with twenty-one guns joined in the fighting here. Battery B, First Ohio Artillery with three guns went into position on the far left of the line. The Third Wisconsin Battery with six guns had originally crossed to the other side of the river with the infantry. When it retreated in came back here and went into position to your right between the Seventh Indiana Battery and Batteries H and M. The Chicago Board of Trade Battery with six guns took a position to the right of Batteries H and M. The Eighth Indiana Battery with six guns complete the artillery line and went into position to the right of Battery F, First Ohio Artillery.

In addition to the forty-five guns where you are, Mendenhall directed the Twenty-sixth Pennsylvania Battery and the Sixth

Ohio Battery with six guns each, a total of twelve guns, to fire in support of the defense. These batteries were located near the railroad tracks 900 yards to your right. From there they placed flanking fire on the Confederate attack.

With fifty-seven guns in action, more than one hundred artillery rounds were fired per minute. In a classic example of artillery concentration Mendenhall stopped and drove back the Confederate attack in a very short period of time. More than any one person, to him goes the credit for saving the Union left.

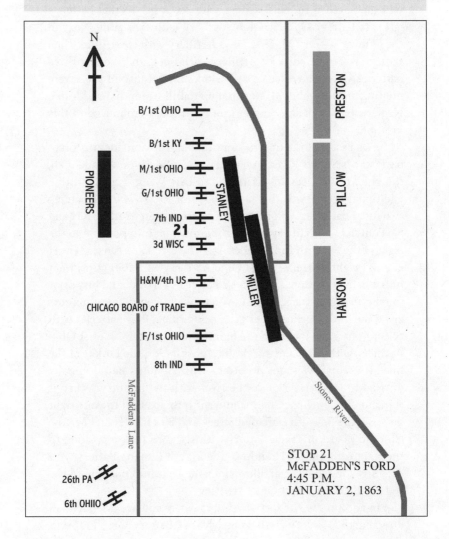

N

B/1st OHIO

B/1st KY

M/1st OHIO

G/1st OHIO

7th IND
21

3d WISC

PIONEERS

STANLEY

MILLER

H&M/4th US

CHICAGO BOARD of TRADE

F/1st OHIO

8th IND

McFadden's Lane

Stones River

PRESTON

PILLOW

HANSON

26th PA

6th OHIIO

STOP 21
McFADDEN'S FORD
4:45 P.M.
JANUARY 2, 1863

Report of Capt. John Mendenhall, USA, Chief of Artillery, Left Wing, Army of the Cumberland

About 4 p.m., while riding along the pike with General Crittenden, we heard heavy firing of artillery and musketry on the left. We at once rode briskly over, and, arriving upon the hill near the ford, saw our infantry retiring before the enemy. The general asked me if I could not do something to relieve Colonel Beatty with my guns. Captain Swallow [Seventh Indiana Battery] had already opened with his battery. I ordered Lieutenant Parsons [Battery H and M, Fourth U.S. Artillery] to move a little forward and open with his guns; then rode back to bring up Lieutenant Estep, with his Eighth Indiana Battery. Meeting Captain Morton, with his brigade of Pioneers, he asked for advice, and I told him to move briskly forward with his brigade, and send his battery [Chicago Board of Trade Battery] to the crest of the hill, near the batteries already engaged. The Eighth Indiana Battery took position to the right of Lieutenant Parsons.

I rode to Lieutenant Stevens [Twenty-sixth Pennsylvania Battery], and directed him to change front, to fire to the left and open fire; and then to Captain Standart [Battery B, First Ohio Artillery], and directed him to move to the left with his pieces; and he took position covering the ford. I found that Captain Bradley [Sixth Ohio Battery] had anticipated my wishes, and had changed front to fire to the left, and opened upon the enemy; this battery was near the railroad. Lieutenant Livingston's [Third Wisconsin] battery, which was across the river, opened upon the advancing enemy, and continued to fire until he thought he could no longer maintain his position, when he crossed over, one section at a time, and opened fire again. The firing ceased about dark.

During this terrible encounter of little more than an hour in duration, [forty-five] pieces of artillery, belonging to the left wing, the Board of Trade Battery of six guns, and the batteries of General Negley's division, about [six] guns, making a total of about fifty-seven pieces, opened fire upon the enemy. The enemy soon retired, our troops following; three batteries of the left wing crossed the river in pursuit. [OR 20, pt. 1, pp. 455–56.]

The attacking Confederates were subjected to this destructive artillery fire because many of them pushed their attacks beyond the high ground on the other side of the river. Spurred on by success, many of the attackers pushed on to Stones River. At such a close range the Union artillery fire was devastating.

Lieutenant *Edwin Porter Thompson*, CSA. *Confederate Veteran*, July 1898.

The Confederate veterans remembered the effect of being on the receiving end of this artillery long after the war was over. *Edwin P. Thompson*, a lieutenant in the Sixth Kentucky Infantry of *Hanson's* Brigade, wrote the best description of this Union cannonade: "The very earth trembled as with an exploding mine, and a mass of iron hail was hurled upon [us]. The artillery bellowed forth such thunder that men were stunned and could not distinguish sounds. There were falling timbers, crashing arms, the whirring of missiles in every direction, the bursting of the dreadful shell, the groans of the wounded, the shouts of the officers, mingled in one horrid din that beggars description. Some rushed back precipitately, while others, walked away with deliberation, and some even slowly and doggedly, as though they scorned the danger or had become indifferent to life." [E. P. Thompson, *History of the Orphan Brigade* (Louisville, 1898), 181–82.]

In addition to the artillery, Colonel Timothy R. Stanley's Second Brigade and Colonel John F. Miller's Third Brigade of Negley's division and Captain James Morton's Pioneer Brigade bolstered the defense. These brigades added their rifle fire to the defenses. As the Confederate attack faltered, Miller, supported by Stanley, counterattacked across the river.

Report of Col. John F. Miller, USA, Commanding
Third Brigade, Second Division, Center
Wing, Army of the Cumberland

About 4 p.m. a furious attack was made by the enemy upon General Beatty's division, then across the river. The fire of the enemy was returned with spirit for a time, when that division retired across the river and retreated through my lines, which were then formed near the bank of the river, my men lying down partly concealed behind the crest of a small hill in the open field.

As soon as the men of Beatty's division had retired entirely from our front, I ordered my command forward—the Seventy-eighth Pennsylvania on the right; the Twenty-first Ohio on the left, to advance under cover of the hill along the riverbank; the Thirty-seventh Indiana and Seventy-fourth Ohio in the center. [Stanley's] Second Brigade moved forward in the same direction, the Eighteenth Ohio on the right, and formed partly in the intervals between the regiments of my right wing. The enemy advanced rapidly, following Beatty's division, and gained the riverbank, all the time firing rapidly across at my line. My troops opened; the enemy halted and began to waver. I then ordered the men forward to a rail fence on the bank of the river. Here a heavy fire was directed upon the enemy with fine effect, and although in strong force, and supported by the fire of two batteries in the rear, he began to retreat. Believing this an opportune moment for crossing the river, I ordered the troops to cross rapidly, which they did with great gallantry under fire from front and right flank.

Here the Eighteenth Ohio, part of the Thirty-seventh Indiana, and part of the Seventy-eighth Pennsylvania were ordered by some one to proceed up the river on the right bank, to repel an attack from a force there firing on my right flank. The colors of the Seventy-eighth Pennsylvania, and, I think, Nineteenth Illinois, were the first to cross the river; the men followed in as good order as possible. While my troops were crossing, a staff officer informed me that it was General Palmer's order that the troops should not cross. [Too late!] The enemy was then retiring, and many of my men [were] across the stream.

I crossed in person and saw the enemy retiring. Taking cover behind a fence on the [east] bank, the men poured a heavy fire into the ranks of the retreating force. The Twenty-first Ohio had crossed the river on the left, and was ascending the bank and fast going into the woods. When in this position I received another order, purporting to come from General Palmer, to recross the river and support the line on the hill. The force on the right of the river was then advancing in the cornfield and driving the enemy, thus protecting my right flank, and, having no inclination to turn back, I ordered the troops forward. Colonel Stoughton, of the Eleventh Michigan, formed his regiment and moved along the bank of the river, while the other troops moved forward to his left. The Twenty-first Ohio came in on the extreme left, and advanced in splendid style.

In crossing the river the men of the different regiments had, to some extent, become mixed together, yet a tolerable line was kept on the colors of the Seventy-eighth Pennsylvania, Nineteenth Illinois, Sixty-ninth and Seventy-fourth Ohio, and the men moved forward with spirit and determination.

The enemy's batteries were posted on an eminence in the woods near corn-field in our front, and all this time kept up a brisk fire, but without much effect. His infantry retreated in great disorder, leaving the ground covered with his dead and wounded.

When within about 150 yards of the first battery, I ordered the Seventy-eighth Pennsylvania Volunteers to charge the battery, which was immediately done by the men of that regiment, and the Nineteenth Illinois, Sixty-ninth Ohio, and, perhaps, others. The Twenty-first Ohio coming in opportunely on the left, the battery, consisting of four guns, was taken and hauled off by the men. [The artillery is *Wright's* or *Semple's* batteries or both being mistaken for one battery.]

Union counterattack across McFadden's Ford on January 2, 1863. Library of Congress.

The colors of the Twenty-sixth Tennessee [of *Pillow's* Brigade] at the time of the charge were near the battery, and were taken by men of the Seventy-eighth Pennsylvania and brought to the rear. Another battery, farther to the front, all this time kept up a heavy fire of grape and canister upon our forces, but without much effect.

Seeing my troops in the disorder, which follows such success, and being nearly out of ammunition, I sent a staff officer back to General Negley for re-enforcements with which to pursue the enemy. I ordered the troops to halt and reform, so as to hold the ground until relieved by other troops. [*OR* 20, pt. 1, pp. 434–35.]

Joining in this counterattack were Hazen's brigade and several regiments of Cruft's brigade, all from Palmer's division. Regiments from Price's and Grider's brigades of Van Cleve's division that had rallied upon retreating across the river recrossed with the counterattack.

Breckinridge's attack had a good chance of success, as demonstrated by the infantry capturing the first Union defensive position on the high ground east of the river. In addition, the attack was timed close to sunset so as to severely limit the daylight left for Union reaction.

Three factors combined to turn *Breckinridge's* early success into defeat. First, the Confederate artillery was poorly handled. There were thirty-four guns in eight batteries available to support the attack. Five of these batteries were under *Breckinridge's* control, while the other three came under control of Captain *Felix H. Robertson,* a battery commander in *Withers's* Division. *Breckinridge* and *Robertson* argued about the employment of the artillery. *Breckinridge* wanted the artillery placed between the two lines of infantry and to accompany the attack. *Robertson* thought this compressed the batteries too close and placed them in a dangerous position. He wanted to hold the artillery back until the infantry had captured the high ground and then rapidly bring the guns forward. Both concepts had merit. However, the argument was not resolved for one concept or the other, and as a result *Breckinridge* placed part of his divisional artillery with the infantry making the assault while *Robertson* held his back until the objective was captured. This divided command and control resulted in many of the batteries going into action piecemeal. In addition, there was no preattack bombardment to either support the infantry assault or neutralize the Union artillery. Even worse, some Confederate artillery was used earlier in the afternoon against the Union position. This only succeeded in alerting the defenders that something was about to happen on their left.

Second, the Union artillery was superbly controlled. It was positioned to provide concentrated fire in defense of the ground on both sides of McFadden's Ford. As the fighting progressed, Captain Mendenhall brought additional artillery into action. Nine months later, on September 20 at Chickamauga, Mendenhall would attempt to do the same massing of artillery. There he arranged twenty-nine guns from six batteries, five of which had been with him at McFadden's Ford, on the high ground west of Dyer's Field in an attempt to check the Confederate penetration of the Union defenses. On that day, however, he was not successful, as only a few infantry regiments supported the artillery and the Confederate attack was able to flank the artillery position.

Third, the Confederate attack went too far. The objective of *Breckinridge's* attack was to capture the high ground east of McFadden's Ford. Whoever controlled this ground had two tactical advantages. First, they could enfilade the other's defensive line with artillery. Second, occupying or controlling this ground denied an enemy the advantage of enfilading artillery fire. The attack was timed so that the ground would be captured just before sunset. This would give Rosecrans a minimum, if any, amount of time to counterattack before it became dark. Additionally, *Breckinridge's* brigades would have the entire night to organize and strengthen their defensive position.

Breckinridge's attack captured the high ground east of McFadden's Ford and Stones River and drove the Union defenders in retreat in the first thirty minutes of the attack. At this point *Breckinridge's* soldiers had accomplished their mission. Although they were now within range of Union artillery above McFadden's Ford, there were many depressions and folds in the ground where they could be protected from this fire and hold their position. Also, they were out of range of effective Union rifle fire. Rather than stop and consolidate on the objective, many attacking regiments pursued the retreating Union regiments toward the river. At this point the attacking force began to loose cohesion. As this occurred, command and control began to break down and many units became commingled. This pursuit also brought them closer to the defending artillery and infantry. As they came closer, the artillery was able to fire canister and the infantry's rifle fire became effective. All of the advantages of the defense were given to the Union artillery and infantry. When the defending infantry counterattacked back across the river, the loss in unit cohesion, commingling of the regiment, and breakdown in command and control prevented an effective response by *Breckinridge's* brigades.

Two months after the battle Lieutenant General *William J. Hardee* wrote a distinct appraisal of the strengths and weaknesses of the Army of Tennessee and the Army of the Cumberland as exemplified by the fighting on January 2: "It is worthy of remark that at Murfreesboro, whenever the fight was confined principally to musketry, and the enemy had no advantage in artillery, we were successful. It was only when they had massed heavy batteries that we were repulsed. In every form of contest in which mechanical instruments, requiring skill and heavy machinery to make them, can be used, the Federals are our superiors. In every form of contest in which manly courage, patient endurance, and brave impulse are the qualities and conditions necessary to success, we have invariably been successful. Long-range cannon and improved projectiles can be made only by great mechanical skill, heavy machinery, and abundant resources. The enemy is, therefore, superior in artillery. Infantry constitutes the great arm of the service, and its appointments and equipments are simple. The Federal infantry, unsupported by artillery, has not in a single instance fought successfully with ours when the odds were less than three to two." [*OR* 20, pt. 1, p. 778–79.]

As the Union counterattack swept across the river and reoccupied the ground they had been on only an hour earlier, the Battle of Stones River came to an end.

Chapter 5

THE AFTERMATH

Neither the commanders nor the soldiers realized it at the time, but the Battle of Stones River ended with the Union counterattack across McFadden's Ford.

Concerned that Rosecrans might follow up the counterattack on Friday with an attack against his right, on the night of January 2–3 *Bragg* redistributed his divisions. *Cleburne's* and *McCown's* Divisions were moved to the east side of the river and placed in a position to support *Breckinridge. Cheatham's* and *Withers's* Divisions continued to occupy the Confederate line west of the river. *Hardee* controlled the divisions east of the river and *Polk* those west of the river.

That night *Cheatham* and *Withers* became concerned over the lack of Confederate forces west of the river and sent the following message, endorsed by *Polk,* to *Bragg.*

Murfreesboro, Tenn.
January 3, 1863 -12.15 a.m.

General *Bragg,*

We deem it our duty to say to you frankly that, in our judgment, this army should be promptly put in retreat. You have but three [divisions] that are at all reliable, and even some of these are more or less demoralized from having some brigade commanders who do not possess the confidence of their commands. Such is our opinion, and we deem it a solemn duty to express it to you. We do fear great disaster from the condition of things now existing, and think it should be averted if possible.

Very respectfully, general, your obedient servant,

J. M. Withers,	*B. F. Cheatham,*
Major-General	Major-General,

[*OR* 20, pt. 1, p. 700.]

Lieutenant *W. B. Richmond* of *Polk's* staff delivered this note to *Bragg* at 2:00 a.m. *Bragg* woke, read half the message, then told Lieutenant *Richmond* to inform *Polk,* "We shall maintain our position at every hazard." [*OR* 20, pt. 1, p. 700.]

Throughout the night and into the morning a steady cold rain fell. The runoff from this rain and that of the previous day began to raise the water level and rate of flow of Stones River. The rising water made the potential for *Bragg's* army to be divided by the river a real and immediate threat. Taking this into consideration, along with reports that Rosecrans was receiving reinforcement and an overestimation of the Union strength, *Bragg* called his subordinate commanders to his headquarters and announced the army would retreat that night.

Report of Gen. *Braxton Bragg,* CSA, Commanding Army of Tennessee

On Saturday morning, the 3d, our forces had been in line of battle for five days and nights, with but little rest, having no reserves; their baggage and tents had been loaded and the wagons were 4 miles off; their provisions, if cooked at all, were most imperfectly prepared, with scanty means; the weather had been severe from cold and almost constant rain, and we had no change of clothing, and in many places could not have fires. The necessary consequence was great exhaustion of officers and men, many having to be sent to the hospitals in the rear, and more still were beginning to straggle from their commands, an evil from which we had so far suffered but little. During the whole of this day the rain continued to fall with little intermission, and the rapid rise in Stone's River indicated it would soon be unfordable. Late on Friday night I had received the captured papers of Major-General McCook, commanding one *corps d'armée* of the enemy, showing their effective strength to have been very near, if not quite, 70,000 men [a large overestimation]. Before noon, reports from Brigadier-General *Wheeler* satisfied me the enemy, instead of retiring, was receiving re-enforcements. Common prudence and the safety of my army, upon which even the safety of our cause depended, left no doubt on my mind as to the necessity of my withdrawal from so unequal a contest. My orders were accordingly given about noon for the movement of the trains, and for the necessary preparation of the troops.

The only question with me was, whether the movement should be made at once or delayed for twenty-four hours, to save a few more of our wounded. As it was probable we should lose by exhaustion as many as we should remove of the wounded, my inclination to remain was yielded. The whole force, except the cavalry, was put in motion at 11 p.m., and the army retired in perfect order to its present position behind Duck River without receiving or giving a shot. Our cavalry held the position before Murfrees-boro until Monday morning, the 5th, when it quietly retired, as ordered, to cover our front.

We left about 1,200 badly wounded, one-half of whom we learn have since died from the severity of their injuries; about 300 sick, too feeble to bear transportation, and about 200 well men and medical officers as their attendants. [*OR* 20, pt.1, pp. 668–69.]

> *Bragg's* army retreated south into Middle Tennessee. Initially *Bragg* issued orders to retreat and establish defensive positions along the Elk River, fifty miles south of Murfreesboro. When he realized Rosecrans was not pursuing, he ordered the army to cut the retreat short and take up positions along the Duck River, thirty miles south of Murfreesboro.
>
> The Army of Tennessee spent the next six months in the Duck River Valley recovering from Stones River. *Bragg's* army had taken just over ten thousand casualties, 27 percent of its effective strength. Losses of brigade and regimental commanders were as follows: two brigade commanders killed or died of wounds and three wounded; ten regimental commanders killed or died of wounds, sixteen wounded, and two captured. This was the equivalent of the brigade and regiment leadership structure for a division. There were no division commander losses. During the remainder of winter and throughout the spring these loses in men and commanders were replaced.
>
> *Bragg's* reputation suffered greatly as a result of Stones River. After the first days fighting he sent a telegram to Richmond.

THE AFTERMATH

Murfreesboro, Tenn.,
December 31, 1862

We assailed the enemy at 7 o'clock this morning, and after ten hours hard fighting have driven him from every position except his extreme left, which [where] he has successfully resisted us. With the exception of this point, we occupy the whole field. We captured 4,000 prisoners, including 2 brigadier-generals, 31 pieces of artillery, and some 200 wagons and teams. Our loss is heavy; that of the enemy much greater.

Braxton Bragg,
General,
Commanding

[*OR* 20, pt. 1, p. 662.]

His premature telegram suggesting victory came back to haunt *Bragg.* His telegram was released by the government and news of his victory announced in many newspapers throughout the Confederacy. When it became known that he had retreated from Murfreesboro, many of these newspaper publishers attacked him in their editorials. Coming after his retreat from Kentucky in late 1862, the retreat from Murfreesboro did irreparable damage to *Bragg's* position as the army commander, both within and without the army.

As his army went into winter quarters, *Bragg* and his subordinate commanders, *Hardee* and *Polk,* and several of their subordinates engaged in their favorite pastime of fighting and scheming against one another. A simmering argument after Perryville developed into a full-blown conflict after Stones River that challenged *Bragg's* competence to continue in command. *Bragg* prevailed in this fight, however, and remained in command. He then set out to exact his revenge. Using their actions at Stones River as an excuse, *Cheatham* was censured in writing, *McCown* was court-martialed and transferred to Mississippi, *Breckinridge* was transferred to Mississippi, and in July *Hardee* followed him. A deep distrust developed between *Bragg* and many of the remaining division and brigade commanders. This absence of confidence and loyalty would plague the army as long as *Bragg* remained in command.

Contrary to what *Bragg* believed, Rosecrans was not contemplating an immediate renewal of offensive operations on January 3. However, on that day Rosecrans's supply situation began to improve when a 303-wagon supply train escorted by Brigadier General James G. Spears's brigade arrived. The arrival of the supplies and the reinforcement of Spears's brigade along with the earlier arrival of another brigade began to increase Rosecrans's combat capability.

Late Sunday afternoon, January 4, Rosecrans ordered Colonel Timothy R. Stanley to conduct a reconnaissance with his brigade toward Murfreesboro. Stanley proceeded along the east bank of the river to the edge of town. Early the next morning Negley was ordered to move his entire division into Murfreesboro. By mid-morning Negley had occupied Murfreesboro.

The next day Rosecrans officially announced his victory with a telegram to Halleck in Washington.

> Headquarters Department of the Cumberland,
> Via Nashville, Tenn., January 5, 1863
>
> We have fought one of the greatest battles of the war, and are victorious. Our entire success on the 31st was prevented by a surprise of the right flank; but have, nevertheless, beaten the enemy, after a three-days' battle. They fled with great precipitancy on Saturday night. The last of their columns of cavalry left this morning. Their loss has been very heavy. Generals *Rains* and *Hanson* killed. *Chalmers, Adams,* and *Breckinridge* are wounded.
>
> W. S. Rosecrans,
> Major-General
>
> H. W. Halleck
> General-in-Chief
> [*OR* 20, pt. 1, p. 186.]

Almost immediately he received a congratulatory telegram from a relieved president.

> Executive Manson,
> Washington, January 5, 1863.
>
> Maj. Gen. W. S. Rosecrans,
> Murfreesboro, Tenn.:
>
> Your dispatch announcing retreat of enemy has just reached here. God bless you, and all with you! Please tender to all, and accept for yourself,

the nation's gratitude for your and their skill, endurance, and dauntless courage.

A. Lincoln

[*OR* 20, pt. 1, p. 186.]

Stones River cost Rosecrans's army 30 percent of it effective strength. Among division, brigade, and regimental commanders the losses were severe. Two division commanders were wounded. Three brigade commander were killed, one wounded, and one captured. Eighteen regimental commanders were killed or died of wounds, twenty were wounded, and seven were captured. This was the equivalent of the leadership structure for almost two divisions.

Rosecrans lost 20 percent of his artillery, 28 of 137 guns (*Bragg* lost three guns). Two hundred and twenty-nine wagons were captured, destroyed, or damaged. In addition 2,108 cavalry, artillery, and draft horse and mules had to be replaced. The artillery had fired 20,307 rounds, and the infantry had used 2 million rounds of ammunition. The Army of the Cumberland needed to pause, regain its strength, reequip, and resupply. Further, the roads and weather from January on continued to get worse. Confirming that *Bragg* had retreated, Rosecrans called a halt to active campaigning.

Colonel John Beatty, commander of the Second Brigade of Rousseau's division left a very descriptive account of the battlefield after the fighting was over. "During the forenoon the army crosses Stones River, and with music, banners, and rejoicings takes possession of the old camps of the enemy," Beatty wrote. "So the long and doubtful struggle ends. I ride over the battlefield. In one place a caisson and five horses are lying, the latter killed in harness, and all fallen together. Nationals and Confederates, young, middle-aged, and old are scattered over the woods and fields for miles. Poor [Private James] Wright, of my old company [I, Third Ohio], lay at the barricade in the woods. Many others lay about him. Further on we find men with their legs shot off; one with brains scooped out with a cannon ball; another with half a face gone; another with entrails protruding; young [Private Charles A.] Winnegard, of [Company D] the Third [Ohio], has one foot off and both legs pierced by [canister] at the thighs; another boy lies with his hands clasp above his head, indicating that his last words were a prayer. Many Confederate sharpshooters lay behind stumps, rails and logs, shot in the head. A young boy, dressed in the Confederate uniform lies with his face turned to the sky and looks as if he might be sleeping. How many poor men moaned through the cold nights in the thick woods where the first day's battle occurred, calling in vain to man for help and finally making their last solemn petition to God!" [John Beatty, *The Citizen Soldier; or Memoirs of a Volunteer* (Cincinnati: Wilstach, Baldwin, 1879), 210–11.]

In early January Rosecrans's army was officially named the Army of the Cumberland, a term that had been used unofficially for the preceding several months. The Center, Right, and Left Wings were designated the Fourteenth, Twentieth, and Twenty-first Corps, with Thomas, McCook, and Crittenden as the respective commanders.

Rosecrans's victory was politically and strategically significant for the Union. The last half of 1862 had seen a series of Confederate battlefield victories that threatened to wipe out all previous Union successes. Culminating in a disastrous December, the morale of the population in the North was at an all-time low. Rosecrans provided a victory that helped to bolster that morale, especially in the midwestern states, where a large number of the Army of the Cumberland's soldiers came from.

Eight months later Lincoln was still expressing his appreciation to Rosecrans for the Union victory at Stones River. In a letter to Rosecrans dated August 31, 1863, Lincoln wrote, "I can never forget, whilst I remember anything, that about the end of last year and the beginning of this, you gave us a hard earned victory, which, had there been a defeat instead, the nation could scarcely have lived over." [Roy P. Basler, ed., *The Collected Works of Abraham Lincoln,* 8 vols. (New Brunswick, N. J.: Rutgers University Press, 1953), 6:424.]

Strategically, Stones River provided an irreversible Union penetration into Middle Tennessee. Nashville was secure. Using the Cumberland River and the Louisville and Nashville Railroad, it was turned into a significant supply depot. This depot became the base of supply for the Union advances into southern Tennessee and Georgia. Murfreesboro was turned into a forward supply base and was used by Rosecrans to support his Tullahoma and Chicka-mauga campaigns. Politically, Rosecrans's victory provided in-creased legitimacy to the Emancipation Proclamation, which went into effect on January 1, 1863.

With Stones River, the Army of the Cumberland began a series of campaigns that took it all the way to Atlanta and beyond.

UNION ORDER OF BATTLE

ARMY OF THE CUMBERLAND
    MAJ. GEN. WILLIAM S. ROSECRANS

RIGHT WING
    MAJ. GEN. ALEXANDER McD. McCOOK

FIRST DIVISION
    BRIG. GEN. JEFFERSON C. DAVIS

FIRST BRIGADE
    COL. P. SIDNEY POST
    59th Illinois, Capt. Hendrick E. Paine
    74th Illinois, Col. Jason Marsh
    75th Illinois, Lieut. Col. John E. Bennett
    22d Indiana, Col. Michael Gooding

SECOND BRIGADE
    COL. WILLIAM P. CARLIN
    21st Illinois:
        Col. John W. S. Alexander (w)
        Lieut. Col. Warren E. McMackin
    38th Illinois, Lieut. Col. Daniel H. Gilmer
    101st Ohio:
        Col. Leander Stem (mw and c)

Lieut. Col. Moses F. Wooster (mw and c)
Maj. Isaac M. Kirby
Capt. Bedan B. McDonald
15th Wisconsin, Col. Hans C. Heg

THIRD BRIGADE

COL. WILLIAM E. WOODRUFF
25th Illinois:
Maj. Richard H. Nodine
Col. Thomas D. Williams (k)
Capt. Wesford Taggart
35th Illinois, Lieut. Col. William P. Chandler
81st Indiana, Lieut. Col. John Timberlake

ARTILLERY

2d Minnesota Battery, Capt. William A. Hotchkiss
5th Wisconsin Battery:
Capt. Oscar F. Pinney (mw)
Lieut. Charles B. Humphrey
8th Wisconsin Battery:
Capt. Stephen J. Carpenter (k)
Sergt. Obadiah German
Lieut. Henry E. Stiles

SECOND DIVISION

BRIG. GEN. RICHARD W. JOHNSON

FIRST BRIGADE

BRIG. GEN. AUGUST WILLICH (c)
COL. WILLIAM WALLACE
COL. WILLIAM H. GIBSON
89th Illinois, Lieut. Col. Charles T. Hotchkiss
32d Indiana, Lieut. Col. Frank Erdelmeyer
39th Indiana, Lieut. Col. Fielder A. Jones
15th Ohio:
Col. William Wallace
Capt. Andrew R. Z. Dawson
Col. William Wallace
49th Ohio:
Col. William H. Gibson

Lieut. Col. Levi Drake (k)

Capt. Samuel F. Gray

SECOND BRIGADE

Brig. Gen. Edward N. Kirk (w)

Col. Joseph B. Dodge

34th Illinois:

Lieut. Col. Hiram W. Bristol

Maj. Alexander P. Dysart

79th Illinois:

Col. Sheridan P. Read (k)

Maj. Allen Buckner

29th Indiana:

Lieut. Col. David M. Dunn (c)

Maj. Joseph P. Collins

30th Indiana:

Col. Joseph B. Dodge

Lieut. Col. Orrin D. Hurd

77th Pennsylvania:

Lieut. Col. Peter B. Housum (k)

Capt. Thomas E. Rose

THIRD BRIGADE

Col. Philemon P. Baldwin

6th Indiana, Lieut. Col. Hagerman Tripp

5th Kentucky, Lieut. Col. William W. Berry (w)

1st Ohio, Maj. Joab A. Stafford

93d Ohio, Col. Charles Anderson (w)

ARTILLERY

5th Indiana Battery, Capt. Peter Simonson

1st Ohio, Battery A, Lieut. Edmund B. Belding

1st Ohio, Battery E, Capt. Warren P. Edgarton (c)

CAVALRY

3d Indiana, Companies G, H, I, and K, Maj. Robert Klein

THIRD DIVISION

Brig. Gen. Philip H. Sheridan

FIRST BRIGADE

Brig. Gen. Joshua W. Sill (k)
Col. Nicholas Greusel
36th Illinois:
    Col. Nicholas Greusel
    Maj. Silas Miller (w and c)
    Capt. Porter C. Olson
88th Illinois, Col. Francis T. Sherman
21st Michigan, Lieut. Col. William B. McCreery
24th Wisconsin, Maj. Elisha C. Hibbard

SECOND BRIGADE

Col. Frederick Schaefer (k)
Lieut. Col. Bernard Laiboldt
44th Illinois, Capt. Wallace W. Barrett (w)
73d Illinois, Maj. William A. Presson (w)
2d Missouri:
    Lieut. Col. Bernard Laiboldt
    Maj. Francis Ehrler
15th Missouri, Lieut. Col. John Weber

THIRD BRIGADE

Col. George W. Roberts (k)
Col. Luther P. Bradley
22d Illinois:
    Lieut. Col. Francis Swanwick (w and c)
    Capt. Samuel Johnson
27th Illinois:
    Col. Fazilo A. Harrington (k)
    Maj. William A. Schmitt
42d Illinois, Lieut. Col. Nathan H. Walworth
51st Illinois:
    Col. Luther P. Bradley
    Capt. Henry F. Wescott

ARTILLERY

Capt. Henry Hescock
1st Illinois, Battery C, Capt. Charles Houghtaling
4th Indiana Battery, Capt. Asahel K. Bush
1st Missouri, Battery G, Capt. Henry Hescock

CENTER
Maj. Gen. George H. Thomas

FIRST DIVISION
Maj. Gen. Lovell H. Rousseau

FIRST BRIGADE
Col. Benjamin F. Scribner
38th Indiana, Lieut. Col. Daniel F. Griffin
2d Ohio:
    Lieut. Col. John Kell (k)
    Maj. Anson G. McCook
33d Ohio, Capt. Ephraim J. Ellis
94th Ohio:
    Col. Joseph W. Frizell (w)
    Lieut. Col. Stephen A. Bassford
10th Wisconsin, Col. Alfred R. Chapin

SECOND BRIGADE
Col. John Beatty
42d Indiana, Lieut. Col. James M. Shanklin (c)
88th Indiana:
    Col. George Humphrey (w)
    Lieut. Col. Cyrus E. Briant
15th Kentucky:
    Col. James B. Forman (k)
    Lieut. Col. Joseph R. Snider
3d Ohio, Lieut. Col. Orris A. Lawson

THIRD BRIGADE
Col. John C. Starkweather
24th Illinois, Col. Geza Mihalotzy
79th Pennsylvania, Col. Henry A. Hambright
1st Wisconsin, Lieut. Col. George B. Bingham
21st Wisconsin, Lieut. Col. Harrison C. Hobart

FOURTH BRIGADE
Lieut. Col. Oliver L. Shepherd
15th United States, 1st Battalion:
    Maj. John H. King (w)
    Capt. Jesse Fulmer

16th United States, 1st Battalion, and Company B, 2d Battalion:
    Maj. Adam J. Slemmer (w)
    Capt. Robert E. A. Crofton
18th United States, 1st Battalion, and Companies A and D, 3d
  Battalion:
    Maj. James N. Caldwell
18th United States, 2d Battalion, and Companies B, C, E, and F, 3d
  Battalion:
    Maj. Frederick Townsend
19th United States, 1st Battalion:
    Maj. Stephen D. Carpenter (k)
    Capt. James B. Mulligan

ARTILLERY

CAPT. CYRUS O. LOOMIS
Kentucky, Battery A, Capt. David C. Stone
1st Michigan, Battery A, Lieut. George W. Van Pelt
5th United States, Battery H, Lieut. Francis L. Guenther

CAVALRY

2d Kentucky (six companies), Maj. Thomas P. Nicholas

SECOND DIVISION

BRIG. GEN. JAMES S. NEGLEY

FIRST BRIGADE

BRIG. GEN. JAMES G. SPEARS
1st Tennessee, Col. Robert K. Byrd
2d Tennessee, Lieut. Col. James M. Melton
3d Tennessee, Col. Leonidas C. Houk
5th Tennessee, Col. James T. Shelley
6th Tennessee, Col. Joseph A. Cooper

SECOND BRIGADE

COL. TIMOTHY R. STANLEY
19th Illinois:
    Col. Joseph R. Scott (w)
    Lieut. Col. Alexander W. Raffen
11th Michigan, Col. William L. Stoughton

18th Ohio, Lieut. Col. Josiah Given
69th Ohio:
    Col. William B. Cassilly
    Maj. Eli J. Hickcox (w)
    Capt. David Putnam
    Capt. Joseph H. Brigham
    Lieut. Col. George F. Elliott

THIRD BRIGADE

Col. John F. Miller
37th Indiana:
    Col. James S. Hull (w)
    Lieut. Col. William D. Ward
21st Ohio, Lieut. Col. James M. Neibling
74th Ohio, Col. Granville Moody (w)
78th Pennsylvania, Col. William Sirwell

ARTILLERY

Kentucky, Battery B, Lieut. Alban A. Ellsworth
1st Ohio, Battery G, Lieut. Alexander Marshall
1st Ohio, Battery M, Capt. Frederick Schultz

THIRD DIVISION

Brig. Gen. Speed S. Fry

FIRST BRIGADE

Col. Moses B. Walker
82d Indiana, Col. Morton C. Hunter
12th Kentucky, Col. William A. Hoskins
17th Ohio, Col. John M. Connell
31st Ohio, Lieut. Col. Frederick W. Lister
38th Ohio, Col. Edward H. Phelps

SECOND BRIGADE
(Not at Stones River)

Col. John M. Harlan
10th Indiana, Col. William B. Carroll
74th Indiana, Col. Charles W. Chapman
4th Kentucky, Col. John T. Croxton

10th Kentucky, Lieut. Col. William H. Hays
14th Ohio, Col. George P. Este

THIRD BRIGADE
(Not at Stones River)

BRIG. GEN. JAMES B. STEEDMAN
87th Indiana, Col. Kline G. Shryock
2d Minnesota, Col. James George
9th Ohio, Col. Gustave Kammerling
35th Ohio, Col. Ferdinand Van Derveer

ARTILLERY

1st Michigan, Battery D, Capt. Josiah W. Church
1st Ohio, Battery C, Capt. Daniel K. Southwick
    (Not at Stones River)
4th United States, Battery I, Lieut. Frank G. Smith
    (Not at Stones River)

FOURTH DIVISION
(Not at Stones River)

BRIG. GEN. ROBERT B. MITCHEL

FIRST BRIGADE

BRIG. GEN. JAMES D. MORGAN
10th Illinois, Lieut. Col. McLain F. Wood
16th Illinois, Lieut. Col. James B. Cahill
60th Illinois, Col. Silas C. Toler
10th Michigan, Lieut. Col. C. J. Dickerson
14th Michigan:
    Lieut. Col. Myndert W. Quackenbush
    Lieut. Col. Milton L. Phillips

SECOND BRIGADE

COL. DANIEL McCOOK
85th Illinois, Col. Robert S. Moore
86th Illinois, Lieut. Col. David W Magee
125th Illinois, Col. Oscar F. Harmon
52d Ohio, Lieut. Col. D. D. T. Cowen

CAVALRY

2d Indiana, Company A, Capt. John G. Kessler
5th Kentucky, Maj. John Q. Owsley
3d Tennessee, Col. William C. Pickens

ARTILLERY

2d Illinois, Battery I, Capt. Charles M. Barnett
10th Wisconsin Battery, Capt. Yates V. Beebe

FIFTH DIVISION
(Not at Stones River)

BRIG. GEN. JOSEPH J. REYNOLDS

FIRST BRIGADE

COL. ALBERT S. HALL
80th Illinois, Col. Thomas G. Allen
123d Illinois, Col. James Monroe
101st Indiana, Col. William Garver
105th Ohio, Lieut. Col. William R. Tolles

SECOND BRIGADE

COL. ABRAM O. MILLER
98th Illinois, Col. John J. Funkhouser
17th Indiana, Col. John T. Wilder
72d Indiana, Maj. Henry M. Carr
75th Indiana, Col. Milton S. Robinson

ARTILLERY

18th Indiana Battery, Capt. Eli Lilly
19th Indiana Battery, Capt. Samuel J. Harris

LEFT WING

MAJ. GEN. THOMAS L. CRITTENDEN

FIRST DIVISION

BRIG. GEN. THOMAS J. WOOD (w)
BRIG. GEN. MILO S. HASCALL

FIRST BRIGADE

Brig. Gen. Milo S. Hascall
Col. George P. Buell
100th Illinois, Col. Frederick A. Bartleson
58th Indiana:
  Col. George P. Buell.
  Lieut. Col. James T. Embree
3d Kentucky:
  Col. Samuel McKee (k)
  Maj. Daniel R. Collier
26th Ohio, Capt. William H. Squires

SECOND BRIGADE

Col. George D. Wagner
15th Indiana, Lieut. Col. Gustavus A. Wood
40th Indiana:
  Col. John W. Blake
  Lieut. Col. Elias Neff (w)
  Maj. Henry Learning
57th Indiana:
  Col. Cyrus C. Hines (w)
  Lieut. Col. George W. Lennard (w)
  Capt. John S. McGraw
97th Ohio, Col. John Q. Lane

THIRD BRIGADE

Col. Charles G. Harker
51st Indiana, Col. Abel D. Streight
73d Indiana, Col. Gilbert Hathaway
13th Michigan, Col. Michael Shoemaker
64th Ohio, Lieut. Col. Alexander McIlvain
65th Ohio:
  Lieut. Col. Alexander Cassil (w)
  Maj. Horatio N. Whitbeck (w)

ARTILLERY

Maj. Seymour Race
8th Indiana Battery, Lieut. George Estep
10th Indiana Battery, Capt. Jerome B. Cox
6th Ohio Battery, Capt. Cullen Bradley

SECOND DIVISION

Brig. Gen. John M. Palmer

FIRST BRIGADE

Brig. Gen. Charles Cruft
31st Indiana, Col. John Osborn
1st Kentucky, Col. David A. Enyart
2d Kentucky, Col. Thomas D. Sedgewick
90th Ohio, Col. Isaac N. Ross

SECOND BRIGADE

Col. William B. Hazen
110th Illinois, Col. Thomas S. Casey
9th Indiana, Col. William H. Blake
6th Kentucky, Col. Walter C. Whitaker
41st Ohio, Lieut. Col. Aquila Wiley

THIRD BRIGADE

Col. William Grose
84th Illinois, Col. Louis H. Waters
36th Indiana:
    Maj. Isaac Kinley (w)
    Capt. Pyrrhus Woodward
23d Kentucky, Maj. Thomas H. Hamrick
6th Ohio, Col. Nicholas L. Anderson
24th Ohio:
    Col. Frederick C. Jones (k)
    Maj. Henry Terry (k)
    Capt. Enoch Weller (k)
    Capt. A. T. M. Cockerill

ARTILLERY

Capt. William E. Standart
1st Ohio, Battery B, Capt. William E Standart
1st Ohio, Battery F:
    Capt. Daniel T. Cockerill (w)
    Lieut. Norval Osburn
4th United States, Batteries H and M, Lieut. Charles C. Parsons

THIRD DIVISION

Brig. Gen. Horatio P. Van Cleve (w)
Col. Samuel Beatty

·FIRST BRIGADE

Col. Samuel Beatty
Col. Benjamin C. Grider
79th Indiana, Col. Frederick Knefler
9th Kentucky:
    Col. Benjamin C. Grider
    Lieut. Col. George H. Cram
11th Kentucky, Maj. Erasmus L. Mottley
19th Ohio, Maj. Charles F. Manderson

SECOND BRIGADE

Col. James P. Fyffe
44th Indiana:
    Col. William C. Williams (c)
    Lieut. Col. Simeon C. Aldrich
86th Indiana, Lieut. Col. George F. Dick
13th Ohio:
    Col. Joseph G. Hawkins (k)
    Maj. Dwight Jarvis Jr.
59th Ohio, Lieut. Col. William Howard

THIRD BRIGADE

Col. Samuel W. Price
35th Indiana, Col. Bernard F. Mullen
8th Kentucky:
    Lieut. Col. Reuben May
    Maj. Green B. Broaddus
21st Kentucky, Lieut. Col. James C. Evans
51st Ohio, Lieut. Col. Richard W. McClain
99th Ohio:
    Col. Peter T. Swaine (w)
    Lieut. Col. John E. Cummins

ARTILLERY

Capt. George R. Swallow
7th Indiana Battery, Capt. George R. Swallow

Pennsylvania, Battery B (26th), Lieut. Alanson J. Stevens
3d Wisconsin Battery, Lieut. Cortland Livingston

CAVALRY

Brig. Gen. David S. Stanley

CAVALRY DIVISION

Col. John Kennett

FIRST BRIGADE

Col. Robert H. G. Minty
2d Indiana, Company M, Capt. J. A. S. Mitchell
3d Kentucky, Col. Eli H. Murray
4th Michigan, Lieut. Col. William H. Dickinson
7th Pennsylvania, Maj. John E. Wynkoop

SECOND BRIGADE

Col. Lewis Zahm
1st Ohio:
    Col. Minor Milliken (k)
    Maj. James Laughlin
3d Ohio, Lieut. Col. Douglas A. Murray
4th Ohio, Maj. John L. Pugh

ARTILLERY

1st Ohio, Battery D (section), Lieut. Nathaniel M. Newell

RESERVE CAVALRY

(Under direct command of Brig. Gen. Stanley)
15th Pennsylvania:
    Maj. Adolph G. Rosengarten (k)
    Maj. Frank B. Ward (mw)
    Capt. Alfred Vezin
1st Middle (5th) Tennessee, Col. William B. Stokes
2d Tennessee, Col. Daniel M. Ray

UNATTACHED CAVALRY

4th U.S. Cavalry, Capt. Elmer Otis

PIONEER BRIGADE
  Capt. James St. C. Morton
  1st Battalion, Capt. Lyman Bridges (w)
  2d Battalion, Capt. Calvin Hood
  3d Battalion, Capt. Robert Clements
  Illinois Light Artillery, Chicago Board of Trade Battery,
      Capt. James H. Stokes

ENGINEERS AND MECHANICS
  1st Michigan, Col. William P. Innes

(k) Killed
(w) Wounded
(mw) Mortally Wounded
(c) Captured

[OR 20, pt. 1, pp. 174–82.]

CONFEDERATE ORDER OF BATTLE

ARMY OF TENNESSEE
> Gen. Braxton Bragg

POLK'S CORPS
> Lieut. Gen. Leonidas Polk

FIRST DIVISION
> Maj. Gen. Benjamin F. Cheatham

DONELSON'S BRIGADE
> Brig. Gen. Daniel S. Donelson
> 8th Tennessee:
>> Col. William L. Moore (k)
>> Lieut. Col. John H. Anderson
> 16th Tennessee, Col. John H. Savage
> 38th Tennessee, Col. John C. Carter
> 51st Tennessee, Col. John Chester
> 84th Tennessee, Col. Sidney S. Stanton
> Carnes's (Tennessee) Battery, Capt. William W. Carnes

STEWART'S BRIGADE
> Brig. Gen. Alexander P. Stewart
> 4th Tennessee and 5th Tennessee, Col. Otho F. Strahl

19th Tennessee, Col. Francis M. Walker
24th Tennessee:
>   Col. Hugh L. W. Bratton (mw)
>   Maj. Samuel E. Shannon
31st Tennessee and 33d Tennessee, Col. Egbert E. Tansil
Mississippi Battery, Capt. Thomas J. Stanford

MANEY'S BRIGADE

Brig. Gen. George Maney
1st Tennessee and 27th Tennessee, Col. Hume R. Feild
4th Tennessee (Provisional Army), Col. James A. McMurry
6th Tennessee and 9th Tennessee, Col. Charles S. Hurt
Tennessee Sharpshooters, Capt. Frank Maney
Smith's (Mississippi) Battery, Lieut. William B. Turner

SMITH'S (VAUGHAN'S) BRIGADE

Col. Alfred J. Vaughan Jr.
12th Tennessee, Maj. J. N. Wyatt
13th Tennessee:
>   Lieut. Col. William E. Morgan (mw)
>   Capt. R. F. Lanier
29th Tennessee, Maj. J. B. Johnson
47th Tennessee, Capt. W. M. Watkins
154th Tennessee, Lieut. Col. Michael Magevney Jr.
9th Texas, Col. William H. Young
Allin's (Tennessee) Sharpshooters:
>   Lieut. J. R. J. Creighton (w)
>   Lieut. T. F. Pattison
Tennessee Battery, Capt. W. L. Scott

WITHERS'S DIVISION

Maj. Gen. Jones M. Withers

DEA'S (LOOMIS'S) BRIGADE

Col. John Q. Loomis (w)
Col. J. Coltart
19th Alabama
22d Alabama
25th Alabama, Col. John Q. Loomis

26th Alabama, Col. J. Coltart
39th Alabama
17th Alabama Battalion Sharpshooters, Capt. B. C. Yancey
1st Louisiana (Regulars), Lieut. Col. Frederick H. Farrar Jr. (mw)
Robertson's Battery, Capt. Felix H. Robertson

CHALMERS'S BRIGADE

Brig. Gen. James R. Chalmers (w)
Col. Thomas W. White
7th Mississippi
9th Mississippi, Col. Thomas W. White
10th Mississippi
41st Mississippi
9th Mississippi Battalion Sharpshooters, Capt. Osborn F. West
Blythe's (44th Mississippi) Regiment
Garrity's (Alabama) Battery

WALTHALL'S (ANDERSON'S) BRIGADE

Brig. Gen. James Patton Anderson
45th Alabama, Col. James G. Gilchrist
24th Mississippi, Lieut. Col. Robert P. McKelvaine
27th Mississippi:
    Col. Thomas M. Jones
    Lieut. Col. James L. Autry (k)
    Capt. E. R. Neilson (w)
29th Mississippi:
    Col. William F. Brantly (w)
    Lieut. Col. James B. Morgan
30th Mississippi, Lieut. Col. Julius I. Scales
39th North Carolina, Capt. Alfred W. Bell
Missouri Battery, Capt. Overton W. Barret

ANDERSON'S (MANIGAULT'S) BRIGADE

Col. Arthur M. Manigault
24th Alabama, Col. William A. Buck (w)
28th Alabama, Col. John C Reid
34th Alabama, Col. Julius C. B. Mitchell
10th South Carolina, Lieut. Col. James F. Pressley
19th South Carolina, Col. A. J. Lythgoe (k)
Alabama Battery, Capt. David D. Waters

HARDEE'S CORPS

Lieut. Gen. William J. Hardee

BRECKINRIDGE'S DIVISION

Maj. Gen. John C. Breckinridge

ADAMS'S BRIGADE

Brig. Gen. Daniel W. Adams (w)
Col. Randall L. Gibson
32d Alabama:
    Lieut. Col. Henry Maury (w)
    Col. Alexander McKinstry
13th Louisiana and 20th Louisiana
    Col. Randall L. Gibson
    Maj. Charles Guillet
16th Louisiana and 25th Louisiana
    Col. Stuart W. Fisk (k)
    Maj. Francis C. Zacharie
14th Louisiana Battalion, Maj. John E. Austin
Washington Artillery (5th Battery), Lieut. William C. D. Vaught

PALMER'S BRIGADE

Col. Joseph B. Palmer
Brig. Gen. Gideon J. Pillow
18th Tennessee:
    Lieut. Col. William R. Butler
    Col. Joseph B. Palmer (w)
26th Tennessee, Col. John M. Lillard
28th Tennessee, Col. Preston D. Cunningham (k)
32d Tennessee, Col. Edmund C. Cook
45th Tennessee, Col. Anderson Searcy
Moses's (Georgia) Battery, Lieut. R.W. Anderson

PRESTON'S BRIGADE

Brig. Gen. William Preston
1st Florida and 3d Florida, Col. William Miller (w)
4th Florida, Col. William L. L. Bowen
60th North Carolina, Col. Joseph A. McDowell

20th Tennessee:
    Col. Thomas B. Smith (w)
    Lieut. Col. Frank M. Lavender
    Maj. Frederick Claybrooke
Tennessee Battery:
    Capt. E. E. Wright (k)
    Lieut. J. W. Phillips

HANSON'S BRIGADE

BRIG. GEN. ROGER W. HANSON (mw)
COL. ROBERT P. TRABUE
41st Alabama:
    Col. Henry Talbird
    Lieut. Col. Martin L. Stansel (w)
2d Kentucky:
    Maj. James W. Hewitt (w)
    Capt. James W. Moss
4th Kentucky:
    Col. Robert P. Trabue
    Capt. Thomas W. Thompson
6th Kentucky, Col. Joseph H. Lewis
9th Kentucky, Col. Thomas H. Hunt
Kentucky Battery, Capt. Robert Cobb

JACKSON'S BRIGADE
(Attached to Breckinridge's Division)

BRIG. GEN. JOHN K. JACKSON
5th Georgia:
    Col. William T. Black (k)
    Maj. Charles P. Daniel
2d Georgia Battalion Sharpshooters, Maj. Jesse J. Cox
5th Mississippi, Lieut. Col. W. L. Sykes (w)
8th Mississippi:
    Col. John C. Wilkinson (w and c)
    Lieut. Col. Adin McNeill
Pritchard's (Georgia) Battery
Lumsden's (Alabama) Battery, Lieut. Henry H. Cribbs

CLEBURNE'S DIVISION

Maj. Gen. Patrick R. Cleburne

POLK'S BRIGADE

Brig. Gen. Lucius E. Polk
1st Arkansas, Col. John W. Colquitt
13th Arkansas
15th Arkansas
5th Confederate, Col. J. A. Smith
2d Tennessee, Col. William D. Robison
5th Tennessee, Col. B. J. Hill
Helena (Arkansas) Artillery, Lieut. Thomas J. Key

LIDDELL'S BRIGADE

Brig. Gen. St. John R. Liddell
2d Arkansas, Col. Daniel C. Govan
5th Arkansas, Lieut. Col. John E. Murray
6th Arkansas and 7th Arkansas:
    Col. Samuel G. Smith (w)
    Lieut. Col. F. J. Cameron(w)
    Maj. William F. Douglass
8th Arkansas:
    Col. John H. Kelly (w)
    Lieut. Col. George F. Baucum
Swett's (Mississippi, Warren Artillery) Battery, Lieut. H. Shannon

JOHNSON'S BRIGADE

Brig. Gen. Bushrod R. Johnson
17th Tennessee:
    Col. Albert S. Marks (w)
    Lieut. Col. Watt W. Floyd
23d Tennessee, Lieut. Col. Richard H. Keeble
25th Tennessee:
    Col. John M. Hughs (w)
    Lieut. Col. Samuel Davis
37th Tennessee:
    Col. Moses White (w)
    Maj. Joseph T. McReynolds (k)
    Capt. C. G. Jarnagin

44th Tennessee, Col. John S. Fulton
Jefferson (Mississippi) Artillery, Capt. Putnam Darden

WOOD'S BRIGADE

Brig. Gen. Sterling A. M. Wood
16th Alabama, Col. William B. Wood (w)
33d Alabama, Col. Samuel Adams
3d Confederate, Maj. J. F. Cameron
45th Mississippi, Lieut. Col. R. Charlton
15th Mississippi Battalion Sharpshooters, Capt. A. T. Hawkins
Alabama Battery, Capt. Henry C. Semple

MCCOWN'S DIVISION

Maj. Gen. John P. McCown

ECTOR'S BRIGADE
(Dismounted Cavalry)

Brig. Gen. Matthew D. Ector
10th Texas Cavalry, Col. Matthew F. Locke
11th Texas Cavalry:
    Col. John C. Burks (mw)
    Lieut. Col. Joseph M. Bounds
14th Texas Cavalry, Col. John L. Camp
15th Texas Cavalry, Col. Julius A. Andrews
Texas Battery, Capt. James P. Douglas

RAINS'S BRIGADE

Brig. Gen. James E. Rains (k)
Col. Robert B. Vance
3d Georgia Battalion, Lieut. Col. M. A. Stovall
9th Georgia Battalion, Maj. Joseph T. Smith
29th North Carolina, Col. Robert B. Vance
11th Tennessee:
    Col. George W. Gordon (w)
    Lieut. Col. William Thedford
Eufaula (Alabama) Light Artillery, Lieut. William A. McDuffie

MCNAIR'S BRIGADE

Brig. Gen. Evander McNair
Col. Robert W. Harper

1st Arkansas Mounted Rifles (Dismounted):
    Col. Robert W. Harper
    Maj. L. M. Ransaur (w)
2d Arkansas Mounted Rifles (Dismounted), Lieut. Col. James A.
  Williamson
4th Arkansas, Col. Henry G. Bunn
30th Arkansas:
    Maj. James J. Franklin (w and c)
    Capt. William A. Cotter
4th Arkansas Battalion, Maj. J. A. Ross
Arkansas Battery, Capt. John T. Humphreys

CAVALRY

BRIG. GEN. JOSEPH WHEELER

WHEELER'S BRIGADE

BRIG. GEN. JOSEPH WHEELER
1st Alabama, Col. William W. Allen (w)
3d Alabama:
    Maj. Frank Y. Gaines
    Capt. Tyirie H. Mauldin
51st Alabama, Col. John T. Morgan
8th Confederate, Col. William B. Wade
1st Tennessee, Col. James E. Carter
Tennessee Battalion, Maj. DeWitt C. Douglass
Tennessee Battalion, Maj. D. W. Holman
Arkansas Battery, Capt. J. H. Wiggins

BUFORD'S BRIGADE

BRIG. GEN. ABRAHAM. BUFORD
    3d Kentucky, Col. J. R. Butler
    5th Kentucky, Col. D. Howard Smith
    6th Kentucky, Col. J. W. Grigsby

PEGRAM'S BRIGADE

BRIG. GEN. JOHN PEGRAM
1st Georgia
1st Louisiana

WHARTON'S BRIGADE

Brig. Gen. John A. Wharton
14th Alabama Battalion, Lieut. Col. James C. Malone
1st Confederate, Col. John T. Cox
3d Confederate, Lieut. Col. William N. Estes
2d Georgia:
    Lieut. Col. James E. Dunlop
    Maj. Francis M. Ison
3d Georgia (detachment), Maj. R. DeWitt C. Thompson
2d Tennessee, Col. Henry M. Ashby
4th Tennessee, Col. Baxter Smith
Tennessee Battalion, Maj. John R. Davis
8th Texas, Col. Thomas Harrison
Murray's (Tennessee) Regiment, Maj. W. S. Bledsoe
Escort Company, Capt. Paul F. Anderson
McCown's Escort Company, Capt. Leslie T. Hardy
White's (Tennessee) Battery, Capt. B. F. White Jr.

UNASSIGNED ARTILLERY

Baxter's (Tennessee) Battery
Byrne's (Kentucky) Battery
Gibson's (Georgia) Battery

(k) Killed
(w) Wounded
(mw) Mortally Wounded
(c) Captured

[OR 20, pt. 1, pp. 658–61.]

UNION CASUALTIES

Right Wing

FIRST DIVISION
Brigadier-General DAVIS

Command	Killed and Wounded*
1st Brigade, Colonel Post	161
2d Brigade, Colonel Carlin	619
3d Brigade, Colonel Woodruff	226
Total Division	**1,006**

SECOND DIVISION
Brigadier-General JOHNSON

Command	Killed and Wounded*
1st Brigade, Colonel Gibson	472
2d Brigade, Colonel Dodge	405
3d Brigade, Colonel Baldwin	291
Total Division	**1,168**

THIRD DIVISION
Brigadier-General SHERIDAN

Command	Killed and Wounded*
1st Brigade, Colonel Greusel	479
2d Brigade, Colonel Laiboldt	206
3d Brigade, Colonel Bradley	443
Total Division	1,128
TOTAL RIGHT WING	**3,302**

Center Wing

FIRST DIVISION
Major-General ROUSSEAU

Command	Killed and Wounded*
1st Brigade, Colonel Scribner	208
2d Brigade, Colonel Beatty	281
3d Brigade, Colonel Starkweather	28
4th Brigade, Colonel Shepherd	561
Total Division	**1,078**

SECOND DIVISION
Brigadier-General NEGLEY

Command	Killed and Wounded*
1st Brigade, Brig. Gen. Spears	16
2d Brigade, Colonel Stanley	500
3d Brigade, Colonel Miller	410
Total Division	926
TOTAL CENTER WING	**2,004**

Left Wing

FIRST DIVISION
Brigadier-General WOOD

Command	Killed and Wounded*
1st Brigade, Brig. Gen. Hascall	343
2d Brigade, Colonel Wagner	329
3d Brigade, Colonel Harker	454
Total Division	**1,126**

SECOND DIVISION
Brigadier-General PALMER

Command	Killed and Wounded*
1st Brigade, Brig. Gen. Cruft	255
2d Brigade, Colonel Hazen	336
3d Brigade, Colonel Grose	516
Total Division	**1,107**

THIRD DIVISION
Brigadier-General VAN CLEVE

Command	Killed and Wounded*
1st Brigade, Col. S. Beatty	411
2d Brigade, Colonel Fyffe	288
3d Brigade, Colonel Price	342
Total Division	1,041
Total Left Wing	**3,274**

Pioneer Brigade

Captain Morton

Killed and Wounded*
30

Cavalry

Killed and Wounded*
84

ARMY TOTAL*	**8,694**
TOTAL INCLUDING MISSING	13,249

*Does not include missing in action or detached units for headquarters, guards, and escort.
**Does not include 3,673 missing in action.

[OR 20, pt. 1, pp. 200–01 and 215.]

CONFEDERATE CASUALTIES

Polk's Corps

CHEATHAM'S DIVISION

Command	Casualties*
Donelson's Brigade	700
Stewart's Brigade	399
Maney's Brigade	193
Smith's [Vaughan's] Brigade	707
Total Division	**1,999**

WITHERS'S DIVISION

Command	Casualties*
Deas's [Loomis's] Brigade	591
Chalmers's Brigade	548
Walthall's [Anderson's] Brigade	763
Manigault's Brigade	517
Total Division	**2,419**
TOTAL POLK'S CORPS	**4,418**

Hardee's Corps

BRECKINRIDGE'S DIVISION

Command	Casualties*
Pillow's [Palmer's] Brigade	425
Preston's Brigade	539
Adams's Brigade	703
Hanson's Brigade	401
Jackson's Brigade (attached)	303
Total Division	**2,371**

CLEBURNE'S DIVISION

Command	Casualties*
Staff	2
Wood's Brigade	504
Johnson's Brigade	606
Liddell's Brigade	607
Polk's Brigade	347
Total Division	**2,066**

McCOWN'S DIVISION

Command	Casualties*
No brigades listed	**962**
Total Hardee's Corps	**5,399**

Cavalry

Command	Casualties*
Wheeler's Brigade	167
Wharton's Brigade	264
Pegram's Brigade	None Reported
Buford's Brigade	18
CAVALRY TOTAL	**449**
ARMY TOTAL	**10,266***

*Includes killed, wounded, and missing.
[OR 20, pt. 1, p. 674.]

MONUMENTS

U.S. Regulars Monument

This monument is located near Stop 16, inside the National Cemetery. It is close to the flagpole, which is at the end of the narrow paved road. The monument is a tall, cylindrical shaft with an eagle mounted on top. It was erected in 1882 to honor the soldiers of the Regular Brigade of the Amy of the Cumberland. [Ann Wilson Willett, "A History of Stones River National Military Park," master's thesis, 1958.]

U.S. Regulars Monument.

Hazen Brigade Monument

This monument is located at Stops 17 and 19, next to the Old Nashville Highway, just south of the National Cemetery.

This is one of the first (if not the first) Civil War monuments constructed. Under the direction of Lieutenant Edward Crebbin of Company F, Ninth Indiana Infantry, soldiers from each regiment of the brigade began work on the monument in the summer of 1863. Two of the enlisted men in this construction crew were Sergeant James Murray and Private David Cochran of the Forty-first Ohio Infantry. The majority of the work was done between July and November 1863. In the spring of 1864 two stone cutters, Sergeant Daniel C. Miller and Private Christian Bauhoff of the 115th Ohio Infantry Regiment, inscribed the monument's four faces. Fifty-five soldiers of Hazen's Brigade are buried next to the monument. [Daniel A. Brown, "Marked for Future Generations: The Hazen Brigade Monument, 1863–1929," (Denver: National Park Service Technical Information Center), 1985].

Hazen Brigade Monument.

Artillery Monument

The Artillery Monument is located on the high ground overlooking McFadden's Ford at Stop 21. It is a tall white shaft that stands over thirty-five feet high. At the direction of its president, Major John W. Thomas, the Nashville, Chattanooga and St. Louis Railway placed it there in 1906. [Willett, "History of Stones River."]

Artillery Monument and Estep's battery.

Memorial to Confederate Dead

The memorial monument is located in Murfreesboro's Evergreen Cemetery. It is a four-sided shaft with a ball on top. On it are two inscriptions: "Our Unknown Dead" and "1861–1865." Next to the monument are the graves of two thousand Confederate solders.

Confederate Memorial.

CEMETERIES

National Cemetery

The National Cemetery is located within the National Park Service boundary. The entrance to the cemetery is on Old Nashville Highway, across the highway from the entrance for the Visitor Center.

National Cemetery.

The cemetery was established under an act passed by Congress in 1862 and War Department General Order Number 75, which provided for burial honors for Union soldiers. In June 1864 Major General George Thomas, who also established the National Cemetery at Chattanooga, detailed Captain John A. Means of Company C, 115th Ohio Volunteer Infantry to find and lay out a site for the cemetery. Captain Means was also the first cemetery superintendent.

The first burials were in October 1865. The soldiers buried here are Union dead from the Battle of Stones River and the skirmishes before and after. Of the 7,121 buried, 6,139 are Civil War dead. The last burials were done in 1973, and the cemetery was closed in January 1974 by act of Congress. The National Park Service maintains the cemetery. [Brown, "Marked for Future Generations."]

Grave marker for Thomas S. Miller, Company B, 90th Ohio. He was killed at what is now Stop 18.

Evergreen Cemetery

The cemetery was established in 1873 on land that was once part of Oak-lands Plantation. The Confederate dead were first buried on the battle-field. In 1867 they were moved to an original Confederate cemetery along the Shelbyville Highway, two miles south of Murfreesboro. In 1874 their remains began to be moved to Evergreen Cemetery. Two thousand are buried in a circle where the memorial to the Confederate dead is located. [Mable Pittard, Rutherford County (Memphis: Memphis State University Press, 1984), 96; John C. Spence, Annals of Rutherford County, vol. 2 (Mur-freesboro, Tenn.: Rutherford County Historical Society, 1991), 257–58.]

Confederate burial area in Evergreen Cemetery.

INDEX